This book, a revised and updated version of the books which appeared under the same title in 1976, 1982 and 1987, describes the main features of the systems of government support for export credits in the 22 countries that are members of the OECD Trade Committee's Group on Export Credits and Credit Guarantees (TC/ECG) and, for the first time, the system of Turkey. TC/ECG member countries also participate in the Arrangement on Guidelines for Officially Supported Export Credits (otherwise known as the OECD Arrangement or "Consensus").

Since the publication of the third edition, each country chapter has been thoroughly revised and updated in conjunction with the main national agencies. Therefore, the information on organisation and facilities, as well as all dates and numbers, are the most up–to–date known at the time of publication. In addition, each chapter has been reorganised into four main sections. The first details all main organisations involved in a country's export credit system and describes their structure; the second describes the various available types of insurance and guarantee policies and the conditions of their eligibility together with premium structures; the third is concerned with the forms of official financing support as well as their eligibility conditions and the resulting interest rate structure whilst the fourth comprises for the first time a description of that aspect of national aid finance programmes that have a bearing on export credit activity (e.g. mixed credits, "monobloc" loans, etc.).

The book also contains the full revised text of the Arrangement, which appears as Chapter 25. At their 30th meeting, held in May 1986, the Participants decided that the Arrangement be made available to the public. Annex II has been made available to the public by decision of the OECD Council. The remainder of the text and the chapters on national systems are published on the responsibility of the Secretary General of the OECD.

Also available

DEVELOPMENT CO–OPERATION IN THE 1990s. 1989 REPORT. Efforts and Policies of the Members of the Development Assistance Committe (1989)
(43 89 04 1)ISBN 92–64–13300–3 288 pp.   £18.00   US$32.00   FF150   DM62

TRADE IN SERVICES AND DEVELOPING COUNTRIES (1989)
(22 89 01 1)ISBN 92–64–13278–3 132 pp.   £8.50   US$15.00   FF70   DM29

FINANCING AND EXTERNAL DEBT OF DEVELOPING COUNTRIES – 1988 SURVEY (1989)
(43 89 03 1)ISBN 92–64–13261–9 228 pp.   £14.50   US$25.00   FF120   DM50

EXTERNAL DEBT STATISTICS. THE DEBT AND OTHER EXTERNAL LIABILITIES OF DEVELOPING, CMEA AND CERTAIN OTHER COUNTRIES AND TERRITORIES AT END–DECEMBER 1987 AND END–DECEMBER 1988 (1989)
(43 89 05 1)ISBN 92–64–13305–4 30 pp.   £8.50   US$15.00   FF70   DM29

Development Centre Studies

FINANCIAL POLICIES AND DEVELOPMENT by Jacques J. Polak (1989)
(41 89 01 1)ISBN 92–64–13187–6 234 pp.   £17.00   US$29.50   FF140   DM58

Prices charged at the OECD Bookshop.

The OECD CATALOGUE OF PUBLICATIONS and supplements will be sent free of charge on request addressed either to OECD Publications Service,
2, rue André-Pascal, 75775 PARIS CEDEX 16, or to the OECD Distributor in your country.

The Export Credit Financing Systems

in OECD Member countries

FOURTH EDITION

ORGANISATION FOR ECONOMIC CO-OPERATION AND DEVELOPMENT

Pursuant to article 1 of the Convention signed in Paris on 14th December 1960, and which came into force on 30th September 1961, the Organisation for Economic Co-operation and Development (OECD) shall promote policies designed:

- to achieve the highest sustainable economic growth and employment and a rising standard of living in Member countries, while maintaining financial stability, and thus to contribute to the development of the world economy;
- to contribute to sound economic expansion in Member as well as non-member countries in the process of economic development; and
- to contribute to the expansion of world trade on a multilateral, non-discriminatory basis in accordance with international obligations.

The original Member countries of the OECD are Austria, Belgium, Canada, Denmark, France, the Federal Republic of Germany, Greece, Iceland, Ireland, Italy, Luxembourg, the Netherlands, Norway, Portugal, Spain, Sweden, Switzerland, Turkey, the United Kingdom and the United States. The following countries became Members subsequently through accession at the dates indicated hereafter: Japan (28th April 1964), Finland (28th January 1969), Australia (7th June 1971) and New Zealand (29th May 1973).

The Socialist Federal Republic of Yugoslavia takes part in some of the work of the OECD (agreement of 28th October 1961).

Publié en français sous le titre:

LES SYSTÈMES DE FINANCEMENT
DES CRÉDITS A L'EXPORTATION
DANS LES PAYS MEMBRES DE L'OCDE

QUATRIÈME ÉDITION

TABLE OF CONTENTS

INTRODUCTION

Broadly defined, an export credit arises whenever a foreign buyer of exported goods or services is allowed to defer payment. Export credits are generally divided into short term (usually below two years), medium term (usually two to five years) and long term (usually over five years). They may take the form of "supplier credits", extended by the exporter, or of "buyer credits", where the exporter's bank or other financial institution lends to the buyer (or his bank). Export credit agencies may give official support to both types of credit. This official support may be limited to "pure cover", by which is meant insurance or guarantees given to exporters or lending institutions without financing support. Alternatively, it may be given in the form of "financing support", which is defined as including direct credits, refinancing and all forms of interest subsidies. Official financing support may or may not be given in conjunction with the basic guarantee or insurance facility. Of the twenty–three OECD countries whose export financing systems are described in this book, all but Turkey are members of the Group on Export Credits and Credit Guarantees (ECG) of the OECD Trade Committee.

The ECG members also participate in the Arrangement on Guidelines for Officially Supported Export Credits, which came into being in April 1978. This is an arrangement that was accepted directly among its participants and that was developed in the framework of the OECD. It replaced a less elaborate understanding that had been in effect among a more limited number of OECD countries since early 1976.

The main purpose of the Arrangement is to provide the institutional framework for an orderly export credit market and thus to prevent an export credit race in which exporting countries compete on the basis of who grants the most favourable financing terms rather than on the basis of who provides the highest quality and the best service for the lowest price. The Arrangement does not cover the conditions or terms of insurance or guarantees — only the conditions or terms of the export credits that benefit from such insurance or guarantees. As such, it deals with actions and policies of official export credit and insurance agencies. It sets limits on the terms and conditions for export credits with a duration of two years or more that are officially supported — that is, are insured, guaranteed, extended, refinanced or subsidised by or through export credit agencies. Within these limits, certain "derogations" from the rules and some "deviations" from what is considered normal practice are possible. These must be notified to all other participants in the Arrangement who can then "match" the deviation or derogation. The most important conditions are as follows:

a) At least 15 per cent of the contract is to be covered by cash payments;
b) The maximum repayment term is eight and a half years. This may be extended to ten years for relatively poor and for a limited number of intermediate countries;

c) Minimum rates of interest are set for periods of up to five, up to eight and a half and up to ten years. Since October 1983, these minima, known as the "matrix", have been subject to change every January and July according to an automatic mechanism based on the SDR weighted average of five major currencies. If commercial rates of interest for the currency of a participant fall below these minima, any participant may lend in that currency at "commercial interest reference rates" (CIRRs), which are subject to monthly adjustment to reflect market rates. Since July 1988, matrix minima have not been available for Category I (Relatively Rich) markets. Thus, the appropriate CIRR is the minimum rate for financing support on credit to countries in this category.

This interest rate minima condition applies only to credits benefiting from official financing support (see page 9).

Several sector understandings, setting special terms for the respective sectors, have been developed. In most cases these sector understandings are closely linked to the Arrangement. (Sector understandings have been accepted for nuclear power plants and aircraft. A sector understanding on agriculture commodities is envisaged. A separate understanding on ships is also in effect among eighteen OECD Countries).

In addition to export credit activity, the Arrangement also covers tied or partially untied aid financing: that is to say, credits or grants that are wholly or partly from public funds for development purposes and that are tied to purchases from the donor and from most developing countries. A number of governments combine such development aid with export credit to create "mixed credits" or soft loan facilities. According to the Arrangement guidelines at the time of publication, the conditions for all credits may be more favourable than those listed above for export credits if the overall concessionality level of individual transactions is at least 35 per cent.

A full text of the Arrrangement appears as Chapter 25 of this book.

All twenty–three countries included in this booklet have put in place a system to insure at least the political risk (risk of non–payment because of government imposed restrictions) of providing export credit to foreign buyers and many will also cover the "transfer" risk (risk of non–availability of foreign exchange to meet repayment obligations), although cover may be very restricted in markets with poor payment experience. Most of the institutions providing such insurance will also cover the commercial risks (risks of non–payment because of bankruptcy or default of the buyer) and some reinsure such risks taken by private institutions. In addition to insurance activities, most participants are involved in at least one of the three forms of official financing support described above. Several major agencies are used by their Governments as the instrument for providing interest rate subsidies whilst a smaller number of participants make export finance directly available to borrowers, or will refinance credits extended by the private market.

A variety of solutions have evolved with regard to government involvement. The organisational form of the institutions providing insurance or financing ranges from a section of a ministry (e.g. EID–MITI, Japan), or a government agency (e.g. ECIO, Greece), through independent government agencies (e.g. Mediocredito Centrale, Italy) and semi–public joint stock companies (e.g., COFACE, France) to private institutions operating partly under an agreement with the government (e.g. NCM, the Netherlands). These solutions are reflected in the way these organisations are funded: from the budget, special government funds, loans and capital from the government or shares and bonds.

Arrangement Matrix of Interest Rate Minima 1976–1990[1]
(per cent)

	I. Relatively rich countries	II. Intermediate countries	III. Relatively poor countries
Credits for 2–5 years			
July 1976	7.75	7.25	7.25
July 1980	8.50	8.00	7.50
November 1981	11.00	10.50	10.00
July 1982	12.15	10.85	10.00
October 1983	12.15	10.35	9.50
July 1984	13.35	11.55	10.70
January 1985	12.00	10.70	9.85
January 1986	10.95	9.65	8.80
July 1986	9.55	8.25	7.40
January 1988	10.15	8.85	8.00
July 1988	–	9.15	8.30
Credits for 5–8.5 years			
July 1976	8.00	7.75	7.50
July 1980	8.75	8.50	7.75
November 1981	11.25	11.00	10.00
July 1982	12.40	11.35	10.00
October 1983	12.40	10.70	9.50
July 1984	13.60	11.90	10.70
January 1985	12.25	11.20	9.85
January 1986	11.20	10.15	8.80
July 1986	9.80	8.75	7.40
January 1988	10.40	9.35	8.00
July 1988	–	9.65	8.30
Credits for 8.5–10 years			
July 1976	–	–	7.50
July 1980	–	–	7.75
November 1981	–	–	10.00
July 1982	–	11.35*	10.00
October 1983	–	10.70*	9.50
July 1984	–	11.90*	10.70
January 1985	–	11.20*	9.85
January 1986	–	10.15*	8.80
July 1986	–	8.75*	7.40
January 1988	–	9.35*	8.00
July 1988	–	9.65*	8.30

1. The matrix minima as at July 1988 continued to apply for the six months commencing January 1990

* Available only for countries that were classified in Category III before 6th July 1982.

Another aspect that varies widely is the position of the export credit agency on the market for officially supported (insured or financed) export credits or, conversely, the role played by private organisations such as banks and insurance companies. This is complicated by the fact that some private organisations act partly in the public sphere on behalf of governments and partly in the private sphere on their own account, whilst some public organisations act from time to time as if they were privately owned. Also, in certain cases, the provision of official financing support is dependent upon basic insurance; in others the entry of private banks and insurance companies into the market is forbidden. In some countries, official institutions are required or encouraged to cooperate with the private market, and an increasing number of official agencies are additionally experiencing the pressure of competition from private sector agencies.

Thus, there is a wide range of approaches. At one extreme are those that combine a complete range of insurance and guarantee facilities and additional options such as cost escalation insurance and foreign currency risk insurance with a comprehensive financing support system (including participation in mixed credits). In between are systems that offer the usual insurance cover (pre- and post-shipment cover for political and commercial risks on individual or wholeturnover policies), subsidised credits for matching those extended by other countries, some development aid credits and additional insurance facilities, and credits that the domestic market cannot provide. At the other end of the range would be an approach that provides only the insurance, guarantees and credits that the international market cannot provide, such as political risk insurance for higher risk countries or subsidised credits or guarantees for matching purposes and development aid credits. The move towards a Single European Market by the beginning of 1993 may result in a certain measure of harmonisation of the activities and procedures of European Community member countries' export credit agencies. However, at the time of publication, no firm proposals in this direction had been made.

Chapter 1

European Economic Community Procedures Concerning Export Credits

1. Decisions

The Decisions of the Council of the European Communities of 3rd December 1973 (73/391/EEC) and 27th July 1976 (76/641/EEC) defined the rules for consultation and information procedures in matters of credit insurance, credit guarantees and financial credits.

2. Procedures for Prior Consultation

Under the provisions of Section 1, Member States shall hold a consultation if the State, any other state organisation or any body for credit insurance or finance considers committing itself to extend or to guarantee fully or partially international credits that are linked to exports of goods or services and whose duration exceeds five years calculated from the Berne Union's starting points:
— whether the consultation concerns supplier credits or financial credits;
— whether these credits cover individual contracts or framework credit arrangements;
— whether the credits are purely private or are fully or partially subject to intervention out of public funds.

Detailed information concerning the envisaged operation shall be transmitted by telex to each Member State, the Commission and the Secretariat of the Council.

The consulted Member States or the Commission may give comments, make reservations, express an unfavourable opinion, request a consultative meeting, or indicate that the terms notified do not call for any comments.

This procedure must be initiated within a period of seven calendar days from the date of the notification. The consulting Member State shall reply within five calendar days to requests for additional details. The partners are allowed a maximum period of three working days following receipt of such additional details to express their opinion.

If a consultative meeting on a transaction is requested, it is held at the seat of the Secretariat of the Council on the occasion of a meeting of the Policy Coordination

Group for Credit Insurance, Guarantees and Financial Credits that was set up by the Council Decision of 27th September 1960. If five Member States express an unfavourable opinion, the meeting takes place automatically. The consulting Member State must suspend its decision until the consultative meeting has been held.

If, in the course of a consultation on a framework credit arrangement — whether public or private in nature — a Member State or the Commission requests an oral consultation, and if in the course of this oral consultation five Member States request that all or some of the individual contracts under this framework arrangement be the subject of prior consultations, the consulting Member State shall hold consultations on such contracts.

All partners shall be informed of the final decision taken on each transaction.

3. Information Procedures

A Member State may ask another Member State whether it is considering covering a transaction that has not yet been the subject of a consultation and, in particular, whether the credit terms alleged by an exporter or a financial institution are being considered.

4. Requirement for Automatic Inclusion of Subcontracts in the Cover

In accordance with Paragraph 1 of Section II of the EC Council Decision dated 10th December 1982, subcontracts with parties that are all in one or more Member States shall be automatically included in the cover granted to the principal contractor if the amount of such subcontracts is equal to or less than:

- 40 per cent for contracts of a value less than 7 500 000 ECU;
- 3 000 000 ECU for contracts of a value between 7 500 000 and 10 000 000 ECU;
- 30 per cent for contracts of a value over 10 000 000 ECU.

However, if because the risk of the transaction is particularly heavy, the principal contractor's credit insurer is unable to grant cover for the whole of the transaction, consultation between the interested credit insurance organisations shall take place with a view to resolving the problem by means of joint insurance or, if possible, reinsurance. If export contracts involve subcontracting in both Member States and non–member countries, subcontracting in Member States must be automatically included, up to the percentages and limits fixed in Section II, paragraph 1, by all subcontractors. The principal contractor must be eligible for the same insurance conditions, irrespective of whether he employs subcontractors from his own or from other Member States.

5. Obligations of EC Member States Not to Grant Interest Rate Subsidies

In accordance with Article 92 of the Treaty establishing the European Economic Community, any aid granted by a Member State or through state resources in any form whatsoever is, in so far as it affects trade between Member States, incompatible with the common market. Therefore, subsidising the interest rate of credits that finance trade between Member States is forbidden.

6. **Reciprocal Obligations of official export credit insurance organisations of Member States in the case of joint guarantees for a contract involving one or more subcontracts in one or more Member States of the European Communities**

In November 1984, the Council of the European Communities approved a directive establishing a standard agreement with which Member States are required to comply when their official export credit insurance organisations grant, jointly with an organisation or public department of another Member State, guarantees relating to a contract involving one or more subcontracts in one or more Member States.
The standard specimen agreement describes the scope, as well as the obligations of the principal insurer and each joint insurer in the case of joint insurance.
The specimen agreement also covers the case where the principal contractor enters into a contract with an enterprise situated in a non-member state.

Chapter 2

BELGIUM

1. ORGANISATION AND STRUCTURES

1.1 Insurance and Guarantees

1.1.1 *Representative organisation*

Office National du Ducroire
Square de Meeûs 40
1040 Brussels

Telephone: (32 2) 509 4211
Telex: OND B 21147
Telefax: (32 2) 513 5059

1.1.1.1 *Function*

Government authorities have been assisting in export credit insurance operations since 1921, but it was only in 1939, when the Office National du Ducroire (OND) was set up, that the existing arrangements came into force. OND is a state guaranteed public agency. Its General Manager and two Managers are appointed by the Crown.

OND insures both political and commercial export risks either directly or by reinsuring private insurance companies. It is empowered to take part in financing operations when other financing sources are insufficient. However, this power has only seldom been exercised.

As mentioned above, it also has authority to reinsure private Belgian credit insurance companies. Reinsurance of this kind is usually provided to cover commercial risks in Western European countries. However, since January 1989 OND covers these risks directly.

In 1964, some measures were introduced to enable OND to underwrite for the account of the government, within a certain ceiling, risks that are justified from a national interest point of view of but which are not insurable on the basis of the underwriting criteria usually adopted by OND.

1.1.1.2 *Summary of organisation*

Applications are received, depending on the kind of transaction, either in the Short and Medium Term Department or in the Long Term and Special Transactions Department. While the latter is organised in an underwriting and policies section, the former is structured along the lines of the exporters' sectors of activity.

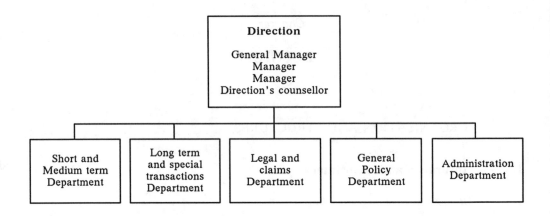

1.1.1.3 *Resources*

OND has its own capital fund, which is made up of various government debentures and at present amounts to BF 12 billion. The capital of BF 12 billion may be increased by a Royal decree discussed in the Council of Ministers to BF 14 billion in successive tranches of 1 billion. A ceiling for OND's liabilities is fixed by the Crown.

OND is required to set aside special reserve funds and provisions that, under its rules, must cover the guarantees given and any loss which they might entail. The premiums received, and the income from the capital fund and reserves, are allotted, after operating costs have been apportioned and deducted, to strengthen the special reserve funds and provisions as necessary. As at 31st December 1988, the general reserve, the special reserve funds and the provisions amounted to respectively BF 1 billion, BF 61 million and BF 10.3 billion.

The capital fund, combined with the general reserves and multiplied by 20, gives the OND's global liability ceiling for its own account. As a consequence, at 31st December 1988, the ceiling for OND's insurance and guarantee commitments for its account totalled BF 260 billion. In the event of the special reserves being exhausted, OND must draw on its capital and general reserve funds. If the available special reserves fall below a level fixed by the Board of Directors (see 1.1.1.4), OND's own funds may be supplemented by borrowing.

At the same time, the ceiling fixed by the government for the risks insured by OND for the government's account is BF 90 billion.

1.1.1.4 *Other organisations involved*

The Board of Directors of OND is composed of one President, one Vice–President and eighten members. Six members represent Ministers of Central State (Prime Minister, Ministers of Economics Affairs and Finance and the Ministers responsible respectively for External Relations, External Trade and Development Cooperation). They convey to OND the broad outlines of the policy to be followed. They have a veto power in every decision to be taken. Six other members represent the Regions and six other represent important business interests (e.g. employers' and employees' organisations, industry organisations etc.). Though it is OND's supreme decision body, the Board of Directors delegates far reaching powers to the management.

1.1.1.5 *Relations with the state*

OND is covered by a final state guarantee for both commercial and non–commercial risks, which it either insures directly or reinsures.

The Board of Directors is responsible for the conduct of OND's affairs. However, any decision involving the underwriting of new types of risk must be referred to the Minister of Economic Affairs. Such a decision only takes effect if no objection is lodged against it within two days.

1.1.1.6 *Relations with the private sector*

There are some private insurance companies operating in Belgium that offer cover of commercial export credit risks. Banks can, but in practice do not, provide export credit cover apart from confirming letters of credit.

1.1.1.7 *Additional structure*

In practice, Creditexport requires an OND policy, but other financial institutions, in particular the Institut de Réescompte et de Garantie, may finance credits without having OND cover.

1.2   **Export finance**

1.2.1   *Representative organisation*

Creditexport
Address: rue du Commerce 78
          B–1040 BRUSSELS

Telephone: (32–2) 511.73.30
Telex:
Telefax: (32–2) 514.34.50

1.2.1.1 *Function*

"L'Association pour la Coordination du Financement à Moyen Terme des Exportations belges", Creditexport in short, is a non–profit making organisation that was set up on a non–profit–making basis in 1959. It comprises the National Bank of Belgium (BNB), l'Institut de Réescompte et de Garantie (IRG), the Office Nationale du

Ducroire (OND) and the members of its financing pool, namely, three public credit institutions (Société Nationale de Crédit à l'Industrie, Caisse Générale d'Epargne et de Retraite and Caisse Nationale du Crédit Professionnel), fifteen banks with a close involvement in foreign trade financing and seven private savings banks.

Day–to–day management is carried out by the Institut de Réescompte et de Garantie (IRG), a state–guaranteed agency, whose capital is held by the banks and which provides the Secretariat for both Creditexport and the pool.

1.2.1.2 *Summary of organisation*

The Boards of Directors of Creditexport is composed of one representative from each of the six public bodies and six representatives from private sector. The representative of the Central Bank of Belgium is "de jure" chairman of the Board of Directors. An official of the Ministry of Finance in charge of matters regarding public credit and the senior ministerial officer in charge of foreign trade may attend meetings of the Board of Directors in a consultative capacity. The Institut de Réescompte et de Garantie acts as the secretariat of Creditexport.

1.2.1.3 *Resources*

The bulk of resources is obtained in the financial market. Revolving discount lines are available from the members of the pool, but are only used as the need arises. Their ceilings are set individually; each increase in the ceilings is negotiated.

Credits of one year or less are also funded in the market, particularly through the Institut de Réescompte et de Garantie and the National Bank of Belgium. Bills are first submitted to the National Bank of Belgium for certification. Paper held by the pool is also traded on the short and medium term markets provided by the Institut de Réescompte et de Garantie.

Credit lines opened by the members of the refinancing pool total BF 115 billion at present.

1.2.1.4 *Other organisations involved*

The executive body for refinancing operations approved by Creditexport is the Société Nationale de Crédit à l'Industrie, which acts as leading underwriter to the pool.

1.2.1.5 *Relations with the state*

The Belgian government may make loans to foreign governments. A loan may be used to finance all or part of the down–payments, the decision in the matter being taken by the recipient of the credit. The appropriations required for such loans are entered in the Budget of the Ministry of Finance.

Applications for interest rate subsidies are submitted to Copromex (Comité pour la promotion des exportations), an advisory committee responsible to the Minister for Foreign Trade, who takes the final decision. The amount of the subsidy is decided in the light of the foreign competition encountered and the interest rate applied by Creditexport. It does not however always bridge the gap between the rates paid by foreign competitors and those applied by Creditexport. In principle, the interest rate may not fall below the minimum level specified in the Arrangement, except in order to match lower rates charged abroad. The subsidy is calculated on the same amount and for the same duration as the export credit extended by Creditexport, and it applies to the whole of the credit. Funds for financing interest rate subsidies are allocated out of the budget, subject to a specified ceiling. Only exports to countries outside the EEC are eligible for interest rate subsidies. A Government decision is required to prolong the authority of Copromex to intervene.

1.2.2   Representative organisation

L'Institut de Réescompte et de Garantie (IRG)

1.2.2.1   Function

In the framework of its fundamental object (the creation of bank liquidities) the Institute opens short and medium–term rediscount credits in favour of commercial and savings banks. This is intended to allow them, in time of liquidity difficulties, to mobilize for short periods advances made to their clients.

The Institute also has wide powers to intervene in case of either a lack of liquidity or of an accident of solvability, in accordance to its serving the public interest.

On the other hand the Institute is operating as an official money market dealer. In this capacity it is actively engaged in all compartments of the Belgium franc money market e.g. the call money market, the interbankmarket and the short–term paper market.

1.2.2.2   Summary of organisation

Since 1935, a Rediscount and Guarantee Institute has existed in Belgium, the capital of which is subscribed by Belgian banks and saving banks. It is co–administrated equally by them and members appointed by the Government.

1.2.2.3   Resources

On one side the State guarantees its commitments, the ceiling of which is legally fixed at 120 billion Belgian francs. On the other side 36 commercial banks and 7 savings banks have subscribed to the capital, at present BEF 1 billion.

1.2.2.4   Other organisations involved

None.

1.3   Aid Finance

1.3.1   Representative organisation

General Administration for Development Cooperation (AGCD)
Address: Place du Champ de Mars 5 bte. 57
Telephone: 02/519.02.11
Telex: 21 376
Telefax: –

1.3.1.1   Function

AGCD is a semi–autonomous agency supervised by the Secretary of State for Development Cooperation.

1.3.1.2 *Summary of organisation*

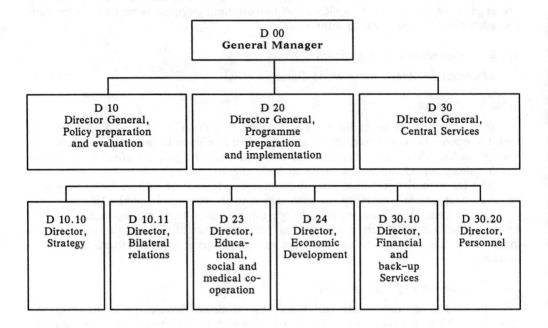

1.3.1.3 *Resources*

Tied aid and partially untied ODA loans are extended from the "Fund for Loans to Foreign States" for which the Finance Ministry is responsible.

1.3.1.4 *Other organisations involved*

A commission chaired by the Ministry of Finance and on which the Secretary of State for Development Cooperation is represented, appraises the projects to be financed by tied and partially untied ODA loans.

2.   INSURANCE PROGRAMMES

2.1   Cover for Exporters

2.1.1 *Policies available*

The insurance and guarantees normally cover risks which arise after the date of delivery or commissioning, but can also cover risks incurred during the period of manufacture.

Exporters can insure contracts only if they have previously contracted one of the following comprehensive insurance arrangements:

— *Comprehensive policy*: (short term business up to 1 year credit)

A distinction between "zone 1" and "zone 2" is made. For exports to "zone 1 countries" (i.e. OECD countries less Turkey) the cover can be limited to the commercial risk. For exports to "zone 2 countries", both political and commercial risks for contracts with private buyers as well as non–payment risks for contracts with government buyers are to be proposed to insurance.

— *Extended comprehensive policy*: covering the same risks as the ordinary comprehensive policy, but for exports of light capital goods with credit up to five years;

— *Comprehensive agreement*: covering supplies of capital goods and services for which the credit period exceeds five years, and special operations (civil engineering contracts, turnkey plants and engineering services for large amounts), whatever the duration of the credit.

OND also covers certain political risks and force majeure losses. In general, exporters must themselves bear risks in respect of arbitration clauses.

The maximum percentage guaranteed by OND policies is 90 per cent for commercial risks in the case of private debtors and 95 per cent for political risks (including nonpayment by a government debtor). It may be increased by 5 per cent for commercial risks when the debtor or his guarantor is a bank. For short term business to category 1 countries, the maximum percentage of guarantee for commercial risk on private debtor is in principle fixed at 85 % (95 % when the guarantor is a bank).

2.1.2   *Eligibility*

Provision of credit depends on the terms requested, and on the creditworthiness of the buyer and country as assessed by OND. Particularly for developing countries, the assessment also takes account of any additional guarantees (from a public body or local bank) that the potential buyer can offer. A distinction is made between credits granted to public and private buyers respectively. In the case of the latter, commercial and noncommercial risks are assessed separately, whereas in the case of governments or governmental organisations, commercial and political risks are combined for purposes of the assessment. When OND considers a risk to be unacceptable according to its normal criteria, it can be referred to the government, which may allow it to be underwritten directly for its own account if the contract is clearly advantageous to the Belgian economy.

The normal terms for insuring or guaranteeing credits are as follows:

— *Maximum credit periods*
    — Consumer goods: in principle six months, with exceptions to twelve months in certain sectors, according to international arrangements;
    — Light capital goods: depending on the amount of the contract, with a maximum of five years;
    — Heavy capital goods: from five to ten years depending on the value of the contract and its destination;

— *Cash payment, repayment schedules and cover of local costs;* in accordance with the Arrangement.

Cover may be extended to foreign goods and services incorporated in Belgian exports. The extension is automatic, is subject to reciprocity and normally covers up to 30/40 per cent of the value of the contract.

An agreement made in 1963 with the Office du Ducroire Luxembourgeois (ODL) empowers OND to re–insure 50 per cent of the risks insured by the Luxembourg agency.

2.1.3   Cost of cover

In principle, premiums are payable in advance. They are calculated according to the amount and duration of the credit, the destination of the exports and the kind of risks insured. They may be modified depending on the exporter, the amount insured, its geographical distribution and the number of claims. They are not subject to the normal taxes on insurance premiums. In most cases premiums range from some tenths of one per cent to rarely more than 2 per cent for short term credits and from 1 to 5 per cent for medium and long term credits.

2.2   Guarantees for banks

2.2.1   Policies available

With the agreement of OND, the proceeds of insurance policies may be assigned to the institution financing the transaction. In the case of supplier credits, such assignment may mean that from the date of delivery, OND will waive, vis–à–vis the assignee, claims which it might have made against the exporter. In many cases of so–called "special" assignments, OND has in principle recourse only to the exporter.

In the case of individual financial credits, the bank is covered by OND for the non–payment risk, while the exporter is covered for the risk of breach of contract.

2.2.2   Eligibility

Rules of acceptance are the same as those described in section 1.2 above. The bank may require the exporter to bear the risk of part of the unguaranteed portion on the understanding that it is itself required to bear a minimum of 2 per cent of risks in respect of the principal amount insured and 5 per cent of risks in respect of contractual interest payment.

2.2.3   Cost of cover

The cost of the guarantee is calculated as stated in section 1.3 above.

2.3   Other insurance programmes

2.3.1   Foreign exchange risk insurance

OND shall insure the risk of foreign currency fluctuations when the contract is payable in foreign currency and financing shall be made in Belgian francs. Such cover shall be granted only if the insured has requested an offer of cover prior to the occurence of the risk. This insurance can be obtained from the time of bid or from the time of signature of the contract. In the latter case, OND may provide cover only for contracts of more than two years of execution and OND may limit its guarantee to the payment falling due after twelve months' from signature of the contract. Realised exchange losses exceeding 3 per cent (franchise) are indemnified, and corresponding gains have to be surrendered to OND.

The premium is 1 per cent annually on the insured principal outstanding.

Cover in foreign currencies

Cover in a foreign currency may be granted in the event of default when financing is made in this currency. Most of the main convertible currencies used in international trading are eligible for this cover which is linked to the credit risk guarantee.

Pursuant thereto, OND shall choose between:

— indemnifying in foreign currency,
— indemnifying in Belgian francs converting the unpaid amount on the basis of the latest official rate quoted on the day on which the claim occurs.

The amount of the extra premium charged for this cover depends on the currency of the contract:

— either 10 % of the insurance premium for the US$ and the currencies with a higher interest rate than the BF,
— either 7 % of the insurance premium for other currencies.

2.3.2   Bond insurance

Under its bond insurance scheme, OND can offer exporters insurance against forfeiture demanded unlawfully or for political reasons of sums deposited as security in connection with tendering, completion of works or return of payments made on account. The base rate of this type of guarantee is 1 per cent, modified by a differentiated coefficient according to the nature of the bond.

2.3.3   Other Facilities

OND also covers the sequestration of equipment or goods, goods on consignment or exhibited at fairs.

3.   EXPORT FINANCE PROGRAMMES

3.1   Direct Credits

3.1.1   Type of financing available

The bulk of export financing is provided by the banking system without any official support. In addition to its insurance programmes, OND is authorised to participate directly in financing export credits. Such participation may take various forms. OND may in particular purchase or accept as collateral foreign commercial paper or make loans directly to foreign debtors. Little use has been made of its powers to provide short and medium term finance for export operations.

3.1.2   *Eligibility*

OND intervention in financing is subject to the following criteria:
— It may be used only for OND–guaranteed transactions;
— It is limited to the total of OND's capital and general reserve fund;
— It must be marginal and complementary, filling a gap in financing available from traditional sources.

Belgian government loans are tied to purchases of Belgian goods and services.

3.2   Refinancing

3.2.1   *Types of financing available*

Export credits of over two years' duration are refinanced by Creditexport. Creditexport examines applications for credit and acts on behalf of a pool of public and private credit institutions. Applications can be made by both the latter institutions and non–members of the pool. Decisions are taken by the Board of Directors.

Credits under BF 35 million are refinanced by the IRG. On request, the IRG buys from the banks, at favourable but unsubsidised rates, Creditexport bills with less than one year to run and other types of export paper with a maximum life of one hundred and twenty days, which are in principle certified by the National Bank. It may charge lower short term discount rates since it obtains a part of its funds on the market for call money, at rates that are in principle below the official discount rate. Bills discounted by IRG are for the most part within the ceilings for rediscounting set for the banks by the National Bank of Belgium.

Refinancing is obtained through normal banking channels. Official support mainly takes the form of an interest rate subsidy scheme. The following section describes the framework of financing and refinancing of Belgian exports.

Short–term export credits are provided by commercial banks at the market rates for bank overdrafts. The exporter's bank may however ask the National Bank of Belgium to certify the commercial paper, thus enabling him to benefit, when the bills are for not more than one hundred and twenty days, from the comparatively favourable financing terms offered by the Institut de Réescomte et de Garantie (IRG). IRG purchases such bills at published rates, provided that the seller still has an unused margin within its ceiling for rediscounting with the National Bank. The same procedure is used for pre–shipment credits. Bills can also be traded at a market rate.

Medium and long–term credits are mainly granted by Creditexport. Their maturity must exceed two years, and the credit must be for exports of capital goods and related services. In most cases, the credit is for a period of between three and five years, but for larger projects, post–shipment credits for up to twelve years may be granted. Both supplier and buyer credits are offered. If the credit terms offered through Creditexport do not enable an exporter to win a given contract because more favourable terms are being offered by a foreign competitor, the exporter may apply to the Ministry of Foreign Trade for an interest rate subsidy before the contract is concluded. Such a subsidy may not, in principle, reduce the interest rate below the OECD Arrangement level.

Pre-delivery financing: Financing during the manufacturing period may be provided by means of short term bank credits. These may be refinanced by IRG. When, however, Creditexport undertakes to provide finance for deferred payments, it may also agree to finance the manufacturing period on the same terms.

3.2.2   *Eligibility*

Short term credits are for up to two years, medium and long term credits have a repayment term of over two years. Creditexport's credits are offered at fixed interest rates, which automatically follow the movements in certain medium term market rates.

3.2.3   *Resulting interest rates*

The rates fixed for the duration of financing contracts are determined according to set criteria established by Creditexport. The rates are linked:

— To the yield, for the financial intermediaries, on the latest loan over five years' duration issued or directly guaranteed by the government, this yield being converted into a rate of interest payable at the end of each half year;
— To the rate charged by the Société Nationale de Crédit à l'Industrie for credits to industry, less the cost of the bank guarantee.

Since July 1988, the interest rate for credits to be reimbursed in maximum 10 half–yearly instalments is reduced by 10 basis points.

The rate fixed applies to the whole of the export credit and is usually below that prevailing on the market for medium and long term credits. The bills or promissory notes for export credits that are guaranteed by the National Bank prior to being used for refinancing at Creditexport command a lower rate. Bills may be refinanced without certification, but an additional 0.50 per cent is then charged. Even the lowest interest rate is usually well above the minimum laid down in the OECD Arrangement. The interest subsidies granted by Copromex may supplement the financing terms applied by Creditexport.

Short term credits

IRG's discount rate for commercial paper issued against export transactions is at present (August 1989) 9.15 per cent maximum for periods up to one hundred and twenty days, for exports within the E.E.C. and 8.15 per cent for exports outside the E.E.C.

In addition, a facility modelled on the Creditexport system was set up by IRG in 1978 in order to assist exports payable within one to two years. The discount rate for this type of paper is 7.65 per cent per annum (August 1989) provided that National Bank of Belgium certification is obtained. IRG acts as broker for paper that is not bankable. Transactions are then concluded at market rates (duration from one to twelve months).

For credits granted directly to a foreign debtor, a bank commission (flat) varying from 0.45 to 1.0 per cent must be added to the rates given above.

The OND premium is between 0.20 and 3.15 per cent depending on the risks covered.

Medium and long term credits

Most medium and long term export credits are financed via Creditexport, which determines the rates to be applied to them throughout their duration. The following table gives examples of the cost of export credits in November 1989:

Length of credit	from 2 to 5 years (per cent)	over 5 years
Rate applied by Creditexport (1)	8.25	8.35
Bank commission	0.45	0.45
Other charges: stamp duty, certification, commitment fee (2)	0.26	0.26

1. Rate for certified paper: interest is payable at the end of each half-year.
2. On the amount of the bill.

3.3   Other credit operations

Foreign currency transactions

OND cover may also be obtained for export contracts payable in foreign currency. A limit for any indemnity payment is nonetheless determined at the time the policy is written. Since 1972, OND has also been allowed in certain circumstances to cover exchange risks arising from contracts providing for payment in a foreign currency.

In practice, the exporter must insure his credit with OND in order to initiate Creditexport participation in the financing of the transactions; the same applies to participation of Creditexport in the financing of medium and long term export credits denominated in foreign currency.

The few contracts that are denominated in foreign currency are refinanced in Belgian francs by the pool members of Creditexport. The exchange risk is then covered by the exporter or his bank. The amount of the credit provided by Creditexport is calculated on the basis of the exchange rate ruling when the contract was concluded.

Bank acceptances in Belgian francs remitted in the course of using up the credit are then refinanced by Creditexport. The exchange risk run by the exporter because of the difference between the currency of the contract and that of the financing operation may be covered by OND. The exporter may also seek refinancing on the international capital market in the same currency as that of the contract. If this is done, the operation is not submitted to Creditexport. Credits in foreign currency may benefit from Copromex intervention in the form of stabilized rates in the same way as Belgian franc credits granted by Creditexport.

4.   AID FINANCE PROGRAMMES

4.1   Associated Financing (mixed credits)

See 1.2.1.5. above.

4.1.1   *Procedures*

ODA loans are occasionally combined with export credits — normally at the initiative of the recipient country which also identifies the projects.

Chapter 3

DENMARK

1. ORGANISATION AND STRUCTURE

1.1. Insurance and Guarantees

1.1.1 *Representative Organisation*

Organisation responsible for major part of policies issued

Eksportkreditradet (EKR) (The Export Credit Council)
Codanhus
Gl. Kongevej 60
1850 Frederiksberg C
Copenhagen

Telephone: (45 1) 31 38 35
Telex: 22910 def dk
Telefax: (45 1) 31 24 25

1.1.1.1 *Function*

EKR is a governmental council responsible to the Minister of Industry. Its operations are based on the 1960 Danish Trade Fund Act, which has been amended periodically, principally to increase its liability ceilings. Since 1960, EKR, which is an autonomous entity but responsible to the Minister of Industry, has provided insurance against the risk of non–payment of Danish exports of goods and services. Two years later, as a complement, the Ministry of Industry set up a special guarantee programme for exports to developing countries in collaboration with the Danish International Development Agency (DANIDA). In 1985, this scheme was transferred to EKR as "Section 2".

EKR receives applications and makes decisions on cover, terms and claims. The Minister of Industry has promulgated standing orders for the Export Credit Council as well as rules governing the Council's activities.

The chairman of the Council is appointed by the Queen. The Minister of Industry appoints representatives from each of the following governmental authorities, organisations, etc.: the Ministry of Industry; the Ministry of Foreign Affairs; the Ministry of

Finance; the Ministry of Fisheries; the Ministry of Agriculture; the Ministry of Housing; the Danish Central Bank; the Danish Bankers Association; the Association of Danish Savings Banks; the Agricultural Council and the Copenhagen Chamber of Commerce (representing the wholesale trade in Denmark); the Federation of Danish Small-holders' Associations (jointly); Denmark's Fishing Industry and Fish Exporters' Association; the Handicrafts Council (representing crafts and small industries); and the Economic Council of the Labour Movement. Members are appointed for four year periods.

1.1.1.2   *Summary of organisation*

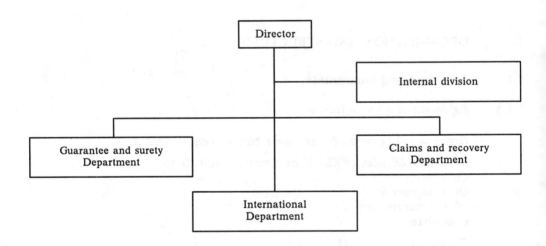

1.1.1.3   *Resources*

EKR

The law creating the EKR provided for the "Danish Trade Fund" of DKr 190 million, which was set up as a guarantee fund for the operations of EKR. As at 31st December 1988 it stood at DKr 433 million. A liability ceiling is fixed by Parliament. Presently the ceiling amounts to DKr 50 billion.

For "Section 2", the ceiling for special insurance for exports to developing countries presently amounts to DKr 30 billion.

1.1.1.4   *Other organisations involved*

The Danish Trade Fund (Danmarks Erhvervsfond) finances EKR, absorbing profits and losses after paid claims and administrative expenses. Pursuant to section 3 (5) of the Danish Trade Fund Act, the Minister of Industry appoints an *Executive Committee* consisting of the Chairman and the Deputy Chairman of the Council and representatives of the Ministry of Finance and the Ministry of Foreign Affairs.

1.1.1.5   *Relations with the State*

The Export Credit Council's decisions are final, except that matters of particular importance in the field of trade policy involving special risk may be submitted to the Minister of Industry for decision. The government is committed to make up any loss exceeding the means of the "Danish Trade Fund".

1.1.1.6   *Relations with the private sector*

The H–Guarantee scheme (see 2.1.1) is administered by private banks on behalf of EKR.

1.2   **Export Finance**

1.2.1   *Representative organisation*

Dansk Eksportfinansieringsfond (Danish Export Finance Corporation) (DEFC)
La Cours Vej 7
DK– 2000 Frederiksberg

Telephone: (45) 38 33 18 88
Telex: 15070 FIH DK
Telefax: (45) 38 33 26 66

1.2.1.1   *Function*

DEFC was established on 19th March 1975 by Danmarks Nationalbank (the Central Bank of Denmark), Den Danske Bankforening (The Danish Bankers' Association) an Danmarks Sparekasseforeining (The Danish Savings Banks' Association).

DEFC's purpose is to provide medium and long term credit facilities for the export of capital goods (excepts ships) manufactured in Denmark and for the export of services and technical expertise provided by Danish entities.

DEFC was established as part of the Danish government's programme to provide finance for Danish industry. Management of DEFC has been entrusted to one of the principal promoters of this programme, Finansieringsinstituttet for Industri og Handvaerk A/S (Finance for Danish Industry A/S).

1.2.1.2   *Summary organisation chart*

Not available.

1.2.1.3   *Resources*

The funds needed for DEFC's financing activities are provided by the Central Bank at a preferential rate and by borrowing on international markets.

On 31st December 1988, DEFC's borrowing totalled DKr 6 049 million, all of which are foreign loans taken up as bank loans or private placements:

Currency	Amount DKr million	%
SF	991	16
DM	2 612	43
JY	674	11
US$	1 772	30
	6 049	100

1.2.1.4   Relations with the State

Although DEFC is self–governing, it is a part of the official programme for export promotion.

1.2.1.5   Relations with the private sector

Applications for and disbursements and repayments of credits financed by DEFC must be channelled through Danish commercial or savings banks.

1.2.2   Danmarks Skibskreditfond (The Ship Credit Fund of Denmark) and its subsidiary,

Aktieselskabet Dansk Skibsfinansiering (Danish Ship Finance Ltd.)
205 Klampenborgvej
DK–2800 Lyngby

Telephone: (45) 42 93 20 20
Telex: 16757 fond DK
Telefax: (45) 42 88 84 33

1.2.2.1   Function

The Danmarks Skibskreditfond (SCFD) was established on 6th June 1961 for the financing of the building, purchase or sale of ships.

1.2.2.2   Summary organisation chart

Not available.

1.2.2.3   Resources

There is no ceiling imposed on the amount of available funds. Loans are financed by bonds issued by Danmarks Skibskreditfond. The bonds are purchased by Danmarks Nationalbank at par less a commission of 5 per cent for the time being paid by the Ship Credit Fund to Danmarks Nationalbank.

1.3   Aid finance

The aid programme is administered by the Danish International Development Agency (DANIDA).

2.   INSURANCE AND GUARANTEE PROGRAMMES

2.1   Cover for Exporters

2.1.1   *Policies available*

Cover from *EKR* is normally available from date of shipment, although in certain cases the manufacturing period can be covered. Cover is available for short–term for individual buyers covering shipments within a 12 month period at a time within a preset maximum, or as general insurance (comprehensive guarantee) covering all claims on an exporter's foreign customers. For longer credit terms cover is available for the individual transaction. Cover includes commercial and political risks, but cover for individual buyers or transactions may be issued as cover for political risks only.

An application for insurance covering the post–shipment risk must reach EKR by the time of shipment. If an exporter wants to cover his pre–shipment during the manufacturating period, he must submit his application by the time the contract is signed.

— Insurance covering commercial post–shipment risks

Commercial risks covered are the buyer's insolvency, his failure to pay within six months of maturity or losses due to the buyer's refusal to take delivery of the goods (repudiation). Compensation is paid as soon as the amount of the loss has been ascertained. It amounts to 80 per cent or 90 per cent of the loss depending on the type of policy (the percentage may be reduced where the commercial risks are greater).

— Cover against political post–shipment risks

Political risks covered are primarily claims that are not settled because of political or economic circumstances beyond the control of buyers and sellers alike. It covers inter alia obstacles to payment transfers, a general moratorium, expropriation and similar government action, imposition of quantitative import restrictions or cancellation of previously issued import licences. In addition, losses caused by war, civil war, revolution or similar unrest abroad and losses arising out of an export embargo imposed in Denmark or revocation of an export licence granted previously are also covered.

Compensation is paid six months after due date, and is 80 per cent or 90 per cent depending on the type of policy and on the risk classification of the buyer country. (The percentage may be lower for high–risk countries).

— General insurance (comprehensive guarantees)

This type of combined guarantee covers commercial as well as political risks and, in principle, all claims on goods sold on credit terms not exceeding three hundred and sixty days for an exporter's foreign customers in countries in category 1, 2 and 3 (out of 4). Another characteristic feature of this policy is that prior approval of the foreign buyer by EKR is not required for transactions within the exporter's individual preset risk ceiling, (normally between DKr 100.000 and 500.000 for buyers in an OECD-member country). Subject to prior approval by EKR, a higher maximum may be fixed for individual customers; in such cases, however, the exporter must submit separate applications for any amounts above the preset maximum. Compensation is 90 per cent within the maximum.

The scheme is presently under review.

— Quick short term cover (H guarantees)

This guarantee is issued by the banks on behalf of EKR and simplifies the processing of applications for individual commercial and political cover. The applicant must have a good credit report on the buyer, the credit period must not exceed one hundred and eighty days and the maximum credit amount is DKr 500.000 otherwise. Compensation is 80 per cent.

— Insurance covering risks both before and after shipment (contract guarantees)

Contracts for major capital goods that are made to meet a buyer's special needs and that, consequently, cannot be sold or are difficult to sell to other buyers, may be covered for the period of manufacturing as well as the period of credit, if any. Normally, it is a condition for cover of pre–shipment risks that the buyer makes a downpayment with the order. A contract guarantee covers the same risks as those indicated above.

Claims after shipment are paid according to the invoice value; before shipment, they are made up according to the direct and indirect costs of production. Thus, if a loss occurs before shipment, the exporter's profit is not covered.

— Cover for sales to public buyers (S guarantees)

No distinction can be made between commercial and political risks in the case of sales made to public authorities (unlike sales to private buyers). "S" guarantees therefore cover losses arising from political or economic conditions in the buyer's country. The compensation percentage is similar to that for political risk cover.

— Insurance covering risks in connection with services and civil engineering projects

A policy issued for performance of services covers losses that arise from work performed and are attributable to commercial or political risks. Claims are paid according to the invoiced amount outstanding less counterclaims, guarantees and agent's commission.

A contractor's policy covers losses due to commercial or political reasons, after contract signature, arising from non–completion of the contract project and from failure to deliver materials and equipment or to make or authorize contractual payments. The cover includes transfer and re–export obstacles for or seizure of local bank deposits and temporarily imported equipment necessary for the contracted work.

Before completion and final delivery of a project, a contractor's policy covers direct and indirect costs including cost of demobilisation of personnel and organisation plus profit calculated in proportion to the invoiced part of the sum of the contract less payments received. After completion and final delivery of a project, claims are paid according to the invoiced amount outstanding.

2.1.2 *Eligibility*

— Nationality requirements

The Export Credit Council normally covers only Danish goods and services. Cover is available for foreign goods in special cases where no competition with Danish goods is involved, e.g. in subcontracting of services. Commercial risks cannot be insured if the buyer is or may be regarded as an affiliate of the Danish exporter or if the buyer is otherwise financially dependent on the exporter. If, however, the Danish parent company covers only a limited part of the capital of the subsidiary company, commercial risks may be covered to a certain extent. Political risks in connection with export to a foreign subsidiary can be covered with the normal per cent of cover. Policies are issued only to firms domiciled in Denmark.

EKR has agreements with EKN (Sweden), GIEK (Norway) and VTL (Finland) on reciprocal treatment of foreign content.

— Credit conditions

Consumer goods to one hundred and eighty days; capital goods up to five years but longer in the case of ships and officially supported foreign competition. Credit conditions to comply with the Arrangement on Guidelines for Officially Supported Export Credits. Local costs payment can in principle be insured in accordance with the Arrangement rules. Local costs thus covered are also eligible for financing with the Dansk Eksportfinansieringsfond. Minimum loan amount for buyer's credit DKr 10 million. Acceptance of business is subject to satisfactory creditworthiness of buyer/country as shown by exporters' reports and eventual EKR investigation. A public or local bank guarantee may be required as supplementary security.

— Section 2

Cover is provided for larger export transactions to developing countries. In extending cover creditworthiness criteria are somewhat less stringent than those applied by EKR under Section 1. Conditions comply with the Arrangement on Guidelines for Officially Supported Export Credits. Minimum order amount is DKr 10 million. Credit lengths are between six and ten years. Local costs payments can in principle be guaranteed in accordance with the Arrangement rules. Local costs thus covered are also eligible for financing with Dansk Eksportfinansieringsfond. The percentage of cover is 95. Central Bank or similar guarantee is always required.

2.1.3 *Cost of cover*

Premiums are payable on the value of the credit and vary according to the risks covered, the securities offered, the length of credit, the type of buyer, and the creditworthiness of the buyer/country. EKR classifies countries in four categories. Some examples of the premia are: the premium charged for insuring an individual transaction against commercial and political post–shipment risks varies normally between 0.40

and 1.40 per cent of the maximum outstanding amount covered for terms of credit up to and including one year. For political risks, the premium for a guarantee is between 0.15 and 0.90 per cent for credit periods of up to and including one year. For a transaction with 5 years of credit the premium will normally range between 1.47 and 4.45 per cent on a private buyer and 0.95 and 3.92 per cent on a public buyer depending on the risk classification of the buying country. (For Section 2 guarantees, similar premiums are charged).

2.2   Guarantees for banks

2.2.1   *Policies available*

— Guarantees for financing

EKR insurance may, with its approval, be transferred to a financing institution to enable financing of the covered portion of the transaction. The maximum percentage of guarantee is 90 per cent for commercial risks with 65 per cent as a minimum. Political risk cover attains 90 per cent but may be 85 per cent in the case of poorer country risks. The coverage may be raised by 5 per cent if the party taking out the guarantee, i.e. the bank, does not stipulate recourse to the exporter (the beneficiary).

Guarantees issued under *Section 2* in the framework of the programme for developing countries provide for 95 per cent cover of the commercial and political risks.

Reimbursement under the documentary credit will normally be effected not later than one hundred and eighty days after payment . EKR may, however, guarantee documentary credits with longer periods to reimbursement, if this is justified by the description of the goods or the terms of payment.

— Guarantees to banks for loans to foreign buyers (financial/buyer credit guarantees)

This type of guarantee covers non–payment for any reason other than faults of the party for whom the guarantee was issued. Liability under such guarantees cannot take effect until payments are made under the loan for shipments or work performed.

Contracts may be financed for delivery of Danish capital goods — e.g. machinery, complete manufacturing plant, civil engineering projects, etc. — and related services. The borrowing requirement, i.e. the amount of the order less prepayment, must be for not less than DKr. 10 million and the credit period must not be less than five years.

A buyer credit guarantee may be issued to a Danish bank even if the latter, through membership of an international consortium of lenders, bears the risk of only a minor part of the whole loan, provided that the Danish bank manages the loan on behalf of all the lenders. Exchange rate losses are generally not covered by this type of guarantee, but loans contracted in a foreign currency shall be repaid at the rate of exchange quoted on the date of maturity. A buyer credit guarantee may cover up to 90 per cent of the guaranteed amount in default. The cover may be increased to 95 per cent if the borrower is a bank approved by EKR.

Section 2 guarantees for exports to developing countries are issued for specific contracts. The contract usually involves capital goods on relatively long credit terms. Cover for buyer credits under credit lines is also available.

— Guarantees to banks for credit lines (credit line guarantees)

This type of guarantee may be issued in connection with credit lines established to finance exports of Danish capital goods and related Danish services sold on credit for periods of two years or longer. The credit line must have been established under a credit ceiling agreement concluded by EKR with authorities of the borrower's country. The credit line must also have been established under a loan contract approved in advance by EKR. The guarantee covers the same risks as those referred to above (financial/buyer credit guarantees). Cover is 90 or 85 per cent, depending on EKR's classification of the borrower's country.

— Guarantees with recourse

Guarantees may be issued for export loans serving as operational credit. This type of guarantee is intended to supplement the normal credit facilities available to exporters in Danish banks and may be issued as risk–sharing with the lending bank. In addition to other finance, exporters may thus obtain bank loans secured by guarantees.

Such guarantees can be:

— *Shipment credit guarantees*, to cover a credit for the time between shipment and payment;
— *Manufacturing guarantees*, to cover a credit for the time between manufacturing and payment;
— *Loans for potential exports*, to cover a credit for potential exports, e.g. in the case of seasonal adjustment of export production, manufacturing of stocks for rapid execution of export orders as well as cases where the exports consist of a large number of small orders.
— *Guarantees for special purpose loans*, examples being:

In the case of exports of major projects and related services, the buyer may require the exporter to contribute part of the buyer's risk capital, i.e. to enter into a joint venture with the buyer. If the exporter can submit evidence to show that a capital contribution to such a joint venture is a necessary condition for the export transaction, EKR may guarantee loans to finance the capital contribution.

In the case of exports of ships, EKR may issue a guarantee for financing both the building period and the credit period. Such guarantees will normally be issued to Denmark's Ship Credit Fund.

2.3   Other insurance programmes

2.3.1   *Exchange risk cover*

EKR offers two types of cover for foreign currency risk to Danish exporters holding contracts with payment in a major foreign currency acceptable to EKR.

— Foreign exchange risk insurance

For Danish exporters refinancing themselves in DKr EKR offers an exchange risk insurance scheme covering all yields exceeding a margin of + 3 per cent, from contractual commitment until actual dates of payments, for payments due more than one year from commitment. However the terms of credit must exceed two years. The premium, 0,7 per cent per annum, is due on date of the issue of the guarantee.

— Supplementary exchange risk guarantee

For Danish exporters refinancing themselves in the contracted foreign currency EKR offers a supplementary guarantee scheme insuring payment of compensation from EKR under a nonpayment cover at the official rate of exchange on the date the compensation become due. The premium is a surcharge to the cover premium. As examples are the surcharges 10 per cent for credit terms of one year, and 30 per cent for credit terms of five years.

2.3.2   Bond insurance

Bid bonds, prepayment bonds and performance bonds can be insured. Bid bond guarantees cover unjustified calling of the bond. The bonds must contain a date of validity. The cover is 90 per cent. The premium charged for such guarantees is 0.14 per cent per quarter. The degree of utilisation has been steadily growing as more and more countries are demanding bonds.

2.3.3   Counter guarantees

When an exporter who makes a bid for a contract with a foreign buyer is required to provide a bid bond or who, in connection with an export contract, is required to give a guarantee for prepayment or a performance bond, the Export Credit Council may issue a guarantee covering the Danish banker's guarantee.

3.   EXPORT FINANCE PROGRAMMES

3.1   Direct Credits

There is no programme for direct credits.

3.2   Refinancing

3.2.1   Types of contract available

DEFC finances exports by lending to Danish exporters or financial institutions against the security of their claims on buyers or financial institutions abroad. Export credits to suppliers account for approximately 28 per cent of the Corporation's loan portfolio, as at December 31st, 1988. In special cases, the Corporation may purchase exporters' claims against foreign importers or foreign banks.

3.2.2   Eligibility

Financing by DEFC is normally conditional upon the following terms:
1) The credit conditions must be in compliance with the Arrangement on Guidelines for Officially Supported Export Credits;
2) The exports must be capital goods (except ships) produced in Denmark or services provided by Danish entities;

3) The terms of payment must be customary for the merchandise in question;

4) The export credit must be repaid in equal semi–annual, quarterly or monthly instalments;

5) The maturity of the export credit must exceed two years but not four years.

6) The total contract price less advance payment must exceed DKr 500 000.

DEFC finances exports by means of buyer credits granted directly to importers abroad or to the buyer's bank. As at december 31st, 1988, buyer credits accounted for approximately 65 per cent of the balance of DEFC's loan portfolio, and refinancing from the banks 7 per cent. Buyer credits are normally extended in connection with export contracts in excess of DKr 10 million. The extent of coverage is as follows:

Pre–shipment financing (only by the banks) of the exporter may be covered to 100 per cent by EKR under guarantee with recourse, within a financial need not exceeding 75 per cent of the order amount. Pre–shipment guarantees are available for 85 to 90 per cent from EKR. Financing is granted for the manufacture of Danish exports of products whose normal credit period exceeds six months.

Post–shipment financing is granted for exports of Danish produced capital goods and covered for 85 or 95 per cent by guarantees from EKR. The residual guarantee coverage comes from banks, when DEFC finances.

3.2.3   *Resulting interest rates*

The Danish bank interest rate as at end–August 1989 were : 8,5 to 10,0 per cent per annum for Danish kroner. LIBOR plus 1 to 1.5 per cent per annum for other currencies. DEFC interest rate: Arrangement rates to which should be added the premium for EKR and the guarantee commission for the bank guarantee. There is no commitment fee, but a management fee of 1/4 per cent for supplier credits and 5/8 per cent for buyer credits are charged for medium and long post–shipment financing. A stamp duty of 3 pro mille is charged for short term credits. Loans from DEFC are not liable to stamp duty.

3.3   **Interest subsidies**

There is no instrument for interest rate subsidies.

3.4   **Other credit operations**

3.4.1   *Foreign currency transactions*

Most of DEFC's loans are normally denominated in Danish kroner, but in some cases loans are denominated in other currencies. On 31st December 1988, the Corporation's currency loans amounted to 2.1 per cent of its disbursed portfolio.

3.4.2   *The Ship Credit Fund of Denmark (SCFD) loans*

SCFD issues special bonds which the builder (borrower) can sell within a certain time limit to the Danmarks Nationalbank at par. The Ship Credit Fund may finance vessels contracted by foreign shipowners at Danish yards in accordance with the terms of the OECD Understanding on Export Credits for Ships. These OECD loans can cover up to 80 per cent of the building price with an amortization period of 8 1/2 years and an interest rate of 8 per cent per annum.

In order to meet intensified international competition among shipyards, especially in financing, it is possible under the rules of the Understanding to offer matching loans in cases where a shipyard runs a risk of losing an export order because the foreign owner from a third country has been offered officially subsidised financing which is more favourable than the current OECD terms. Whether matching will take place is decided by the Ministry of Industry on a case by case basis.

The Ship Credit Fund receives insurance coverage where needed. The fund may also contribute to the financing of conversion of vessels at Danish yards if conversion considerably increases the net tonnage of the vessel or substantially changes its nature. It is not possible to provide general information on borrowing facilities and terms in connection with the financing of conversions.

Combination loans

To supplement loans given on OECD terms, the Ship Credit Fund is able to offer owners domiciled within the EEC contracting at Danish shipyards combination loans in Danish kroner of up to 80 per cent of the contract price along the following lines.

- For contracts concluded before the end of 1989 with delivery before the end of 1991, 14 year index–linked loans with 4 years' grace may be granted of 60 per cent of the contract price as well as an 8 1/2 year OECD loan of 20 per cent of the contract price.
- For contracts concluded before the end of 1990 with delivery before the end of 1992, 14 year index–linked loans with 4 years' grace may be granted of 45 per cent of the contract price as well as an 8 1/2 year OECD loan of 35 per cent of the contract price.

Discount loans

Loans to finance building, rebuildings or purchases of secondhand vessels that are not in accordance with the Understanding can be advanced as discount loans.

These loans are repayable in six monthly equal instalments over a maximum of eight and a half years at the most at an interest rate of 8 per cent per annum to be paid to the Ship Credit Fund. As the bonds issued in these cases are to be sold on ordinary market conditions, a loss on the sale of the bonds must be allowed for, thus bringing the net yield of the loans to a level with the market value prevailing at the time of sale.

4.   AID FINANCE PROGRAMMES

4.1   Associated Financing

4.1.1   Funds available

If a recipient country requests financial assistance for a project that cannot be financed solely by ODA, the Danish authorities will draw the attention of the recipient country to the possibility of combining aid with export credits. In this case, DANIDA administers the ODA component and appraises the project to be financed. The recipient country negotiates and concludes the contract with the supplier under its own responsibility; however, the contract is subject to approval by DANIDA, which can thus check prices and conditions.

Danish aid may also be part of co–financing arrangements with international development finance institutions.

4.1.2   *Eligibility*

Only creditworthy developing countries with a per capita GNP of less than $1 290 in 1987 are eligible for associated financing, and the contract value of a transaction must be at least $3 million. Matching is excluded.

4.1.3   *Resulting terms and interest rates*

For such low–income countries, the ODA component shall be a loan covering 40 per cent of the transaction.

Chapter 4

FRANCE

1. ORGANISATION AND STRUCTURE

1.1 Insurance and Guarantees

1.1.1 *Representative organisation*

Compagnie Française d'Assurance pour le Commerce Extérieur (COFACE)
12 Cours Michelet
La Défense 10, Cédex 51
92065 Paris La Défense

Telephone: (33 1) 4902 2000
Telex: 614884 F
Telefax:

1.1.1.1 *Function*

The formulation of government policy and the coordination of official support in this area are the province of the Direction des Relations économiques extérieures (DREE — External Economic Relations Directorate) of the Ministry of Economic Affairs and Finance.

The Compagnie Française d'Assurance pour le Commerce Extérieur (COFACE), set up in 1946, is a semi–public, joint stock company. It covers short term commercial risks on its own account, while operating the medium and short term credit insurance service on behalf of the government, though in this latter case only for major transactions or insurance against political risks.

1.1.1.2 *Summary of organisation*

Governing board

— Chairman Managing Director
— Director General
— Deputy Director General

— General Financial Control
— Technical Studies Department
— Legal Department

Technical Directorates

— Short term
— Medium term
— Market development insurance

Operational Directorates and Departments

— Marketing and Communications
— Public Relations and Administration
— Finance and Development.

1.1.1.3 *Resources*

COFACE's capital, totalling FF 10 million, is held by the Caisse des Dépôts et Consignations, the Crédit National, the Banque Française du Commerce Extérieur (BFCE), the Société Française d'Assurance pour Favoriser le Crédit and the major nationalised banks and insurance companies.

1.1.1.4 *Other organisations involved*

The Director of External Economic Relations of the Ministry of Economic Affairs and Finance is advised by the Commission des Garanties et du Crédit au Commerce Extérieur (CGCE). The CGCE is made up of representatives from the Ministry of Economic Affairs and Finance, the Ministry of Foreign Affairs, the relevant technical ministries, the Banque de France, COFACE and BFCE.

1.1.1.5 *Relations with the state*

COFACE keeps separate sets of accounts for two types of business. For short term transactions covered by COFACE on its own behalf (short term commercial risk), the French Treasury gives COFACE excess–of–loss cover in consideration of an annual payment of 0.5 per cent of the premiums received. For these short term risks, COFACE is free to make decisions up to a certain ceiling.

For all other risks, COFACE acts on behalf of the government up to the country risk ceilings that may be set each year; decisions are taken by the Director of External Economic Relations of the Ministry of Economic Affairs and Finance upon receipt of a concurring opinion from the CGCE. Some powers of decision, however, have been delegated to COFACE.

1.2   Export Finance

1.2.1   *Representative organisation*

Banque Française du Commerce Extérieur (BFCE)
21 Boulevard Haussmann
75009 PARIS

1.2.1.1   *Function*

The government participates in the financing of export credits with maturities over two years through the BFCE in order to stabilise the financing cost of credits granted in francs or foreign exchange.

In France, export credit financing involves close co-operation between the commercial banks and two public institutions: the BFCE and COFACE (see section 1.1). Like COFACE, the BFCE acts both on its own behalf, and is hence subject to general banking rules, and on behalf of the government, either as the manager of the stabilisation mechanism, when this is applied, or as the direct supplier of credits with maturities exceeding seven years for countries in Consensus Categories II and III.

1.2.1.2   *Summary organisation chart*

Not available.

1.2.1.3   *Resources*

The BFCE raises the necessary resources on national and international financial markets. The government provides surety and, if need be, a subsidy.

Private banks draw the necessary funds from their normal resources, either from the surplus of deposits on credits arranged or raised on the French money market or on national and international financial markets.

1.2.1.4   *Other organisations involved*

Not applicable.

1.2.1.5   *Relations with the state*

Responsibility for framing government export credit policy and coordinating official assistance in this area lies with the Directorate for External Economic Relations (DREE) of the Ministry of Economic Affairs and Finance.

1.3   Aid Finance

The Ministry for Co-operation is responsible for capital grants and technical assistance to some 40 independent countries in sub-Saharan Africa, the Indian Ocean and the Caribbean. ODA loans to these countries (and a few others) are administered by the Caisse centrale de coopération économique (CCCE). ODA to countries not covered by the CCCE is extended by the "Trésor" (Treasury) in the Ministry of Economic Affairs and Finance.

2.   INSURANCE AND GUARANTEE PROGRAMMES

2.1   Cover for Exporters

2.1.1   *Terms of cover*

COFACE offers a wide range of insurance schemes covering commercial and political risks, both during the period of manufacture and the period of the credit. COFACE insurance policies are always conditional (compensation is paid only if damage through one of the risks covered occurs) and the proportion covered is always less than 100 per cent.

For heavy capital goods and major projects, the insurance provided by COFACE takes the form of individual policies covering commercial and political risks. For all these policies, the proportion covered in the case of supplier credits is 85 per cent for commercial risks and 90 per cent for political risks. In the case of buyer credits, it is 95 per cent for all risks.

For mass–produced light manufactured goods, there are two possibilities: a comprehensive policy covering commercial and political risks, leaving the exporter nonetheless free to decide the country of destination to be covered by the guarantee, or an open policy covering political risks and, if required, commercial risks. In both cases, the proportion covered is usually 90 per cent for political risks and 85 per cent for commercial risks. Cover of commercial risks may be raised to 90 per cent where the transaction is guaranteed by a bank approved by COFACE.

Insurance for exports of *consumer goods, raw materials and equipment* is usually given by COFACE on its own account rather than on behalf of the government. A short term comprehensive policy exists for short term credits up to six months. For certain heavy capital goods (e.g. lorries) this cover may be given for up to two years. The maximum proportion covered in the case of commercial and political risks combined is 90 per cent, whereas for commercial risks alone, cover is limited to 85 per cent. If cover of political risks alone is requested, COFACE permits the insured party to select the countries to be covered.

Normally, the insurance or the guarantee covers post–shipment risks, but there are special provisions for pre–delivery financing, especially in connection with capital goods requiring substantial manufacturing lead times.

In accordance with the rules of the Arrangement, the best terms for private credits guaranteed by COFACE are in principle the following:

— Repayment period
  — For heavy capital goods and major projects: five years for developed countries, eight and a half years for intermediate countries and ten years for developing countries (unless otherwise specified);
  — For consumer goods: six months.
— Repayment of principal in *equal half yearly instalments* with no grace period.
— Generally, *minimum cash payments* of 15 per cent. This may be increased up to 20 or 25 per cent depending on the country and the buyer.

— *Local costs* are covered and financed up to the amount of the cash payments and on the same terms as the export credit for the portion that may be repatriated. Assistance with local costs is provided only in exceptional cases and in accordance with the Arrangement.

2.1.2   *Eligibility*

— Criteria for accepting cover

In principle, premiums for individual policies are calculated on a case by case basis according to a scale which, for each type of risk covered (manufacture, credit, cover of the bid and performance bond, company supplies), embodies such parameters as the buyer's standing, the country and the period of guarantee.

— Nationality requirements

Transactions insured by COFACE may, in principle, include a foreign content equivalent of up to 40 per cent of the contract value provided the foreign component originates from another EEC country. Foreign content originating from a non EEC country may constitute up to 30 per cent of the total contract price if there is a reciprocal agreement between France and that country, otherwise a maximum of 10 per cent is allowed.

2.1.3   *Cost of cover*

In the case of cover against political risk during the period of the credit for a private buyer, the premium for a five year credit may be from 0.67 per cent to 2.96 per cent of the amount of the credit depending on country risk. If application is also made for cover against commercial risk for the same credit, the premium may be from 1.34 per cent to 5.54 per cent.

2.2   Guarantees for Banks

COFACE may issue guarantees to French exporters or to resident or non–resident credit institutions financing French exports. French exporters generally receive supplier credit terms; i.e., during the construction period, 85 per cent cover and during the credit period, 85 per cent commercial risk and 90 per cent commercial risk cover. Institutions that extend buyer credits usually receive 95 per cent cover. COFACE may also guarantee financing raised on international bond markets when exports of French goods and services are concerned. The guarantee is then issued to the borrowing institution and covers the repayment of the credit accorded to the foreign buyer, provided this credit is in conformity with the general provisions of the Consensus.

In certain circumstances, COFACE can agree to private insurers covering the portion that it itself does not guarantee, when this portion is smaller than that specified under ordinary law (provided that the total amount guaranteed does not exceed that which would have been covered by COFACE if it had not accorded a reduction).

2.3   Other Insurance Programmes

2.3.1   *Foreign exchange risk insurance*

French exports may be denominated in foreign currencies. At end June 1986, outstanding amounts in foreign currency accounted for 8 per cent of total export credits. For this reason, COFACE offers exchange risk insurance, which is, however, subsidiary to that obtained on the forward market.

A French exporter may apply for exchange risk insurance only when he is unable to negotiate a contract denominated in French francs and cannot fully cover the transaction on the forward market. Exchange risk insurance is available with or without COFACE credit insurance. Realised exchange losses may then be compensated by COFACE; but it equally receives any foreign exchange gains that may accrue. There is no ceiling on the amount paid out. The guarantee covers the period between the date of tender and that of the contract's entry into force (supply guarantee) or the period between the signing of the contract and its entry into force (signature guarantee). The insurance is valid for a period of twelve or six months, at the exporter's choice.

Most of the main convertible currencies can be covered by COFACE. The premium comprises a flat rate sum, payable for all types of contracts and ranging from 0.2 per cent to 0.4 per cent of the amount insured and a pro rata temporis premium of 0.6 per cent per year.

2.3.2   *Cost escalation insurance*

There are two cost escalation insurance schemes: a general scheme and a special scheme applying to shipbuilding. The former is operated by COFACE, while the latter is administered by the Ministry of Industry. Both schemes operate according to similar rules.

Cover is granted during the production period and is limited to products requiring a manufacturing lead time of at least one year. Actual cost increases are compensated above a threshold that is reviewed annually in the light of expected inflation. The threshold is currently 4.35 per cent per year. The premium is 1.15 per cent per year.

In 1977, the claims procedure was tightened up by basing the main part of the claim calculations on a range of indices reflecting actual production costs rather than on the wage index previously used. In 1986, the insurance base was widened to include optional cover for subcontracting originated in other EEC member countries.

2.3.3   *Bond insurance*

Performance bonds are guaranteed by COFACE under its standard credit insurance policy and on the same terms as the latter; COFACE normally covers the exporter against unjustified calling.

Bid and performance bonds are issued by banks, insurance companies and an association of insurance companies (SOFRASCAU). COFACE guarantees the bonds but retains right of recourse against the exporter.

3.   EXPORT FINANCE PROGRAMMES

3.1   **Direct Credits**

Not applicable.

3.2   **Refinancing**

N/A.

3.3   **Interest Subsidies**

3.3.1   *Types of contract available*

Two separate procedures, depending on the term of the credits, apply to export credit financing. Credits for periods of between two and seven years are treated as medium term credits and those for a period of more than seven years as long term credits. Short term credits are not extended on concessional terms and are entirely financed and refinanced by commercial banks at market rates.

Medium term export credits and the medium term portion of long term credits financed in French francs are stabilised by the BFCE on behalf of the Treasury. Long term credits in French francs or foreign currencies are financed by the BFCE either, in the case of supplier credits, through refinancing by banks discounting the commercial claim or, in the case of buyer credits, by direct financing.

3.3.2   *Eligibility*

Entitlement is confined to exports to non EEC countries.

3.3.3   *Resulting interest rates*

The BFCE compensates the difference between a reference rate (TRIBOR) to which is added the current bank margin and the cost of financing (the "taux de sortie") in accordance with the Arrangement. This stabilisation system is symmetrical since the BFCE recoups any gains from refinancing; it is also optional, with the bank free to decide whether to exercise this option before the credit is first used.

The cost of financing (the "taux de sortie") for medium and long term credit varies depending on whether or not the rate is officially subsidised:

— In the case of medium or long term French franc credits for Consensus Category II (post–shipment period only) and Category III countries, or foreign currency credits for all categories, irrespective of the currency in which they are denominated, the cost is the rate applicable under the Arrangement, including the bank margin, to which should be added the credit guarantee premium and the initial commission and management charges levied by the banks;

— In the case of medium or long term French franc credits (for the pre–shipment period) for Category I and Category II countries, the banks receive no official financing subsidy and are free to set the interest rate at the level they deem appropriate. The cost of the credit hence depends on that rate, to which should be added a margin, the credit guarantee premium, the initial commission and management charges.

Short term credits are generally extended at rates akin to money market rates or the bank base rate (which corresponds to the "prime rate") plus an average of 1 per cent for bank charges and the cost of the COFACE premium when these credits are insured. The base rate is adjusted fairly frequently. In September 1986, it stood at 9.60 per cent.

3.4   Other Credit Operations

Commercial banks and exporters are permitted to extend credits denominated in a foreign currency. Since 1983, these credits may be stabilised by the BFCE on behalf of the government; this stabilisation offsets the difference between a reference rate (PIBOR), increased by the prevailing bank margin, and the cost of financing in line with the Arrangement. Since here too the procedure is symmetrical, the refinancing gains are again recouped. At end June 1986, outstanding amounts in foreign currency accounted for 8 per cent of total export credits.

4.   AID FINANCE PROGRAMMES

4.1   Associated Financing (mixed credits)

Funds from the Treasury are generally associated with officially guaranteed private export credits under a scheme for mixed credits that was established in the early 1960s. Mixed credits are extended under agreements ("protocoles") negotiated with the recipient government, which fix the amount and terms of aid available, as well as the purpose (list of projects) and, where appropriate, the respective shares of aid funds and export credits.

The Treasury funds the development aid component on concessional terms. The private credit is extended on Arrangement terms. The ratio of the two parts (Treasury/private) ranges from 30 to 55 per cent and up to 65 per cent for the least developed countries. The overall grant element of these tied aid credits must be in line with the Arrangement guidelines. The BFCE administers the private credit portion on behalf of the commercial banks and specifies the financial conditions.

In principle, mixed credits cannot be used for matching purposes, because their terms and conditions are settled by the protocoles before the offers of competing foreign exporters are known. Projects are appraised by the Treasury in consultation with other parts of the French administration, based on reports from French diplomatic posts. Developmental criteria are applied during this process. Funds involved are tied to procurement in France but can, in certain cases, be used to finance local costs.

4.2   Integrated Credits

In response to requests by some recipient countries, the Treasury has begun to extend single credits as "monobloc" loans. This scheme combines budget funds and market resources in a single loan package put together jointly by le Crédit national and the BFCE. Criteria and procedures for appraising projects and taking decisions are essentially the same as for traditional mixed credits. The Treasury is responsible for the negotiation of the credit with the recipient country. The monobloc loan is tied to procurement of goods from France in the same way as a mixed credit. The intention is to extend such loans only exceptionally.

4.3   Other Tied or Partially Untied Aid

The Caisse Centrale de Coopération Economique (CCCE) provides concessional loans to some 40 independent countries in sub–Saharan Africa, the Indian Ocean and the Caribbean, which are funded from the official development aid budget, as well as commercial loans at Arrangement terms. It also provides mixed credits, which combine both types of loan. The CCCE also cofinances development aid projects in association with the various international financial institutions.

Chapter 5

GERMANY

1. ORGANISATION AND STRUCTURE

1.1 Insurance and Guarantees

1.1.1 *Representative organisation*

Consortium consisting of:

Hermes Kreditversicherungs–Aktiengesellschaft
(Leading partner in the consortium)
Postfach 50 07 40
D–2000 Hamburg 50

Telephone: (49 40) 887...(0)
Telex: 212631–90
Telefax: 887 9175

Treuarbeit Aktiengesellschaft–
Wirtschaftsprüfungsgesellschaft–
Steuerberatungsgesellschaft
Address: as above

1.1.1.1 *Function*

Under the official export credit insurance scheme[1], the federal government carries both the political and the commercial risks. A mandatary consortium is authorised to provide and manage the insurance business in the name and for the account of the government. This consortium consists of a private insurance corporation, Hermes Kreditversicherungs AG (Hermes) — the leading partner in the consortium — and Treuarbeit AG — a corporation in which public bodies hold a minority stake.

Applications for cover are first checked and processed by the mandatory consortium. Hermes normally evaluates and takes decisions itself on applications covering a value of up to DM 2 million, based on guidelines of an Interministerial Committee for Export Guarantees (see 1.1.1.4). On larger contracts, decisions are taken by the Federal Ministry of Economics after discussion in the Interministerial Committee.

---

1. Treuarbeit maintains a separate scheme for intra–German transactions, which mainly corresponds to the rules of the German insurance scheme.

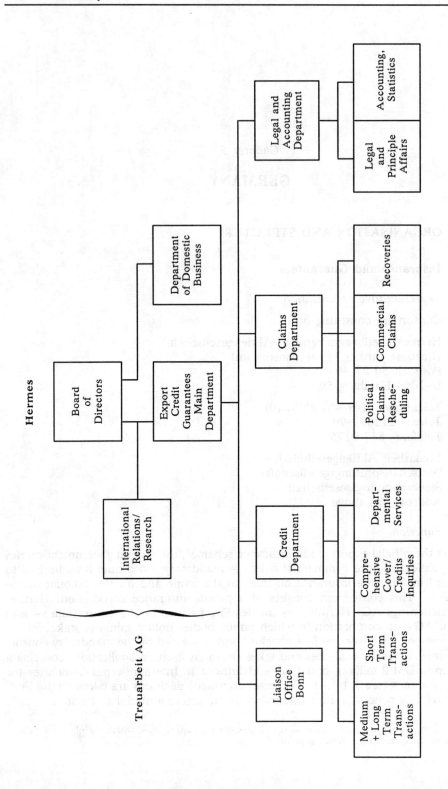

Before conclusion of an export contract, the Federal Ministry of Economics is prepared to give its provisional opinion on the prospects for providing cover, on the understanding that the factual and legal situation remains unchanged. After the conclusion of the contract at the conditions approved by Hermes, the exporter may apply for final approval of cover. On the basis of this approval, an export guarantee will be granted provided that cover is still available under the statutory liability limit. The Federal Republic is only liable for an export guarantee if it has been approved by the "Bundesschuldenverwaltung" (Federal Debt Administration).

1.1.1.2 Summary of organisation

See page 54.

1.1.1.3 Resources

The federal government can grant cover only within an exposure limit on total commitments fixed annually by Parliament. The ceiling for export credit insurance in the 1986 budget year was fixed at DM 195 billion. Thus, the authority for new cover essentially depends on the commitments already existing at the beginning of the fiscal year (about DM 133 billion at the beginning of 1989). Claims are paid from the budget, which is credited with premium payments and any recoveries from earlier claims.

1.1.1.4 Other organisations involved

An Interministerial Committee (Interministerieller Ausschuß) comprises representatives of the Federal Ministries of Economic Affairs (which has functional responsibility), Finance, Foreign Affairs and Economic Cooperation. The Committee is advised by representatives of the Bundesbank, the Kreditanstalt für Wiederaufbau (KfW) (see 1.2.1), the Ausfuhrkredit–Gesellschaft mbH (AKA) (see 1.2.2) and a number of experts from the export trade and the banking business.

The Committee is the central decision making body for underwriting questions and cover techniques; e.g. types of cover, general conditions, premium rates, cover policy and international agreements.

The Committee determines the directives for decisions on cover and indemnification concerning delegations to other ministerial bodies and to the mandatory consortium. It discusses applications for cover of more than DM 2 million before a decision is taken by the Federal Ministry of Economics.

1.1.1.5 Relations with the state

The consortium acts only in the name and on the account of the state.

In the budget law provision on export cover, a distinction is made between cover for promotion of exports and cover for exports of national interest. However, there are no preferential conditions for either exports of national interest or for exports destined for developing countries.

Least developed countries qualify for genuine aid facilities. Transactions that are of particular government interest may involve increased risks compared with normal standards. They are classified separately but are not subject to special ceilings.

1.1.1.6 Relations with the private sector

Apart from government facilities, export credit insurance is provided by private insurance companies for their own account. However, this cover is limited to commercial risks and involves trade almost exclusively with other industrialised countries.

1.1.1.7 Additional structure

Before finance of credits with a period of more than 24 months can be obtained from AKA, government export credit insurance should first be taken out. Such insurance is also a prerequisite for any financing under KfW's export promotion funds and for mixed credits granted by KfW.

Government insurance also facilitates mobilisation of other refinancing sources. However, this is without any appreciable reduction in interest charges. Any reduction in financing charges will be about the same as the insurance premium. Hermes cover enables financing of up to 90 per cent of the exporter's own costs during the manufacturing period.

1.2   Export Finance

1.2.1   Representative organisation

Kreditanstalt für Wiederaufbau (KfW)
Postfach 11 11 41
D–6000 Frankfurt/Main 11

Telephone: (49 69) 74 310
Telex: 41 52 56–0
Telefax: (49 69) 74 31 29 44
Teletex: 69 98 04

1.2.1.1 Function

Kreditanstalt für Wiederaufbau (KfW) was established in 1948. Its initial task was to finance the reconstruction of Germany's post–war economy by means of low–interest investment loans. These domestic activities were expanded, however, in subsequent years to other areas: since 1955, KfW has provided finance for German exports. Since 1961, KfW has extended loans and grants on behalf of the federal government within the framework of German financial cooperation with the developing countries.

The aforementioned three main activities have continued up to the present. Of KfW's annual loan commitments, the largest share is for domestic investment loans for small and medium sized enterprises, environmental protection and other structural measures. In the field of export financing, KfW concentrates on medium and long term loans primarily for supplies to developing countries.

KfW's loan commitments in 1988 in million DM:

I.	Domestic investment loans	12.327
II.	Export credits (and other foreign loans)	5.161
III.	Financial Cooperation	2.132
	Total	19.620

KfW was established by law as a corporation under public law. Eighty per cent of its capital is provided by the Federal Republic and 20 per cent by the "Lander" (federal states).

The executive bodies of KfW are the Board of Management (Vorstand) and the Board of Directors (Verwaltungsrat, see 1.2.1.4 below). The Board of Management is responsible for the conduct of business and the administration of assets.

1.2.1.2   Summary of organisation

Export finance in KfW is handled in two of its Sectoral Departments:

> B II (Sectoral Department II) is responsible for KfW's general export financing, B IV (Sectoral Department IV) is responsible for KfW's ship financing, aircraft financing and mixed credits.

Both departments report directly to KfW's Board of Management (Vorstand).

1.2.1.3   Resources

For its various activities, KfW raises the required funds by issuing bearer instruments and taking up loans in the domestic and foreign capital markets. A minor part of its loan commitments is also financed from appropriations in various public budgets, mainly for financial co-operation with developing countries and for various domestic investment programmes.

With regard to export financing, KfW can refer to two sources:

— To the *two export promotion funds* that are managed by KfW itself, but for which KfW must obtain approval from the Ministry of Economic Affairs for each loan it proposes to make.
One fourth of the credits out of the export promotion fund are financed from two special government funds that originated in the European Recovery Programme (ERP), namely:
Fund I, which contains a revolving refinancing facility of DM 500 million ERP-funds; and
Fund II, which is fed from a yearly allocation out of the ERP budget. In 1988 it amounted to DM 120 million. The allocation are reimbursed to the government as loans are amortised.
KfW combines the ERP fund in a ratio of one to three (or more) with funds raised on the capital market. The average amount available each year in ERP funds is about DM 200 million, KfW can thus provide about DM 800 million worth of long term credit per year out of these export promotion funds.
— To purely *market funds* that are raised by KfW either on the German or on the international capital markets at the terms and conditions available. The volume of such market funds is dependent on the loans committed on the basis of refinancing at market terms.

1.2.1.4   Other organisations involved

The Board of Directors and the specialist committees set up by it are responsible for harmonising the manifold interests of the federal government, the Lander governments, the various economic sectors and the credit institutions. Such interests have to be taken into consideration in the performance of Kreditanstalt's functions. The

Board of Directors consists of the Chairman and the Deputy Chairman, both appointed by the Federal government, several federal ministers, members appointed by the Bundesrat (Upper House), the president of the Deutsche Bundesbank, representatives of the commercial banks, industry, local authorities, agriculture, crafts, trade, and housing industry, and the trade unions.

1.2.1.5   *Relations with the state*

In the field of export financing, government influence is given when KfW grants official support in the form of credits refinanced either partly or wholly with public funds or in the form of interest subsidies out of public funds. This applies for credits under KfW's export promotion funds for mixed credits granted by KfW, and for loans in connection with ship and aircraft financing for which latter activities, KfW administers interest rate subsidies on behalf of the German government. There is *no* government influence when KfW is acting with funds raised in the markets, i.e. when KfW — having no monopoly whatsoever in export financing — is acting like a commercial bank with funds raised in the markets.

1.2.1.6   *Relations with the private sector*

In its export financing activities KfW very often — especially in the case of larger transactions — cooperates with commercial banks, either by inviting commercial banks to participate in a banking consortium under KfW's leadership or by granting a loan as parallel lender to a banking consortium, thereby restricting its participation as a rule to up to 50 per cent.

1.2.2   *AKA*

AKA Ausfuhrkredit–Gesellschaft mbH
Postfach 10 01 63
D–6000 Frankfurt/Main 1

Telephone: 069/ 20 601
Telex: 44 17 78
Telefax: 069/29 29 28

1.2.2.1   *Function*

Ausfuhrkredit–Gesellschaft mbH (AKA) is a private company set up in 1952 as a syndicate to finance export credits.

1.2.2.2   *Summary of organisation*

AKA now comprises 54 commercial banks. It is subject to the normal supervision of banks. It is not responsible to any governmental body. AKA's main bodies are the Supervisory Board and the Credit Committee.

1.2.2.3   *Resources*

There are three types of loans: lines A, B and C. Funds for lines A and C are draw from member banks' resources. The members have put a ceiling of DM 12 billion on each of the A facility and the C loans. Funds for B loans are obtained through rediscounting by the Bundesbank. The variable interest rate is calculated at 0.75 per cent above its discount rate. An interest rate fixed for a period of up to 2 years is also available. A total of DM 5 billion is made available through this facility.

The A and C funds from member banks are granted at variable or fixed interest rates. The latter are graduated according to the credit period. The determination of these rates follows conditions on domestic capital and money markets.

1.3   **Aid finance**

1.3.1   *Representative organisation*

Kreditanstalt für Wiederaufbau (KfW)
Postfach 11 11 41
D–6000 Frankfurt/Main 11

Telephone: (49 69) 74 310
Telex: 41 52 56–0

1.3.1.1   *Function*

Within the framework of the development policy of the Federal Republic of Germany KfW implements the part of the aid programme concerning bilateral financial cooperation.

1.3.1.2   *Summary of organisation*

(See 1.2.1.2).

1.3.1.3   *Resources*

KfW activities under Financial Cooperation are mainly financed from budget funds provided by the Federal Ministry of Economic Cooperation. In this context, KfW also provides own funds together with Financial Cooperation funds (mixed financing).

1.3.1.4   *Other organisations involved*

KfW administers Financial Cooperation independently and on its own responsibility acting to guidelines established by the Federal Government. Within the Government of the Federal Republic of Germany the Ministry for Economic Cooperation is responsible for steering and monitoring assistance programmes in coordination with other ministries.

2.   INSURANCE AND GUARANTEE PROGRAMMES

2.1   Cover for Exporters

2.1.1   *Types of cover available*

There are three types of cover available:

— *Single transaction cover* for a single short term, medium or long term transaction of a German exporter or for a medium or long term loan given by a German bank tied to a German export transaction;
— *Revolving (multiple transaction) cover* for a German exporter's annual turnover (short term business) with a specific foreign buyer;
— *Comprehensive cover* ("Ausfuhr–Pauschal–Gewahrleistung") for a German exporter's whole short term turnover (up to two years) with a number of buyers abroad.

A significant proportion of cover granted is for single transactions. The German system does not require an exporter to take out insurance for all his business, except in cases of comprehensive cover.

Under the system of comprehensive cover, a German exporter may apply for insurance of his whole turnover in the field of short term business up to two years. Protracted default (non–payment six months after maturity) is covered as well as commercial and political risks (see below). The exporter may include or exclude, by special application for each country in his comprehensive cover, all his transactions:

— With OECD countries;
— With public sector buyers;
— With associated companies; or
— On sight letter of credit payment terms.

Terms of cover

In granting cover, a distinction is made between business with private enterprises abroad ("Garantie" business) and transactions with foreign governments and bodies constituted under public law ("Bürgschaft" business).

Risks covered

In principle, political and commercial risks are always covered together. Only in the case of comprehensive policies, can cover be limited to political risks if the creditworthiness of the foreign buyer is too low to insure the commercial risks as well.

Pre–shipment cover

During the period before shipment of goods or execution of services, cover is granted for the exporter's prime costs (manufacturing risks).

Post–shipment cover

For the period after shipment of goods or beginning of execution of services, cover is granted for the exporter's claim (invoice value) under the export contract.

The private buyer policy provides cover for both political and commercial risk. The public buyer policy provides cover for political risks and the risk of non–payment within a period of between three to nine months after date of maturity (protracted default). Since April 1984, cover for protraced default has been extended to the medium and long term private buyer "Garantie" business. Thus, cover for protracted default is granted:

— For the public buyer transactions;
— For the medium and long term private buyer transactions (with a reduced percentage of cover, normally 75 per cent instead of 85 per cent);
— For buyer credits cover (tied loan cover in favour of German banks) (see 2.2.1.1); and
— For comprehensive cover (short term transactions).

Local cost financing

Local cost financing from German banks at market rates may be covered in accordance with rules laid down in the OECD Arrangement and its Sector Understandings.

Side financing

No cover available.

Cosmetic interest rates

Cover for contracts containing cosmetic interest rates is possible if no official financing support is provided.

Exporter's own risk

Cover cannot be obtained for 100 per cent of the risk. The exporter must share part of it. As a rule, this share will be 10 per cent of the loss for political risks, 15 per cent for commercial risks and 15 to 25 per cent for the non–payment risk. The exporter may apply for partial cover at a reduced premium rate. In these cases cover is limited to a certain quota of each instalment.

2.1.2   Eligibility

— Criteria for accepting cover

Insurance cover may be provided to the exporter or to the bank financing the transaction by a buyer credit (see 2.2.1 below). In principle, all types of goods and services may be insured, including construction projects, consignment contracts, products exhibited at trade fairs and capital investments (under the special capital investment cover scheme).

The basic requirements for granting cover are as follows:

— Creditworthiness of the buying country (in cases of limited creditworthiness, there are liability ceilings in the form of maximum amounts for single transactions or for liabilities incurred in the country concerned);
— The buyer or his guarantor must have a good credit rating (if the buyer or his country's credit rating is doubtful, the uninsured portion of the risk to be

borne by the exporter may be increased or the waiting periods may be extended);
— Regular terms (see below).
— In the case of a project financing the quality of the project and its ability to generate the necessary cash flow are of primary importance.

There is no general waiver of any of these requirements for developing countries in special need of aid, or for transactions of special importance for Germany's export policy.

The terms and conditions of cover for insurable credits are based on and in accordance with an agreement with the Berne Union and the OECD Arrangement on Guidelines for Officially Supported Export Credits.

— Nationality requirements

Cover is normally made available only to German exporters and for goods manufactured in (and services rendered from within) the Federal Republic of Germany. However, certain foreign content of an export contract may be included in the cover. The cover depends on where the foreign content originates and on its share of the total contract value. If it originates from another EEC country, it may amount to between 30 and 40 per cent of the contract value. A foreign component originating in Austria, Sweden or Switzerland, normally may amount to 30 per cent, and for other countries up to 10 per cent.

2.1.3   Cost of cover

For comprehensive cover, on account of the mix of risks covered, a special uniform flat premium is fixed for two years.

For all other cover, the following summary gives the most important insurance premiums charged for the normal medium and long term transactions as far as cover of commercial and political risks is concerned. The premium rates apply to the cover of supplier credits as well as to buyer credits (see 2.2.1). The countries for which cover is being granted have no effect on premium rates (there are no country ratings).

Premium for pre-shipment risk

For both private and public buyers the premium being charged is:
— For all insurabale risks included,
   1 per cent of the amount of covered construction costs;
   1.25 per cent in cases of construction periods longer than one year;
— Only for political risks (political insolvency of private buyers included),
   0.75 per cent of the amount of covered construction costs;
   0.90 per cent in cases of construction periods longer than one year.

Premiums for post-shipment risk

When calculating the premium, distinction must be made between private and public buyers.

— Premiums for transactions with private buyers

A non–recurring *basic premium* is charged on the covered amount (capital and interest), irrespective of the percentage of cover:

- 1.5 per cent for short term unsecured open account or medium or long term credit conditions;
- 1 per cent for documents against payment terms;
- 0.75 per cent for letter of credit payment terms (cover for certain political risks only.

To the basic premium is added a *pro rata temporis premium* of 0.1 per cent per month on the respective outstanding amount of capital, starting six months after shipment. In case of more than one shipment, the weighted average delivery is taken into account.

— Premiums for transactions with public buyers

The *basic premium* calculated on capital and interest, irrespective of the percentage of cover, is:

- 1 per cent for short term unsecured open account, or medium or long term credit conditions or documents against payment terms;
- 0.75 per cent for letter of credit payments (cover for certain political risks only).

The *pro rata temporis premium* is 0.55 per thousand of the respective outstanding amount of capital, calculated from the time of shipment (respectively weighted average delivery) for each commenced month.

2.2   Guarantees for banks

2.2.1   Policies available

2.2.1.1   Buyer credit

Besides the supplier credit cover for the risks incurred by the exporter, there is a buyer credit (tied loan) cover available for German banks giving loans to foreign buyers in connection with an export transaction. Instead of the normal percentage of cover (85 per cent for commercial and 90 per cent for political risks), the bank may choose cover of 95 per cent for both risks (so–called "5 per cent alternative"). In these cases, the bank itself must bear 5 per cent of the losses, for which it may not have recourse to the exporter. Under no circumstances is 100 per cent cover available. The premium for buyer credit cover is the same as for supplier credit cover.

2.2.2   Eligibility

See 2.1.2.

2.2.3   Cost of cover

See 2.1.3.

2.3   Other insurance programmes

2.3.1   *Guarantees for the mobilisation of financing*

Commercial banks financing a buyer credit are able to refinance themselves with special credit institutions (mortgage banks, etc.) that have access to long–term credit with fixed rates on the capital market. This refinancing could reach 100 per cent of the financed buyer credit and is totally insured by Hermes. Recourse for the difference between 100 per cent and the normal percentage covered, however, is claimed from the financing bank.

For this scheme of cover, an additional premium of 0.125 per cent will be charged on the respective remaining refinancing amount.

2.3.2   *Foreign exchange risk insurance*

Since 1972, Hermes has offered exchange risk cover for the account of the federal government but not for transactions with EEC countries. Cover is available for contracts expressed in US dollars, pound sterling, Swiss francs and, under exceptional circumstances, also for other freely convertible currencies negotiable in Germany. It is not available for other EEC currencies.

The exchange risk is covered only after a preliminary period of two years from the date of contract signature. The exporter may cover the exchange risk during the initial two years on the forward exchange market. The official conversion rate prevailing on the foreign exchange market in Frankfurt at the end of the preliminary period is the rate guaranteed for the amount then outstanding. There is a threshold of 3 per cent. Losses of less than 3 per cent are borne by the exporter. Losses exceeding 3 per cent are fully indemnified. Gains have to be entirely surrendered to Hermes if they exceed the margin of 3 per cent.

Exchange risk cover is available in isolation or in combination with export credit cover. The premium is 0.6 (combined insurance) or 0.7 (isolated insurance) per cent per annum on the outstanding amount.

2.3.3   *Cover for leasing*

Cover is available for standard financing lease contracts. The object of this cover must be the total amount of the payments due under the leasing contract, which has to be equivalent to the value of goods to be leased (full pay–out leasing). Payment conditions are generally not different from those of purchase contracts: a down payment of 15 per cent is indispensable, but the leasing contract may (in accordance with the Arrangement) concede equal part payments instead of degressive interest payments. All other rules for export sales are applicable.

2.3.4   *Construction works insurance*

German construction companies may apply for a special insurance scheme for construction works to be executed abroad and construction equipment that is to be used on site. Besides the normal pre– and post–shipment cover, the risk of confiscation of constructional equipment can be covered, the cost of land development can be insured and bonds given by the construction company can be guaranteed. The premium for construction works cover can be the same as for other export cover if pay-

ment under the construction contract is due on credit terms. For contracts on a progress payment basis, there is a uniform flat premium of 1 per cent on the contract
value (or a higher value of construction equipment to be covered) for business with
both private and public buyers.

The percentage of cover is generally the same as for purchase contracts,
i.e. 85 per cent for commercial and 90 per cent for political risks. For progress payment contracts, the contractor may choose instead a uniform 87.5 per cent cover for
all risks.

2.3.5   *Bond insurance*

Exporters may obtain cover against political risks and unfair calling of bonds connected with bidding for or execution of an export contract.

2.3.6   *Investment risks insurance*

Capital investment risks are not included in the export guarantee system. There is
a special programme for capital investment risks that is also handled by the Consortium
of Hermes and Treuarbeit. The latter company is the leading partner in this field.
This programme provides cover against political risks such as nationalisation, seizure,
war, rebellion, payment moratoria, impossibility to convert or transfer and comparable
actions or situations for participations, direct investments and capital goods abroad.
Cover can be provided for up to twenty years and for at most 95 per cent of the
investment. Apart from a flat charge of 0.5 to 1 per cent of the amount covered, a
premium of 0.5 per cent per annum of the amount covered is presently charged.

3.   EXPORT FINANCE PROGRAMMES

3.1   **Direct Credits**

3.1.1   *Type of contracts available*

KfW

KfW may grant its loans in the form of both buyer credits and supplier credits.
The German exporter submits a loan application to KfW for both buyer and supplier
financing. In recent years, however, demand has been almost entirely limited to buyer
credits.

AKA

Plafond A consists of funds pooled by member banks for refinancing suppliers'
credits. Application is made through a member bank. Loans are made available by
AKA directly to the exporter against promissory notes, which are discounted by AKA.
Member banks are then requested to provide the necessary funds for refinancing purposes.

Plafond B mainly provides supplier credits to developing countries with a repayment term between one year and four years from signature of the export contract.
Also, credits to state trading countries are funded through this facility.

Plafond C is another fund provided by the member banks at market rates. The total amount of credit granted under this Plafond was DM 401 million in 1988.

As a rule, all Plafond A, B and C loans covered by Hermes' credit insurance are eligible for financing. Terms are determined by the conditions on the German capital and money markets.

3.1.2   Eligibility

KfW

Credits that benefit from official financing support

With export promotion Funds I and II, KfW only finances contracts of German exporters for the delivery of capital goods to developing countries. These transactions must be officially insured or guaranteed by Hermes. The minimum repayment period for loans made under Funds I and II is four years.

Maximum amounts financed out of KfW's export funds are determined as follows (DM contract value less down and interim payments):

— For contract values of up to DM 50 million: actual value;
— For contract values of more than DM 50 million and up to DM 100 million: DM 50 million contract value;
— For contract value of more than DM 100 million: 50 per cent of the actual value up to a maximum contract value of DM 170 million.

Credits that do not benefit from official financing support

Because of limitations on the government supported export promotion funds, KfW is prepared to provide market funds in two different ways:

— For financing the balance of a transaction not being fully financed out of the export promotion funds but limited to the same maximum credit amounts as described above for the officially supported export funds (i.e. up to a maximum of DM 170 million) at interest rates that can be fixed together with the respective rate for the export promotion funds. These additional market funds are granted in principle under the same financing schemes as applicable for the export promotion funds (especially Hermes cover, credit period);
— For financing transactions without any involvement of officially supported export funds at interest rates that are fixed at disbursement. These rates are based on KfW's funding costs in the market plus a margin. With this mode of interest rate fixing, the borrower carries the risk of interest rate variation during the disbursement period. KfW may also offer floating rates.

The financing schemes for such pure market financing are the same as used by commercial banks. Hermes cover is the rule but is not necessary if the credit risk is good. Loans refinanced from market sources are not restricted to borrowers in developing countries.

AKA

On Plafond A transactions, AKA typically refinances 80 to 85 per cent of the contract value (cash payment being 15 to 20 per cent). A maximum credit period is not stipulated but is determined by the period covered by the credit insurance. There is no government subsidisation of Plafond A financing.

Up to 70 per cent of the contract value can be financed under the B credit. All the payments made by the buyer are used to pay off the B credit first. Thus, the proportion not covered by the B credit increases continuously. However, as the B credit can be combined with a credit from Plafond A, the exporter may receive full financing with a repayment term exceeding four years.

Credits under Plafond C are mainly used to finance buyer credits with a repayment term ranging from two to ten years. They are extended at either fixed or variable rates. They receive no government support.

3.1.3   *Resulting interest rates*

KfW

In the case of *official financing support*, the interest rate is a fixed rate determined predominantly at the date of signing of the loan agreement. In some cases, however, it may be fixed earlier when a firm reservation of the funds has been made in favour of the exporter (possible for a maximum period of six months). Interest rates are fixed for the whole lifetime of the credit. The rates correspond to the Arrangement guidelines (due to Germany's status as a low interest rate country the rates are equal to the Commercial Interest Reference Rate for credits denominated in Deutschemarks.)

The blended interest rate for credits granted out of KfW's export funds (ERP sources and KfW market funds blended in the ratio one to three or more) has always been at or above the agreed Arrangement rates. The maximum financing amount currently available under the KfW/ERP export financing programme is DM 170 million.

On undisbursed amounts of credits extended from the export promotion funds, KfW charges a commitment fee of 0.375 per cent per annum from conclusion of the loan agreement. In exceptional cases, KfW may charge a lump sum handling fee.

Credits *at market conditions* on a pure cover basis or even without cover are granted according to a formula by which the interest rate is fixed during the disbursement period. As a rule, this will be the funding costs of KfW in the capital market for corresponding amounts and maturities plus a margin, which varies according to type, term and risk of the specific loan. The provisions of the Arrangement do not apply, i.e. if market rates are below the Arrangement minimum interest rates, credits totally refinanced in the capital market might carry a rate below the Arrangement minimum rates.

For credits at market conditions, a similar commitment fee is charged. This normally amounts to 0.25 per cent per annum. The fee is lower because the interest rate is fixed at disbursement, so KfW has no interest variation risk. A handling fee is also charged.

AKA

Fees for Amounts approved at a variable Interest Rate only

Free of commission – up to conclusion of the Loan Agreement.

Fee payable on the amount committed from conclusion of the Loan Agreement up to disbursement:

Plafond A   1/4% p.a.
Plafond B   1   % p.a.

(This fee will continue to be charged to the exporter's principal bank for the period during which it refrains from rediscounting.)

Plafond C   1/4% p.a.

Fee for Amounts approved at a fixed Interest Rate

Fee payable on the amount committed from approval of the loan up to disbursement:

Plafond A   1/4% p.a.
Plafond B   1   % p.a.

(This fee will continue to be charged to the exporter's principal bank for the period during which it refrains from rediscounting).

Plafond C   1/4% p.a.

The interest rate charged on plafond B credits is the official discount rate of the Bundesbank plus 0.75 per cent. This results in a lending rate of 5.25 per cent (May 1989). In addition, a 0.6 per cent per annum bill of exchange tax and a 0.1 per cent per annum commitment fee are charged.

The Plafond A portion bears a market interest rate. Credits from plafond B may be combined with plafond A credits at market rate. The composite rate must adhere to the interest rate provisions of the Arrangement as government supported funds are involved. If the composite interest rate (fixed or floating) is below the Arrangement rates, the exporter has to pay the difference to a non profit making organisation named by AKA upon expiry of the credit.

Default interest

If amounts due are not remitted in time, the customary default interest debited by banks is charged.

3.2   Refinancing

In KfW's report financing activities a refinancing programme for banks does not exist.

3.2.1   Types of contract available

KfW

Officially supported export credits may be granted under KfW's promotion funds as described in 3.1. Hermes' cover is a prerequisite. Terms comply with the Arrangement.

AKA

Capital goods and related services for multiple projects are financed. Financing can be broken down as follows:

— 88 per cent to developing countries;
— 7 per cent to state trading countries;
— 5 per cent to other industrialised countries.

3.2.2   *Eligibility*

Plafond A consists of funds pooled by member banks for refinancing supplier credits. Application is made through a member bank and AKA typically refinances 80 to 85 per cent of the contract value (cash payment being 15 to 20 per cent). Member banks are requested to provide AKA with the necessary funds for refinancing purposes.

Plafond B loans are refinanced by rediscounting promissory notes at the Bundesbank.

Plafond C is another fund provided by the member banks at market rates. It is mainly used to finance buyer credits with a repayment term ranging from two to ten years.

As a rule, all Plafond A, B and C loans covered by Hermes' credit insurance are eligible for financing. Terms are determined by the market.

3.2.3   *Resulting interest rates*

Interest rates for A and C funds from member banks may be variable or fixed. The latter are set according to the credit period. When determining these rates, the conditions on the German capital and money markets are taken into consideration.

3.3   **Interest subsidies**

N/A.

3.4   **Other credit operations**

Foreign currency transactions

KfW has extended in the past a number of export credits denominated in a foreign currency — mainly in US dollars — for aircraft sales. For these sales, as an exception, an exchange risk guarantee by Hermes is available. In recent years, however, KfW has also developed the financing in foreign currencies — again mainly in US Dollars — for aircraft and ship sales and export transactions for other capital goods *without* an exchange risk guarantee by Hermes. These financing operations in other currencies than Deutsche Mark are based on a specific matching refinancing in the same currency to avoid any exchange risk.

4.   AID FINANCE PROGRAMMES

4.1   Integrated credits

4.1.1   *Funds available*

In addition to the funds available for development cooperation in the federal budget, mixed financing makes it possible to tap other sources of finance for worthwhile development projects. Under the system of "mixed financing" (Mischfinanzierung), resources from the budget of the BMZ can be associated with KfW's own funds, the financial package being extended as single concessional loans. The volume of loan commitments for mixed financing operations fluctuates from one year to the next depending on the opportunities and requirements. There are no special (extra) funds for mixed financing.

4.1.2   *Eligibility*

Selection criteria and appraisal procedures for mixed financing operations are the same as for projects entirely funded from the BMZ budget (see chapter 1.3): projects are identified in intergovernmental agreements, appraised by the KfW against development criteria, and approved by the BMZ.

4.1.3   *Resulting terms and interest rates*

Mixed financing operations that are concentrated on economic infrastructure projects in middle–income developing countries are normally tied to procurement in Germany, but in some cases third country procurement is possible for partial amounts.

Chapter 6

GREECE

1. ORGANISATION AND STRUCTURE

1.1 Insurance and Guarantees

1.1.1 *Representative organisation*

Export Credit Insurance Organization (ECIO)
57, Panepistimiou Street
Athens, P.O.C. 10564

Telephone: (30 1) 324 42 47, 324 16 47 or 320 30 78
Telex: 215206 BNGR–ECIO or 225746 BNGR for ECIO
Telefax:

1.1.1.1 *Function*

The Export Credit Insurance Organization (ECIO), a legal entity in private law, was established under the law 1796/88. Although it functions on the basis of the principles of a private corporation, it neither seeks nor distributes profits. Premiums are calculated so as to compensate for possible losses and cover administrative expenses.

Its Board of Directors is appointed by a common decision of the Minister of National Economy and the Ministry of Commerce. It is composed of seven Members. The members of Board of Directors and the General and the Deputy General Manager are persons with special knowledge and experience in ECIO activities.

1.1.1.2 *Summary of organisation*

The ECIO is an autonomous organisation.

1.1.1.3 *Resources*

The ECIO does not have a share capital of its own, but its liabilities are guaranteed by the state. The guarantee capital for meeting ECIO liabilities from its insurance or reinsurance activities at present (April 1989) amounts to approximately $252 million. Reserves of the ECIO are comprised of premiums, government or third party grants, and income of its property. Currently (April 1989), these reserves total approximately $38.5 million.

1.1.1.4 *Other Organisations Involved*

N/A.

1.1.1.5 *Relations with the State*

The insurance liabilities of the ECIO are guaranteed by the State. The maximum amount of liabilities guaranteed is from time to time revised by Presidential Decree issued on the recommendation of the Minister of National Economy, the Minister of Finance and the Minister of Commerce.

The ECIO operates under the auspices of the Bank of Greece. According to the law 1796/88, the ECIO is operating as an autonomous organisation.

1.1.1.6 *Other organisations providing cover or reinsurance*

Private banks may not provide export credit insurance.

1.2   **Export finance**

N/A.

2.   INSURANCE AND GUARANTEE PROGRAMMES

2.1   **Cover for Exporters**

2.1.1 *Policies available*

The ECIO offers insurance against political, commercial and catastrophe risks, and reinsures commercial risks. In the latter case, private insurance companies extend insurance against commercial risks and then may reinsure these risks with the ECIO.

The ECIO offers its customers the choice of covering all their exports or only specific contracts, independently of the duration of credit. The exporter can be covered for all his exports under a global insurance policy for short term and long term credits or he can be covered, case by case, for specific transactions under specific insurance policies.

There are no limits as to how much of the export turnover has to be covered. A ceiling is pre–determined, but it can be changed in the course of the insured period. Cover is given for supplier credit only. Coverage takes effect either from the date of the sales contract or the date of shipment.

2.1.2 *Eligibility*

At least 25 per cent of the export value must be of Greek origin.

The granting of insurance coverage depends on: the terms of the sales contract, the buyer's credit standing, the conditions prevailing in the country of destination and the credit standing of the insured.

Credit terms insured or guaranteed are:

— Consumer goods, up to three months (or according to the practice of the market);
— Consumer durables, up to twenty four months;
— Investment goods, generally up to three years and, exceptionally, up to five years if required by the nature of the contract.
— Investments which Greek companies realize abroad according to the nature of the project.

2.1.3   Cost of cover

Premiums are payable in advance and are calculated on the basis of the invoice value of the exported goods. Rates range between 0.3 and 3.5 per cent. The actual level of the premium depends on: the status of the importing country, the risks covered, terms of payment, creditworthiness of the buyer and whether the export contract is covered with the ECIO individually or globally.

2.2   Guarantees for banks

ECIO insurance policies encourage commercial banks to finance exporters.

2.2.1   Policies available

Although the banks do not directly receive any guarantees, insurance with the ECIO facilitates extending export credit to exporters. Insurance or reinsurance (see section 2.1) can cover up to 80 per cent of the invoice value of exports. The rights under an insurance policy can be transferred to the credit institution, subject to the consent of the Board of Directors of the ECIO. Decisions to transfer are made on a case by case basis. The commercial banks themselves grant export credits directly. The interest rate is freely negotiable with a minimum of 17 per cent.

2.2.2   Eligibility

As described in 2.2.1.

2.2.3   Cost of cover

If export credit has been insured, the additional burden of insurance premiums should also be added to the cost of financing. These premiums are: from 0.30 per cent to 3 per cent of the invoice value of exports if the export credit matures in a period of up to nine months and from 0.60 per cent to 3.5 per cent of the invoice value if the export credit matures in a period of up to three years. Premiums on credit maturing in a period of up to five years are determined on a case by case basis. Premiums are generally flat.

2.3   Other insurance programmes

2.3.1   *Foreign exchange insurance*

The ECIO operates an insurance facility by which a form of cover is given against devaluation of a foreign currency. Revaluation is not covered.

Premiums and claims are payable in the currency of the contract, but actual receipts and payments are in drachmas. For example, premiums payable in dollars will be collected in drachmas applying the rate of exchange at the date on which the insurance policy has been signed by the ECIO. If a claim arose, it would be paid in drachmas applying the rate of exchange of the above date.

The ECIO offers the choice to exporters of covering against one or more of a number of political/commercial or catastrophe risks as listed in its insurance policy. Thus, the ECIO under its insurance policies (global or specific), offers cover against one or more risks at different premium rates that fluctuate within a range of 0.3 to 3.5 per cent. Ceilings may or may not be determined depending upon the examination of each application. Under this procedure, the degree of utilisation is very low. So far, there has been no cost to public funds.

2.3.2   *Bond insurance*

Since 1975, the ECIO issues insurance policies, under the law 225/75, to commercial banks (or insurance companies) covering risks arising from bonds issued by them to overseas employers on behalf of Greek contractors undertaking construction work abroad. The types of bonds insured are: bid bonds, performance bonds, bonds covering advance payments and bonds covering exemption of customs duty on machinery imported in the employer's country.

The ECIO covers up to 80 per cent of the issuer's loss in case the forfeiture of the bond is due to political reasons or to "acts of God", and up to 50 per cent of the loss in case the forfeiture is due to any fault of the Greek contractor. The ECIO and the banks retain the right of recourse to both the exporter and the foreign buyer.

Bond insurance policies are issued usually for countries in the Middle East and North Africa. Premiums fluctuate within a range of 0.3 to 3.5 per cent.

2.3.3   *Foreign currency transactions*

All export financing is made in the national currency/or in foreign exchange. Neither exporters nor banks are authorised to refinance export credits in international markets. The Export Credit Insurance Organization — the ECIO (see section 1) can only assume liabilities and pay out claims in domestic currency. Export contracts may, however, be concluded in a foreign currency, and repayments may be received in that currency. The exporter can cover the exposed foreign exchange risk with the ECIO or the Central Bank. There is no domestic forward exchange market, and neither banks nor exporters have access to international forward markets. Exporters are obliged to import the value of exported goods and services within a period not exceeding six months from the time the credit is granted.

3.   EXPORT FINANCE PROGRAMMES

3.1   **Direct Credits**

Because of its narrowness, the Greek capital market has traditionally been regulated by the authorities. In fact, interest rates on deposits as well as on loans and credit advances are determined by a government agency, the Currency Committee. The banks provide the funds necessary to finance export sales requiring short or longer term credits.

The public sector does not provide direct export credits.

4.   AID FINANCE PROGRAMMES

Greece has no programme for associated financing.

Chapter 7

IRELAND

1. ORGANISATION AND STRUCTURE

1.1 Insurance and Guarantees

1.1.1 *Representative organisation*

Insurance Corporation of Ireland plc – (ICI)
Burlington House
Burlington Road
Dublin 4

Telephone: (353 1) 601377
Telex: 93618 INCO EI
Telefax: (353 1) 609220

1.1.1.1 *Function*

The Insurance Act, 1953 (as amended) empowers the Minister for Industry and Commerce to extend State guarantees in order to promote exports of Irish goods and certain services. Under the terms of a 1987 Agreement between the Minister for Industry and Commerce and ICI, that Company issues export credit insurance and guarantees policies for export credit finance as agent for and on behalf of the Minister, with whom the ultimate risk resides. ICI is a wholly owned subsidiary of Sealuchais Arachais Teoranta (Insurance Holdings Ltd.), a holding company controlled by the Minister for Industry and Commerce.

1.1.1.2 *Summary of organisation*

1.1.1.3 *Resources*

Export credit insurance premiums received by ICI, less the Company's remuneration expenses and brokerage fees, are remitted to the Minister and surrendered to the Exchequer. Export credit insurance claims are paid by ICI, which is reimbursed by the Minister out of monies voted by the Oireachtas (parliament). The Agreement between the Minister and ICI provides that the scheme will be operated so that, taking one year with another, no net loss to State funds will result. The limit of the Minister's liability for principal monies in respect is currently set at Ir£500 million. This ceiling is adjusted periodically by amending legislation as proves necessary.

1.1.1.4 *Other organisations involved*

N/A.

1.1.1.5 *Relations with the state*

ICI provides export credit insurance and guarantees for export credit finance on behalf of the government. Issuance of export credit insurance policies other than short term policies must be approved by the Department of Industry and Commerce. All policy decisions are the concern of the Department.

1.1.1.6 *Relations with the private sector*

Two separate schemes involving one Irish bank and one credit control agency allow those organisations to provide cover for commercial risks, subject to certain restrictions imposed by ICI, under the umbrella of general policies held by them with specially increased discretionary limits.

1.1.1.7   *Additional structure*

Cover is mandatory for all export credits benefitting from official financing support.

1.2   Export Finance

1.2.1   *Representative organisation*

None.

2.   INSURANCE AND GUARANTEE PROGRAMMES

2.1   Cover for Exporters

2.1.1   *Policies available*

There are five basic policies available under the scheme. Policies cover political and/or commercial risks. A maximum of 95 per cent cover applies to political risks and 90 per cent to commercial risks. The policies are as follows:
— Comprehensive Shipments Policy;
— Comprehensive Services Policy;
— Comprehensive Contracts Policy;
— Specific Contracts Policy;
— Specific Services Policy.

For short term credits (up to one hundred and eighty days), cover used to be available only for the insured exporter's entire export turnover. However, an element of flexibility has been adopted with regard to the "whole turnover" concept. The aim of this is to make the scheme more attractive and useful to exporters and to increase the total proportion of Irish exports insured under the scheme. Inter company sales do not usually qualify for insurance, but cover for sales against political and transfer risks is available. Onward sales cover is also available to those companies that sell through a foreign subsidiary or associate. The Comprehensive Contracts Policy provides cover from date of contract as opposed to date of shipment.

Under the Specific Contracts Policy, cover is provided for pre- and post-shipment risk for sales of capital goods on extended credit terms. Normally, cover is available for up to five years but can be provided for up to eight and a half years in accordance with the terms of the Arrangement.

The Comprehensive Services Policy provides cover for the supply of services on short term credit. Cover is available from date of contract or date of invoice. The Specific Services Policy covers larger services contracts.

Down payments of from 15 to 20 per cent are required for credits of one year or more. Repayments are made in consecutive equal semiannual amounts, commencing six months from date of shipment, with no grace period. Interest, the rate of which is fixed over the credit duration, is payable in outstanding declining balances. The credit duration allowed is linked directly to the value of the contract.

2.1.2   *Eligibility*

— Criteria for accepting cover

Under the standard turnover policies covering short–term credits, the exporter may trade on a discretionary limit basis and be covered by his policy without reference to the ICI. The maximum discretionary limit is currently Ir£ 43 000. Credit limits in excess of the discretionary limit may be approved by ICI at the request of an exporter but are subject to the establishment of the creditworthiness of the buyer. Approved credit limits are designated in the currency of the contract, and the validity of the limits applies only to transactions in the designated currency.

An exporter who has obtained an approved credit limit from ICI on a particular buyer may trade up to the level of the limit plus 25 per cent, provided he has had no unsatisfactory trading experience with that buyer in the year preceding date of ship-ment/contract.

For medium and long term export contracts, provision of cover will depend on establishment of the creditworthiness of the buyer, provision of state, bank or parent company guarantees where necessary, the political and economic state of the buyer's country and the acceptability of the risk as a whole.

— Nationality requirements

To be considered eligible for export credit insurance and finance, goods and serv-ices must have a reasonable Irish content (defined by the Department of Industry and Commerce on a case by case basis). There are no bilateral agreements on favourable treatment of foreign content.

2.1.3   *Cost of cover*

Premiums for short term cover are payable at a flat rate per cent of the face value of contracts or of the gross invoice value of shipments. The rate of premium applied depends on the country of the risk, the creditworthiness of the buyer, the payment terms and the country of destination of the exports. For short–term business, a first deposit premium on the exporter's estimated annual turnover for the coming year is payable at the beginning of the insurance year. When the actual export turnover is known, refunds or excesses are paid.

For medium and long term cover, the premium rate is determined by the mean risk period, the country grading and the status of the buyer. Premiums are payable in advance, at the time of issue.

2.2   **Guarantees for Banks**

2.2.1   *Policies available*

Under arrangements with banks for provision of export credit finance, ICI issues 100 per cent guarantees to the funding banks for particular policies. The guarantee becomes active on presentation of shipping documents. No arrangements exist for issuance of such guarantees to provide for pre–shipment finance. However, policies that indemnify against pre–shipment risk can be assigned to a bank as sole or support-ing security for an advance of funds. Post shipment finance can also be arranged on the basis of a simple assignment of the exporter's policy rights. ICI's (the state's) liability to the exporter remains unchanged, i.e. 90 per cent cover is provided, but the exporter undertakes to reimburse the insurer for any amount which is paid to the bank in excess of the normal liability under the terms and conditions of the policy. At present, no such arrangements exist where policies covering the export of services are concerned. A percentage of every risk is thus assumed by the exporter. Risk sharing with the banks is allowed, in principle.

2.2.2   *Eligibility*

See 2.2.1

2.2.3   *Cost of cover*

The exporter pays a premium on the export credit insurance policy calculated as a percentage of the value of the contract (less the amount paid with order) plus the amount of the interest charges. The rate of premium will depend on the classification of the buyer's country, the mean risk period and the quality of the buyer.

2.3   Other Insurance Programmes

2.3.1   *Bond insurance*

In 1976, the export credit insurance scheme was extended to provide cover against the risk of the unfair calling of conditional performance bonds that exporters may be required to provide in connection with foreign contracts.

An additional premium is payable for this extension of cover.

3.   EXPORT FINANCE PROGRAMMES

3.1   Direct Credits

There are no funds or public financial institutions that directly finance export credits. Formerly, such finance was provided for ships. In 1982, this mechanism was discontinued due to lack of demand.

3.2   Refinancing

All export credit finance is provided by the commercial banks. There are no refinancing arrangements in operation in Ireland.

3.3   Interest Subsidies

3.3.1   *Types of contract available*

A scheme for providing export financing at concessionary rates of interest was introduced in 1975 under an arrangement between the Minister for Industry and Commerce and the four major Irish banks. This arrangement was revised in 1981 and subsequently expanded in 1983 to include other Irish and international banks based in Ireland. The scheme is operated in conjunction with the export credit insurance scheme that is underwritten by the state.

3.3.2   *Eligibility*

Concessionary rates of interest for credits of up to five years are in line with those of the Consensus. They are not available for intra–EEC exports. These rates remain fixed for the duration of the credit and are subsidised by the Department as appropriate. The interest subsidy is provided out of monies voted by the Oireachtas (parliament). In practice, credit finance is available for five years but may be provided for up to eight and a half years for large scale projects.

3.3.3   *Resulting interest rates*

Against the security offered by the 100 per cent guarantee, the banks provide export credit finance at concessionary rates that are in line with Arrangement rates. In addition to the basic interest rate, the banks charge commitment and negotiation fees.

3.4   **Other Credit Operations**

— Short term credits

A scheme for the financing of non capital goods exports sold on short term credit (up to one hundred and eighty days) was introduced in 1981. This scheme, which is operated by the various banks in conjunction with the export credit insurance scheme, is designed to assist, in particular, small and medium sized exporters of non capital goods in easing access to borrowed funds. Finance for short term exports is provided up to a maximum of 90 per cent of the payments due from abroad under bills of exchange. The security for the finance, which refers to the exporter's credit insurance policies, is a 100 per cent guarantee or a simple assignment of the exporter's policy rights. The scheme is a post–shipment one, and funds are only made available to the exporter on production of evidence of shipment. On receipt of payment from the foreign buyer, the bank deducts the amount already advanced, the interest payment and all other costs. It pays the balance to the exporter in foreign or Irish currency, whichever is appplicable. In the event of default, the bank may claim on the guarantee six months after the maturity date of the bill of exchange. The exporter is liable for the interest charges that accrue during that six month period at the relevant preferential rate.

Rates of interest for short term financing are:
— For Irish pound denominated exports, the AAA overdraft rate;
— For foreign currency lending, the appropriate Eurocurrency interest rate plus a fixed margin.

A negotiation fee is also payable. For foreign currency financing, a commitment fee is levied on any undrawn facilities.

— Foreign currency transactions

Ireland's accession to the EMS (30th March 1979) and the consequent break in the link between the Irish pound and Sterling necessitated financing in foreign currency (since most contracts were expressed in Sterling). Under the terms of the arrangement between the banks and the Department of Industry and Commerce, export credit finance is available in domestic or any freely convertible currency. Denomination in low interest rate currencies is preferable from the state's point of view insofar as it reduces subsidisation costs.

4.   AID FINANCE PROGRAMMES

Ireland has no programme for associated financing.

Chapter 8

ITALY

1.   ORGANISATION AND STRUCTURE

1.1   Insurance and Guarantees

1.1.1   *Representative organisation*

Sezione Speciale per l'Assicurazione del Credito all'Esportazione
Casella Postale 253 Roma Centro
00100 Roma

Telephone: (39 6) 67 361
Telex: SACE I 613160
Telefax: (39 6) 673 62 25

1.1.1.1   *Function*

The Special Section for Export Credit Insurance (SACE) was set up in 1977 by an Act regulating export financing (Act No. 227 of 24th May 1977), which made it responsible for the administration of government insurance and export credit guarantee programmes.   SACE is an autonomous section of the "Istituto Nazionale delle Assicurazioni" (National Insurance Institute — INA).   Up to 1977, the INA administered export credit insurance schemes directly at the same time as other types of insurance (life, fire, etc.).   SACE has its own management and assets, but its links to the INA are very close.   The Chairman of the INA is also Chairman of SACE.

SACE is empowered to insure and reinsure political risks, natural disasters, economic and commercial risks as well as exchange rate risks.

1.1.1.2   *Summary of organisation*

SACE is divided into several services:

— General affairs, legal and personnel services,
— International studies and relations service,
— Medium term policies service for Latin America and Asia,
— Medium term policies services for Africa, OECD countries and Europe,
— Short term and commercial risks policies service,
— Claims services and
— Automation, accounting, rescheduling and recoveries service.

1.1.1.3 *Resources*

The resources available for the settlement of claims derive, in principle, from premiums paid, recoveries, reserves and other assets and from an endowment fund (at present L 2 964 billion), which is financed by the state.

1.1.1.4 *Other organisations involved*

The Treasury is SACE's guardian authority. Decisions concerning terms of cover, payment of claims, etc., are taken by the Management Committee, which is composed of representatives of the Ministries concerned, the INA and Mediocredito Centrale. Members are appointed by Decree of the Minister for the Treasury in agreement with the Minister of Foreign Trade. This Committee meets once a week to take the major policy decisions and to authorise insurance transactions that do not fall within the competence of the Director of SACE.

1.1.1.5 *Relations with the state*

Insurance liabilities of SACE are guaranteed by the state within the limits of a revolving fund of L 12 000 billion for guarantees not exceeding 24 months, and a ceiling fixed annually under the Act approving the State budget for guarantees when they are for a longer period. In 1989, this ceiling was fixed at L 10 000 billion.

1.1.1.6 *Relations with the private sector*

Private insurance companies may insure export credits without action by SACE. The only private company with which SACE has signed a reinsurance agreement is the Societa Italiana Assicurazione Credita s.p.d. — SIAC (General Credit Insurance Company). Under this agreement, SACE undertakes to reinsure 45 per cent of all short term commercial risks and 95 per cent of all short term political risks covered by SIAC. SIAC resources are entirely private.

1.1.1.7 *Additional structure*

In October 1st, 1988 the previous foreign exchange regulations were revised. Under the new regulations, foreign exchange transactions no longer require official authorisation, except those concerning goods subject to special permission. The responsibility of foreign transactions lies with the Italian exporter through the issue of a "Foreign exchange statement", which has to be handed over by the exporter to the Bank which takes note of its content.

In the context of the new discipline, the foreign exchange control, delegated by the Ministry of Foreign Trade to SACE, concerns only the authorisation to Italian firms to open accounts abroad and deposits connected with commercial transactions insured by SACE not exceeding 50 billion of liras.

A SACE guarantee or insurance is not an absolute requirement in order to qualify for preferential refinancing by Mediocredito Centrale or for any other public financial support. In practice, however, a large proportion of the credit transactions receiving preferential treatment are insured by SACE. In the case of associated financing, it is in principle requested by banks and exporters.

1.2   Export Finance

1.2.1   *Representative organisation*

Mediocredito Centrale
Via Piemonte, 51 – 00187 ROMA

Telephone: (396) 47911
Telex: 621699 MEDIOC
          626496 MEDCEN

1.2.1.1   *Function*

Mediocredito Centrale is a public financial institution, set up in 1952 to provide refinancing for credits to small and medium sized enterprises and subsequently given the task of helping to finance medium and long term export credits.

Act No. 227 of 24th May 1977, which superseded Act No. 131 of 28th February 1967, changed the Italian system from the institutional standpoint, as well as insurance and financing procedures. It makes a clear distinction between commercial credits and aid credits extended to developing countries.

1.2.1.2   *Summary of organisation*

Mediocredito is divided into several departments: Personnel and General Affairs, Legal Affairs, Treasury and Financial Dept., External Relations, Direct Export Credits, Assisted Export Credits, Credit to Small and Medium Italian Enterprise Aid Credits.

1.2.1.3   *Resources*

Mediocredito Centrale has an endowment fund of L 1 414.6 billion, set up and financed by the Treasury in the framework of current legislation; the Treasury also supplies it with funds for the disbursement of interest subsidies on export credits.

In order to avoid or limit shortages of resources available to support export transactions, the Minister of the Treasury submits, together with the draft state budget, estimates of the insurance commitments to be contracted the following year by SACE and of the financial requirements of Mediocredito Centrale — i.e. for interest rate subsidies and allocations for Mediocredito's endowment fund.

Furthermore, in order to finance its own credit transactions, Mediocredito Centrale is empowered to borrow from Italian and foreign banks. Since 1977, a large proportion of Italian medium and long term exports has been financed by the international financial market.

1.2.1.4   *Other organisations involved*

A General Council, appointed by Presidential Decree on the proposal of the Minister of the Treasury, is composed of fifteen members designated by the Interministerial Committee for Credit and Saving and by the Ministers of Treasury and Industry. The Council is responsible for determining the Mediocredito's general policy. A Board of Directors is responsible for routine transactions; its members are appointed by a Decree of the Prime Minister on the proposal of four Ministers (Treasury, Industry, Trade and Crafts, Foreign Trade and Foreign Affairs).

1.2.1.5 *Relations with the state*

Given that Mediocredito is a public financial institution, the State is represented in the General Council and on the Board of Directors.

In all its activities, Mediocredito must comply with rules, directives and limits dictated by the State through the competent Ministries.

Like any other credit institution Mediocredito is subject to the surveillance of the Bank of Italy.

1.2.1.6 *Relations with the private sector*

Under the 1936 Bank Act, export credits for a period exceeding eighteen months may be granted only by medium and long term credit institutions, including Mediocredito Centrale, and by the special services of certain large commercial banks.

Medium term credit institutions finance credits for periods exceeding eighteen months in lire or foreign currency. They may not use the rediscounting facilities of the Central Bank, which are reserved for four month bills, but they may ask for support from Mediocredito Centrale, if the operation financed is eligible for such support.

1.3   **Aid Finance**

1.3.1   *Representative organisation*

Directorate General for Development Co-operation
Ministry of Foreign Affairs
Address: Piazzale della Farnesina, 1
              00100 Roma – Tel. 3691 – 4215

Telex: 614066 DIPCSI
Telefax: 3691 – 4193

1.3.1.1 *Function*

The Directorate General is responsible for negotiating with recipient countries, preparing the projects, proposing them for approval by the Steering Committee or by the Interministerial Committee, implementing, controlling and monitoring cooperation projects.

1.3.1.2 *Summary of organisation*

The Directorate General headed by the Director General is divided into a Central Technical Unit and twenty offices, of which six are geographical and three administrative. Other offices deal with legal matters, cooperation through the E.E.C., cooperation through multilateral agencies, non governmental organisations, soft loans and emergency projects. The Central Technical Unit is responsible for the technical and economic evaluation of projects.

1.3.1.3 *Resources*

O.D.A. bilateral funds are mainly composed of grants (budget of the Ministry of Foreign Affairs) and soft loans (budget of the Ministry of the Treasury). Each year the State Budget law determines, for the following three years, the amount of the allocations for grants and soft loans. Contributions to multilateral agencies are allocated to various parts of the State Budget.

1.3.1.4   *Other organisations involved*

Ministry of the Treasury;
Ministry for Foreign Trade;
Ministry of the Budget;
Steering Committee and Interministerial Committee.

1.3.1.5   *Relations with the state*

The Directorate General was set up within the Ministry of Foreign Affairs and is an integral part of that Ministry.

1.3.1.6   *Relations with the private sector*

Private enterprises, or state–owned enterprises may act as executing agencies for cooperation projects financed through grants and soft loans, under the control and monitoring of the Directorate General. The control in the field is fulfilled through the local Technical Units, located in the recipient countries of Italian cooperation assistance.

The law favours the constitution of joint ventures between enterprises of the donor and the recipient country, by means of contributions granted to the Italian enterprises.

2.   INSURANCE AND GUARANTEE PROGRAMMES

2.1   Cover for Exporters

Under law 227, SACE may insure directly or reinsure political, catastrophic and commercial risks for short, medium and long term buyer and supplier credits.

2.1.1   *Policies available*

Types of policies at present available:
— Exports of goods and services, goods for sale stocked abroad, feasibility studies, design, bonds, leasing;
— Short term comprehensive policies for exports of goods and services.
— Short term comprehensive policies including pre–shipment, credit and bond risks (RCF policies);
— Documentary credit and revolving short term lines of credit;
— Exchange risk;
— Civil works policies.

SACE covers commercial and political risks for medium and long term credits (exceeding twenty four months). The proportion insured against political risks may be as much as 90 per cent for supplier credits, and 95 per cent for buyer credits, exchange risks guarantees and direct bank guarantees.

The percentage guaranteed for commercial risks is established on a case by case basis in the light of the information available concerning the buyer or the guarantor. Political risks and (since 1979) commercial risks for short term credits (under twenty-four months) may be covered by either comprehensive or individual policies. Short term guarantees provided by private insurance companies may be reinsured by SACE.

Cover is provided on the conditions set out in the Arrangement.

2.1.2 *Eligibility*

— Criteria for accepting cover

Account is generally taken of the nature and volume of the exports as well as the solvency of the buyer and the buyer country. A government or bank guarantee may be required. There are, generally speaking, no predetermined ceilings for individual countries apart from the annual global ceiling. In the event of a claim, the exporter must supply documentary proof of the initial transaction.

— Nationality requirements

SACE may insure up to 30 per cent of the value of contract components coming from other EEC countries or countries that have concluded reciprocity agreements with Italy. In all other cases, a ceiling is fixed at 15 per cent. If it is exceeded, the normal percentage of cover is reduced accordingly.

2.1.3 *Cost of cover*

Levels of medium and long term insurance premiums are calculated on the basis of three categories, varying according to the repayment term of a credit and the type of cover offered (political or commercial risk, comprehensive or individual policy). For short term as well as medium and long term credits, the cost and scope of commercial risk cover vary mainly according to whether they are backed by a bank guarantee.

The combined cost of insurance for cover of political and commercial risks may vary between 6.45 per cent and 8.84 per cent in the case of a long term credit (10 years) to a developing country.

For supplier credits all premiums are normally payable in advance. For buyer credits 30 per cent of the premium is payable in advance and 70 per cent at each draw-drown.

2.2   Guarantees for Banks

2.2.1 *Policies available*

— Medium/long term buyer credits,
— Documentary credit and credit lines that can be renewed at short notice,
— Direct guarantees to banks (short term only) and
— Buyer credits granted by foreign banks for the financing of Italian exports (triangular transactions).

SACE may guarantee short term credit lines extended to foreign banks by Italian commercial banks.

Short term financing provided by national banks to Italian exporters is also eligible for a guarantee.

2.2.2   Eligibility

The proportion insured against political risks may be as much as 95 per cent for buyer credits and triangular transactions and 100 per cent for buyer credits involving intergovernmental agreements. (See also 2.1.2).

SACE may accept liabilities and pay out claims in foreign currencies.

2.2.3   Cost of cover

See 2.1.3.

2.3   Other Insurance Programmes

2.3.1   Foreign exchange risk insurance

A foreign exchange risk insurance scheme has been operating since June 1979. The guarantees have the following characteristics:

Cover is limited to credits in convertible currency for a period exceeding eighteen months, granted for transactions for which payment must be made more than six months after the date of signature of the contract (supplier credits) or the date on which the funds are made available (financial credits). For the moment, the only transactions covered are those denominated in US dollars, Deutschemark, Swiss Fr., Yen and ECU. Transactions in other EC currencies are not covered.

The exchange rate guaranteed is the official rate applying in Italy on the date the contract is signed or the funds are made available, provided that the application for guarantee is submitted to SACE within 45 days after the above–mentioned dates.

The cover has now been extended to the period from the offer to the award of the contract and its validity is subject to the actual signature of the contract.

The indemnity, proportional to the amount guaranteed, covers losses resulting from an increase in the value of the lira in relation to the guaranteed exchange rate and to the currency in which the offer contract was established. In the event of depreciation of the lira, the insured party is required to pay the corresponding exchange profit to SACE.

2.3.2   Bond insurance

SACE extends cover to banks and exporters and to their guarantors up to 90 per cent of the value against "unfair" calling of bid and performance bonds. Only callings for political reasons are covered. Claims are settled within four months. Most of the guarantees have been for exports to the Middle East and Latin America. Premiums are the same for all countries. Provision is made, however, for an increase in the premium for those countries that have made unfair use of bonds during the previous two years.

SACE also guarantees advance payment bonds issued by commercial banks or other institutions. If the bond is called for political reasons, the bond issuer is reimbursed for 90 per cent of the bond value. SACE also extends cover against non–payment of bonds issued by banks.

2.3.3   *Insurance for direct investments abroad*

Insurance for direct investments abroad has been available since July 1979. The scheme is applicable for any direct investment abroad, whether in the form of transfer of funds, supply of capital goods, technology, licences or patents, or for research and development activities and mineral production. The risks covered are: nationalisation, expropriation with inadequate compensation, confiscation, sequestration or any other measure or decision taken by foreign authorities, as well as political developments and natural disasters that may result in a loss or make it impossible for the Italian firm to continue its activities or be paid the sums due to it. The maximum cover is 70 per cent of investment value plus an annual 8 per cent of income from investments; the premium is 0.8 per cent per annum.

2.3.4   *Insurance of market surveys*

Since 1983, there has been a scheme providing insurance for market surveys; including market research, demonstrations and advertising, stocks and samples, permanent agencies, operation of offices and/or sales and service networks and establishment of sales and service networks in countries other than those of the European Community.

The insurance is available on condition that these costs have been entered in a budget certified by an approved audit company. Insurance cover is available for non amortization or incomplete amortization of costs, but only following political events or natural disasters in foreign countries, for example: war, revolution, riot, earthquake, etc. or acts or facts that can be attributed to the public authority in the foreign countries. Non amortization resulting from economic or commercial events is not covered.

Cover may not exceed five years. The premium is payable in advance on an annual basis, taking into account the budget for the programme for the following financial year, which the insured person is required to submit to SACE under pain of cancellation.

2.3.5   *Cover for public works contracts subject to periodic progress reports*

The general terms of policies have recently been amended to replace the system of differential cover by type of risk (payment default, manufacturing risks, destruction of equipment) by a maximum limit, which is fixed in advance and within which the exporter is covered against all the risks provided for in other types of policies and incurred in carrying out the contract.

The percentage covered is normally 60 per cent of the amount of the contract, but the exporter may request a higher or lower percentage according to requirements. The policy is valid for the period of fulfilment of the contract. Any changes that may be made during that period in accordance with the clauses of the contract are included within the limit fixed in advance. In the event of a claim, the insured is indemnified up to the amount insured.

3.   EXPORT FINANCE PROGRAMMES

3.1   Direct Credits

N/A.

3.2   Refinancing

3.2.1   *Types of contract available*

Mediocredito Centrale may provide financial support for exports in the form of advances and rediscounting and/or interest subsidies. (See 3.3.1). The type of aid that it gives for a specific transaction depends on the resources that it is able to make available for refinancing operations and interest subsidies at the time of the transaction. Support in the form of refinancing is limited to export credits financed in lire.

3.2.2   *Eligibility*

See 3.2.1

3.2.3   *Resulting interest rates*

The minimum rates applicable are those established by the Consensus and by other international agreements on export credits. In accordance with Article 92 of the EEC Treaty, the above–mentioned rates are not applicable to transactions with Community countries, which may be refinanced only at the official discount rate (12 per cent).

3.3   Interest Subsidies

3.3.1   *Types of contract available*

In principle, all export credits with a repayment period exceeding eighteen months are eligible for support from Mediocredito Centrale. This may be partly in the form of refinancing and partly in the form of interest subsidies, in such a way that the borrowing rate of the credit is competitive internationally. (See 3.2.1). Foreign currency financing only benefits from interest subsidies.

3.3.2   *Eligibility*

See 3.3.1

3.3.3   *Resulting interest rates*

Mediocredito Centrale support corresponds to the difference between the above–mentioned rates and a "reference rate" represented by the rate of return to medium and long term credit establishments. The reference rate may be fixed or floating during the life of the credit, depending on whether the collection operations of the financing institutions are carried out at a fixed or a floating rate.

The fixed reference rate is established every month by the Treasury on the basis of the average cost of fixed rate borrowing by medium and long term credit institutions, plus a maximum commission of 0.50 per cent.

The floating reference rate is established every six months on the basis of the average cost of floating rate borrowing by medium and long term credit institutions, plus a maximum commission of 0.50 per cent.

Through refinancing or interest rate subsidies, Mediocredito Centrale brings down the cost of credit to the level of the contractual rate, which must not however be lower than the rates fixed by the Arrangement.

3.4   Other Credit Operations

Foreign currency transactions

Medium and long term export credits eligible for official support are largely financed in foreign currencies. A certain number of measures have been taken to facilitate international financing. Ordinary banks may only finance export credits in foreigh currency exceeding eighteen months if they utilise for that purpose funds in foreign currency. Mediocredito Centrale grants interest subsidies for financing foreign currency transactions. Exporters may conclude contracts with a buyer whose resources come from a third country. In these cases, Mediocredito Centrale may grant an interest subsidy directly to the buyer or to the foreign financial institutions.

The preferential rate of officially supported credit financed in a foreign currency may not be below the rates fixed by the Arrangement, while the "reference rate" is fixed taking into account the rate at which funds are obtained abroad, whether it be floating or fixed.

Mediocredito Centrale may provide official support for financing in foreign currencies of the following transactions:

— Export credits financed by Italian medium and long term credit institutions,
— Export credits financed by Italian commercial banks,
— Financing obtained abroad by Italian enterprises,
— Loans obtained directly abroad by foreign buyers and loans granted by foreign credit institutions and banks and
— Discounting abroad of credit instruments delivered by deferred–payment beneficiaries.

4.   AID FINANCE PROGRAMMES

4.1   Associated Financing (mixed credits)

4.1.1   Funds available

ODA can be associated with export credits if a project requires additional finance or, occasionally, in support of Italian exporters in matching situations. Each year a part (up to a maximum of 25 per cent) of the funds available for aid credits can be allocated for mixed credits.

4.1.2   *Eligibility*

With few exceptions, only developing countries with $ 2,500 or less GNP per capita are eligible for this kind of mixed credit.   Projects proposed for associated financing are screened by the Directorate General. If developmental criteria are satisfied and the soft loan component is approved by the relevant bodies (Steering Committee and Interministerial Committee), the request is passed on to the Ministry of Treasury for the necessary authorization.   Associated financing is tied to procurement in Italy, except for some local cost financing for projects in poor countries. Whenever possible, Italian suppliers of goods and services are selected by international competitive bidding or projects are co-financed with international development finance institutions.

Chapter 9

LUXEMBOURG

1. ORGANISATION AND STRUCTURE

1.1 Insurance and Guarantees

1.1.1 *Representative organisation*

Office du Ducroire
L–2981 Luxembourg

Telephone: (352) 43 58 53
Telex: CH COM LU 60174
Telefax: (352) 43 83 26

1.1.1.1 *Function*

Luxembourg supports export credits through an official credit insurance system run by an official agency ("Office du Ducroire") set up by the Act of 25th November 1961, and incorporated as a public body benifiting from the guarantee of the State.

The Agency co–operates closely with the Belgian Credit Insurance Department within the framework of a technical co–operation and reinsurance agreement, concluded between the two bodies on 1st July 1963.

1.1.1.2 *Summary of organisation*

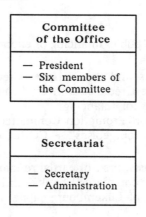

Requests for insurance are addressed to the Secretariat of the Office.

1.1.1.3   *Resources*

On 31st December 1988, Ducroire had at its disposal an appropriation of LF 742 million plus miscellaneous reserves of about LF 690 million. The current law authorises an appropriation increasing progressively up to a ceiling of LF 800 million.

The ceiling on commitments Ducroire may undertake on its own behalf is ten times the sum of appropriations plus the Agency's reserve fund. The ceiling on commitments undertaken on behalf of the State varies depending on the Agency's actual commitments and may not exceed 20 per cent thereof. A grand–ducal decree of 1986 fixed the limit of commitments on behalf of the State to LF 580 millions.

1.1.1.4   *Other organisations involved*

Ducroire is administered by a committee comprising a Chairman and equal numbers of representatives of Government and exporters. The Chairman is appointed by the Minister of Finance; the representatives of the Ministries of Finance, Economic Affairs and Foreign Affairs are nominated by their respective Ministers. Exporters' representatives are designated by the government in council.

The Committee of Ducroire has all the administrative and decision–making powers needed to fulfil the agency's aims.

1.1.1.5   *Relations with the state*

Ducroire operates under state guarantee. In 1981, an Act set up a special state credit insurance fund. Risks covered from this fund on behalf of the state are those that, by reason of their duration, amount or intensity are technically impossible for the Department to take on but whose insurance the government in council deems worthwhile.

1.1.1.6   *Relations with the private sector*

Private insurance companies operate in Luxembourg and may co–operate with Ducroire.

1.2   Export Finance

A particular feature of the public financing of export credits in Luxembourg is the close collaboration between:

— The commercial banks and the National Credit and Investment Company ("Société Nationale de Crédit et d'Investissement" — SNCI) with regard to making funds available for financing;
— The Luxembourg Export Promotion Committee ("Comité pour la promotion des exportations luxembourgeoises" — COPEL) with regard to interest subsidies.

Public sector support consists, first, of partial refinancing by SNCI, on preferential terms, of loans granted by the commercial banks, and second, interest subsidies for certain credits covering export of Luxembourg capital goods.

1.2.1   Representative organisation

Société Nationale de Crédit et d'Investissement (SNCI)
(National Credit and Investment Corporation)
7 rue du St Esprit
L-1475 Luxembourg

Telephone: (352) 46 19 71-1
Telex: 60664 SNCI Ch
Telefax: (352) 46 19 79

1.2.1.1   Function

The National Credit and Investment Company (SNCI), a national banking body, was set up by an Act of 2nd August 1977. Section 7 of this act provides that SNCI may take action, where appropriate, with the help of other bodies to arrange for export loans and credits.

1.2.1.2   Summary of organisation

The SNCI is administered by a board of twelve members appointed by the Government.

The daily work is supervised by the Executive Committee composed of the Chairman, the Vice-Chairman of the Board and the Director.

1.2.1.3   Resources

SNCI raises needed funds through the public or semi-public sector or by borrowing on domestic and international capital markets. For debenture loans, SNCI benefits from the same preferential terms as the Luxembourg state. This enables it to refinance a proportion of export credits at reduced cost.

1.2.1.4   Other organisations involved

For all export credits the SNCI works in close collaboration with the private credit institution established in Luxembourg and the Office du Ducroire.

1.2.1.5   Relations with the state

The SNCI is wholly State-owned.

1.2.1.6   Relations with the private sector

All applications for export credits have to be made through a private banking establishment approved by SNCI for export credit purposes.

1.2.2   COPEL

COPEL Secretariat
c/o Ministry of the Economy
L-2914 Luxembourg

Telephone: (352) 47 94 231
Telefax: (352) 46 04 48

1.2.2.1 *Function*

The "Comité pour la promotion des exportations luxembourgeoises" — Luxembourg Export Promotion Committee — is a body created by a Ministerial regulation of 27th March 1974. The responsible Ministers are the Minister of Foreign Affairs and Foreign Trade, the Minister of Finance and the Minister of Economy.

1.2.2.2 *Summary of organisation*

Not available.

1.2.2.3 *Resources*

Budgetary appropriations are made each year to finance the subsidies.

1.2.2.4 *Other organisations involved*

All COPEL decisions require approval from representatives of the Ministers of Foreign Affairs and Foreign Trade, Finance and Economy.

1.2.2.5 *Relations with the state*

COPEL acts as the agent of the state in administrating interest rate subsidies.

1.2.2.6 *Relations with the private sector*

Applications are introduced by the credit institution of the exporter.

2.   INSURANCE AND GUARANTEE PROGRAMMES

2.1   **Cover for Exporters**

2.1.1 *Policies available*

Transactions to be insured against commercial and/or political risks are classified by Ducroire on the basis of a criterion that at the same time determines the relevant insurance mechanism:
— Comprehensive policies:
   Contracts involving consumer or producer goods on which payment is generally due in the short term (twelve months);
— Comprehensive agreements:
   Contracts for capital goods and services not giving rise to any particular problem and on which payment is due within a maximum of five years; all contracts involving credit for a period exceeding five years, special contracts whatever the period of credit (construction works, turn—key factories, engineering services, etc.).
The various circumstances giving rise to claims include the following:
— Risk of default on the part of the debtor or commercial risk

This refers to debtors who are unable to perform their obligations or who refuse to do so without good reason. When default is the result of a private debtor's insolvency, it is held to be established when recognised in law (bankruptcy, discharge in bankruptcy or other judicial proceedings of a similar nature) or when the policyholder produces evidence that the debtor's situation makes any payment unlikely and that enforced performance or a petition in bankruptcy might lead to increased loss.

— Political risks and risks treated as equivalent

These risks, which for the policyholder or debtor involve a *force majeure* aspect, are essentially:

— Political developments such as wars, revolutions or riots;
— Natural disasters such as earthquakes, volcanic eruptions or tidal waves;
— Economic difficulties such as shortages of foreign exchange leading to delays in transfers;
— Obligations arising from acts, decisions or failures to act by the public authorities.

When the debtor is a public body, the Credit Insurance Department always provides joint cover for default by the debtor and political risks under the heading "public debtor risks". When the debtor is a private body, the risk of default is called a "commercial risk".

Contracts concluded with private debtors must be insured against both political and commercial risks. However, insurance against solely the political risks is possible on an exceptional basis Ducroire refuses to cover the commercial risks, for example when it has doubts as to the financial capacity of the debtor or because the debtor is a subsidiary of the policyholder.

Insurance for the period between conclusion of the contract and delivery (pre-shipment) is known as cover for cancellation claims ("assurance des sinistres de résiliation"). After delivery, the exporter can insure against the non–recovery of debts arising from performance of the contract by means of cover for non–payment claims ("assurance des sinistres de non–paiement").

The Department may authorise cover in a foreign currency, thus granting credit insurance denominated in the currency used in the export contract.

It should be noted that the Department asks the exporter to sign an undertaking to obtain cover for all extra–European transactions; however, it is possible to exempt certain features from this undertaking, for example different methods of payment.

2.1.2   *Eligibility*

— Criteria for accepting cover

Extension of cover depends on the terms requested and on the creditworthiness of the buyer and the buyer country. This assessment takes account of additional guarantees (by public bodies or local banks) offered by the potential buyer. Where Ducroire considers a risk unacceptable according to its normal criteria, it may refer the matter to the government, which may authorise the agency to underwrite the risk directly on its behalf if the contract at stake is of significant importance to the Luxembourg economy. Ducroire provides cover for credits that are in accordance with terms normal for the trade in question.

— Nationality requirements

Foreign content can only be accepted under the rules of:
— The Decision of the Council of the European Community of 10th December 1982 (see chapter 1);
— The bilateral conventions with the Belgian Office National du Ducroire (OND) and with the Compagnie Française d'Assurance du Commerce Extérieur in France (COFACE).

2.1.3   *Cost of cover*

Premiums are as a general rule payable in advance. They are calculated according to the duration of the credit, the destination of the exports and the nature of the risks insured. They are not subject to normal taxes on insurance premiums. The cost of covering short term transactions (up to twelve months credit) is generally less than 1 per cent whereas the premium for medium and long term transactions depends on the credit period as well as the nature and degree of risk.

2.2   Guarantees for Banks

2.2.1   *Policies available*

The Office du Ducroire may provide cover to Luxembourg banks extending financial credits related to export transactions.

Furthermore, the exporter may assign the proceeds of his policy to a bank providing financing.

2.2.2   *Eligibility*

See 2.1.2.

2.3   Other Insurance Programmes

— The Agency may insure against the seizure of or damage to goods and equipment and against the arbitrary seizure of bank guarantees.

— Ducroire may accept liabilities in a foreign currency and pay claims in the same currency.

— Investment insurance (political risks) it also available.

3.   EXPORT FINANCE PROGRAMMES

3.1   Direct Credits

N/A.

3.2   Refinancing

3.2.1   *Types of contract available*

Funds required for export financing are supplied by the commercial banks in the form of supplier credit or buyer credit. The banks take the necessary funds from their normal resources. In the case of credits for a period longer than that of normal commercial credits, the banks may be refinanced in part (normally up to 50 per cent) by preferential–rate deposits made by SNCI.

In addition to the refinancing scheme, there is a pooling arrangement by the major commercial banks to cover very large transactions. SNCI participates in this directly on the same footing as the other banks involved.

3.2.2   *Eligibility*

SNCI participates together with the commercial banks in financing export credits for Luxembourg capital goods. Exports qualifying for support may also include assembly and start–up costs in the country of destination.

Requests for export credits are made to SNCI by the bank with which the exporting firm usually deals. SNCI's participation is limited to a portion, to be fixed by its Board of directors, of between 25 and 75 per cent of the total value of the transaction concerned. In practice, the SNCI's share normally accounts for 50 per cent of the credit. In the absence of special authorisation from the Ministers concerned, export credit for a given transaction may not exceed LF 100 million.

3.2.3   *Resulting interest rates*

The rate of interest on SNCI's share of the export credit depends on the cost of refinancing by SNCI.

3.3   Interest Subsidies

3.3.1   *Types of contract available*

In order to enable Luxembourg exporters to offer their foreign customers (outside the EEC) financial terms similar to those of foreign competitors, the Government introduced in 1974 a system of interest rate subsidies for exports of Luxembourg capital goods in accordance with the terms of the Arrangement.

Applications for interest rate subsidies are submitted to COPEL

3.3.2   *Eligibility*

Only exports to markets outside the EEC qualify for interest rate subsidies.

3.3.3   *Resulting interest rates*

The subsidy amount is fixed with reference to foreign competition and to the rate of interest applied by the bank, or the rate is jointly fixed by the bank and SNCI where the latter participates. The final rate must comply with the level fixed in the OECD Arrangement.

4.   AID FINANCE PROGRAMMES

4.1   Associated Financing (mixed credits)

4.1.1   *Funds available*

Under an Act of 4th December 1981, the Government is authorised, for purposes of promoting foreign trade and with special reference to development co-operation, to grant States or foreign organisations loans that may be tied to the supply of goods or services of Luxembourg origin.

4.1.2   *Eligibility*

The general loan conditions must comply with the following provisions:

a) The total loan period may not exceed 30 years;
b) Loans may include an amortization–free period of not more than ten years;
c) In exceptional cases, the rate of interest may be zero;
d) The principal, interest and ancillary costs of loans to foreign organisations must be jointly and irrevocably guaranteed by the Government, central bank or institution responsible for implementing the development policy of the foreign state.

4.1.3   *Resulting terms and interest rates*

There are in accordance with Arrangement guidelines.

Chapter 10

NETHERLANDS

1. ORGANISATIONS AND STRUCTURE

1.1 Insurance and Guarantees

1.1.1 *Representative organisation*

Nederlandsche Credietverzekering Maatschappij N.V.,
P.O. Box 473
1000 AL Amsterdam
The Netherlands

Telephone: (31 20) 5539111
Telex: NCM NL 11496
Telefax: (31 20) 5532811

1.1.1.1 *Function*

The Nederlandsche Credietverzekering Maatschappij N.V. (NCM), a privately owned insurance company, has provided export credit insurance since 1925. An agreement with the Dutch government in 1932, broadened in 1946 and renewed in 1961 and 1983, provides for reinsurance with the Dutch government of non-commercial risks and commercial risks that fall outside the scope of private insurance. NCM is a private company owned by several Dutch banks and seventeen insurance companies of which two are foreign credit insurance companies.

NCM insures commercial risks for its own account and reinsures with the Dutch government non-commercial risks as well as such medium and long term commercial risks that it can take neither for its own account nor for the account of its private reinsurers. As the agreement with the Dutch government is based on a reinsurance arrangement, NCM handles all matters relating to credit insurance, including the processing and payment of claims.

1.1.1.2 Summary of organisation

NCM is managed by a Managing Board, comprising two members:

President in charge of general policy, finance, reinsurance, organisation and automation
Member in charge of insurance techniques, underwriting, sales promotion, marketing policy

— Short Term Credits Underwriting Department

Responsible for credits of up to twelve months.

— Medium Term Credits Underwriting Department

Responsible for credits exceeding twelve months up to ten years from delivery.

— Claims Department
— Information Department
— Credit Investigation Department
— Sales and External Relations Department
— Management Staff Group/Economic Research Department.
— Financial Administration, Reinsurance and Investment Department
— Personnel

1.1.1.3 Resources

NCM's activities for its own account are supported by its share capital (Gld 11.5 million), guarantee funds amounting to Gld 98.4 million and technical reserves amounting to Gld 559.6 million (1988 figures).

1.1.1.4 Other organisations involved

— *Export and Import Credits Guarantee Department of the Central Bank of the Netherlands* (Afdeling Export–en importgaranties van de Nederlandsche Bank)

A division of the Central Bank that has the authority to approve cover up to Gld 25 million for account of the Dutch government for transactions that cannot be accepted for cover by NCM.

— *Export Credit Insurance and Investment Guarantee Department of the Ministry of Finance and the Division for Exports Policy and Export Finance of the Ministry of Economic Affairs*

These departmental sections share the authority to approve cover for single transactions that exceed the authority of NCM and the Export and Import Credits Guarantee Department of the central bank.

— *State Committee for Export, Import and Investment Guarantees*
(Rijkscommissie voor Export– Import– en Investeringsgaranties)

The State Committee for Export, Import and Investment Guarantees is a committee established by the Minister of Finance and the Minister for Foreign Trade to advise the Minister of Finance on matters concerning export credit insurance. The Members are representatives of banks, insurance companies, trade and industry and representatives of the Ministries of Finance, Economic Affairs and Agriculture and Fisheries.

1.1.1.5   *Relations with the state*

NCM is authorised by the Minister of Finance to issue policies and addenda to policies if the cover extended is in line with general policy and the maximum liability does not exceed Gld 10 million per policy for buyers in all countries. For amounts between Gld 10 and Gld 25 million, approval of the Export and Import Credits Guarantee Department of the central bank is required. For amounts exceeding Gld 25 million, the approval of the Minister of Finance and the Minister of Foreign Trade is required.

Co–operation between the government and NCM is based upon the principle that commercial risks are usually covered for account of NCM and private reinsurers. Non–commercial risks are covered for account of the government by way of reinsurance.

The following risks are covered for account of the government:
— Political risks (including transfer risk),
— Payment risks attached to transactions with government buyers,
— Protracted default risks on private buyers in developing countries and also — if the credit period exceeds two years — private buyer insolvency risk,
— Protracted default risks and insolvency risk incurred with private buyers in industrialised countries where the credit term exceeds five years,
— The unfair calling of bonds,
— Foreign exchange risks, and
— Political risks in connection with investments in developing countries covering such risks as expropriation without adequate compensation, transfer delays, war, etc.

As far as business insured for account of the Netherlands government is concerned, premiums and recoveries received are paid to the government and claims are paid by the government. An annual fee is paid by the government to NCM for the work it carries out on behalf of the government.

1.1.1.6   *Relations with the private sector*

NCM is the only credit insurance company in the Netherlands that provides cover for both commercial and non–commercial risks. Only institutions registered in the Netherlands as insurance companies are allowed to operate as insurers.

1.1.1.7   *Additional structure*

There is no obligation for exporters in the Netherlands to take a credit insurance policy. The only exception to this rule was where the financing bank applied for the facilities offered under the Export Financing Arrangement (see 3.2) managed by the Central Bank.

1.2   Export Finance

With the exception of aid financing, export finance in the Netherlands is provided for by private banks exclusively.

1.2.1   *Other Representative organisation*

Ministry of Economic Affairs
Hoofdafdeling Exportbeleid en Export
financieringsaangelegenheden
P.O. Box 20101
Besuidenhoutseweg 6
2500 EC The Hague
The Netherlands

Telephone: (31 70) 79 63 97

1.2.1.1   *Function*

The Ministry of Economic Affairs operates an interest subsidy scheme for matching purposes (Export Finance Facility) (See 3.3).

1.3   Aid Finance

1.3.1   *Representative organisation*

Ministry of Foreign Affairs
Directorate General for International Co–operation
Besmidenhautserweg 67 P.O. Box 20061
2594 AV The Hague 2500 EB The Hague

Telephone: (31 70) 48 64 86
DAC contact point for Associated Financing, tel: (31 70) 48 60 24.

1.3.2   *Function*

The Directorate General for International Co–operation (DGIS) of the Ministry of Foreign Affairs handles the Netherlands development aid budget (about Gld 4,2 billion in 1988). Only a very small part of this budget (Gld 220 million in 1988) is destined to be used as the prime finance source for exports from the Netherlands (see paragraph 4).

2.   INSURANCE AND GUARANTEES

2.1   Cover for Exporters

Both commercial and non–commercial risks are covered, including transfer risk, payment risks in connection with sovereign buyers and protracted default. Cover is given for the post–shipment (payment) risk only or for pre–shipment (fabrication) and post–shipment risk together.

A very small part of Dutch export credits are expressed in a foreign currency. Exporters and banks may finance and refinance export credits in foreign currencies and may insure such transactions with NCM against the risk of non–payment. However, claims are settled in Dutch guilders. The exchange risks for such transactions sometimes can be covered on the forward exchange markets or with NCM (see 2.3.1).

2.1.1   Policies available

— Short term transactions

Cover is given for consumer goods, raw materials and semifinished goods as well as services. Normal credit terms are up to six months; consumer durables may be covered up to twelve months. Cover for short term business is normally given on a wholeturnover basis. In exceptional cases, cover is also possible for one or more countries or for special business sectors. Percentage of cover is usually 75 per cent; the maximum is 95 per cent.

— Medium term transactions

Cover is available for light and heavy capital goods, construction works and engineering services. For light capital goods, maximum maturity is three years; heavy capital goods and construction works contracts may be covered with credit terms up to ten years, depending on the size of the contract and country of destination. Percentage of cover is usually 95 per cent. A minimum cash payment of 15 per cent is required, of which 5 per cent is payable at date of contract. Cover of local costs is possible up to the amount of the cash payments. Cover for medium term transactions is generally through specific policies.

During the negotiation period of a contract, an exporter may apply for a commitment to cover in which the conditions of insurance are laid down. Such a commitment to cover has a validity of six months but may be extended.

Insurance cover may either be on a supplier credit basis or on a buyer credit basis (see 2.2.1). The supplier credit policy covers the payment risk when the exporter has extended credit to the buyer and is thus issued to the exporter; the buyer credit policy is issued to the bank.

2.1.2   Eligibility

— Criteria for accepting cover

Before underwriting the risk, NCM investigates the creditworthiness of the buyer as well as of the buyer's country. In some cases, NCM may decide that cover for a particular transaction can only be given if the exporter obtains additional payment guarantees from the buyer, e.g. bank guarantee (private buyer) or guarantee from the central government where the buyer is a sovereign (state controlled) organisation.

NCM does not interfere with normal trade practices. However international agreements, such as Arrangement conditions, are to be observed. As far as interest rates subsidised by the government are concerned, NCM's concern is that the actual costs of the credits are in conformity with Arrangement terms.

Side financed transactions are not eligible for cover under NCM policies.

— Nationality requirements

Any exporter established in the Netherlands is eligible for cover under NCM schemes. Cover for buyer credits is given to any bank established in the Netherlands and operating under Dutch laws and regulations (see 2.2.1).

The foreign content of the medium term transaction is in principle restricted to 30/40 per cent of the contract amount. Bilateral reciprocal foreign content (up to 30 per cent) agreements are in force with a number of countries.

2.1.3   Cost of cover

For premium purposes, all countries are classified into four grades. In each grade, there is a different rate for public buyers, private buyers and banking institutions, acting as either debtor or guarantor. Premium rates are further influenced by the risk period, percentage of cover, amount of down payment, etc. For short term transactions only the minimum premium is Gld 5 000. A global indication of the premium for a short term turnover for sales of several million guilders with some tens of creditors that are considered good credit risks and with a cover percentage of 75 is as follows:

Debtor Country	Repayment period		
	Cash against documents	Up to 60 days	60–90 days
The Netherlands		0.3 – 0.8 %	0.45 – 1.0 %
Other industrialised countries		0.4 – 0.8 %	0.7 – 1.1 %
Developing countries	0.6 – 0.7 %	0.9 – 1.2 %	1.0 – 1.4 %

The cost for a medium term policy, including pre–shipment risk (for one year) at an interest rate of the credit of 8 per cent with 90 per cent coverage could be globally indicated as follows:

Debtor		Repayment period			
		2 years	3 years	5 years	8 years
		Per cent			
Private debtor	Country Category I	2.6	3.1	3.9	4.9
	Country Category II	3.2	3.7	4.7	5.9
	Country Category III	4.6	5.4	6.9	8.6
	Country Category IV	6.1	7.0	9.1	11.3
Private bank	Country Category I	1.5	1.7	2.2	2.8
	Country Category II	1.9	2.2	2.8	3.6
	Country Category III	2.9	3.4	4.3	5.4
	Country Category IV	4.0	4.6	5.9	7.4
Sovereign debtor	Country Category I	0.5	0.6	0.8	1.0
	Country Category II	1.1	1.2	1.6	2.0
	Country Category III	2.0	2.3	2.9	3.7
	Country Category IV	3.0	3.5	4.5	5.7

2.2   Guarantees for Banks

2.2.1   *Policies available*

— Buyer credit policies

A buyer credit policy is issued to the financing bank and covers the payment risk where a bank has given a loan to the buyer from which the supplier is paid in full upon delivery of the goods. Cover of progress payments however is also possible. A buyer credit can only be insured if the underlying export transaction is in excess of Gld 4 million.

— Bank guarantees related to supplier credits

NCM may also give a direct guarantee to banks for drafts or promissory notes discounted by them for Dutch exporters, provided the underlying transaction is covered by a supplier credit risk policy. As regards the discounting bank, the direct guarantee is irrevocable and unconditional. NCM retains the right of recourse vis-à-vis the exporter.

— Guarantees for foreign banks

In 1986, a new facility was created that enables foreign banks to receive NCM cover when they are providing medium or long term finance in US dollars at a fixed rate, for Dutch exports of capital goods, or the construction of works by Dutch contractors. In such cases, claims will be honoured in Dutch guilders at the rate of exchange in force on the date of payment of the indemnity. Banks may additionally take out reverse exchange risk cover (see 2.3.2).

2.2.2   *Eligibility*

See 2.1.2.

2.2.3   *Cost of cover*

See 2.1.3.

2.3   Other Insurance Programmes

2.3.1   *Exchange risk cover*

This insurance covers losses, due to exchange rate fluctuations on contracts not denominated in Dutch guilders, of more than 3 per cent on an instalment. Cover is available for currencies listed on the Amsterdam Exchange and for the Japanese Yen and the Saudi Arabian Riyal. The risk period must be two years or more. Indemnification is 100 per cent of the loss; exchange gains must be paid in full to NCM if the gain is more than 3 per cent on an instalment.

2.3.2   *Reverse exchange risk cover*

This insurance may be taken out by banks that provide buyer credits denominated in US dollars. Indemnification is paid to the bank if the buyer defaults and the indemnification paid under the financing policy in Dutch guilders is not sufficient for the bank to cover its dollar obligations under the loan. This cover is only given in combination with a buyer credit policy.

2.3.3   Supplementary cover and counter guarantees

Supplementary cover and counter guarantees protect the exporter's bank as well as the exporter against losses due to unfair calling of bonds. For example, when a contract is concluded where cash or advance payments are agreed upon, the buyer may ask for a bank guarantee in the form of a bond. The exporter may suffer a loss if bonds are unfairly called. This risk may be covered under the so-called supplementary cover, which is an extension of the normal pre-shipment and payment risk cover. To the bank issuing the bonds, a counter guarantee may be given provided the exporter has obtained a policy for the pre-shipment and payment risk and has also obtained supplementary cover.

2.3.4   Investment insurance

Cover may be given for political risks in respect of new investments in developing countries provided that an investment protection agreement is signed with the country and the investment contributes to the economic development of that country. The government of the country where the investment is made has to approve the investment in order for it to qualify for insurance. Investment insurance has a maximum term of fifteen years after completion of the investment or twenty years after issuance of the policy.

2.3.5   Constructional works cover

Cover is given to a contractor for non-payment for services, or for his inability to recover his costs where the contract cannot be completed for reasons beyond his control.

2.3.6   Construction equipment cover

This policy covers the loss of equipment used in the buyer's country for the execution of a construction contract due to seizure of the equipment or to the impossibility of re-exporting the equipment.

3.   EXPORT FINANCE PROGRAMMES

3.1   Direct Credits

There exists neither a special institution nor a programme to provide for direct officially supported export credits in the Netherlands. Exports of Netherlands goods and services sold on short, medium or long term credit conditions are financed and refinanced by exporters and commercial banks at market rates only.

3.2   Refinancing

The Export Financing Arrangement (EFA) has existed since 1967. This arrangement is an agreement between de Nederlandsche Bank (the Central Bank of the Netherlands) and the domestic commercial banks under which the Central bank offered certain discount facilities in exchange for a below–market interest rate charged by the commercial banks for export transactions.

As the European Community regards these discount facilities of the Central bank as official support, the EFA can only be used when the Dutch guilder rate is above the matrix rate and when matching is used outside the EEC. The EFA has not been effective during recent years and may be abolished in the near future.

3.3   Interest Subsidies

3.3.1   *Types of contract available*

In 1988, the Matching Fund was replaced by an Export Finance Facility which enables Netherlands exporters and their bankers to benefit from the same level of official support to reduce financing costs that is enjoyed by their foreign competitors. Within the Export Finance Facility, two different features can be distinguished:

a) an *interest–support scheme* which operates within the framework of the Arrangement. Under the rules of this scheme, the Netherlands exporter has to prove that he has foreign competition receiving official financing support on Arrangement terms.

b) a *matching scheme*, which allows Netherlands exporters to offer export credits with interest rates below the Arrangement minimums in the event of proven foreign competition on similar terms. This scheme may be used for the financing of mixed credits (see 4.1.3).

The costs of the Export Finance Facility are paid for out of the budget. In 1988, Gld 30 million was available.

3.3.2   *Eligibility*

Interest subsidies will only be given to export credits on a matching basis; proof of foreign competition is a prerequisite for support.

Only credits exceeding two years are eligible.

As a rule, the transaction concerned must have a Netherlands content of more than 70 per cent. (Exceptions will be made to comply with EEC rules). The financing institution that receives the support need not be of Netherlands origin as long as the transaction includes the prescribed Netherlands content.

The financing to be supported must be either in Dutch guilders or in the same currency that the competitor is offering. If there is more than one officially supported competitor or if one officially supported competitor is offering different currency options, a subsidy can only be given in one currency. In any case, the funding should originate from the domestic capital market of the currency involved.

3.3.3   *Resulting interest rates*

See 3.3.1.

3.4   Other credit operations

The special interest rate subsidy schemes for ships were abolished in 1988. There are no other interest subsidy schemes currently operational.

4.   AID FINANCE PROGRAMMES

4.1   Associated Financing (mixed credits)

4.1.1   *Funds available*

Official Development Assistance loans are occasionally combined with officially guaranteed export credits under the Programme for Export Transactions Relevant to Development (see also 4.3).

Since 1988, Gld 220 million in ODA–loans has been available on a yearly basis for this programme.

In addition to this programme, other Official Development Assistance loans are occasionally combined with officially guaranteed export credits if an aid project requires additional finance.

Furthermore, the interest subsidy under the Export Finance Facility (see 3.3) can, under certain circumstances and conditions, be transformed into an Official Development Assistance grant of a mixed credit.

Except for the Export Finance Facility, which is administered by the Ministry of Economic Affairs, all requests for mixed credits are to be submitted to the Ministry of Foreign Affairs (Directorate General for International Co–operation), which will make a developmental appraisal of the projects to be partially financed with ODA funds by the Netherlands when it is the initiating donor country.

4.1.2   *Eligibility*

The funds from the Programme for Export Transactions Relevant to Development, the Export Finance Facility and export credits are tied to procurement in the Netherlands; all three sources, however, can be used to finance third country procurements to a limited extent.

The development funds will only be made available for transactions that further the realization of the development assistance policy of the Netherlands and of the recipient country involved. Thus, transactions are appraised for their contribution to the long term development of the recipient country and for their compatibility with the general principles of Netherlands development co–operation policy. Since account is also taken of Dutch interests in terms of exports and employment, the mixed credits are largely tied. As a rule, 70 per cent of the work involved in manufacturing goods or providing services must be undertaken in the Netherlands or by personnel posted abroad by Dutch firms. In terms of value added the criteria stipulate that the "bulk of work" should be done in the Netherlands or by Dutch personnel posted abroad.

Under the Programme for Export Transactions Relevant to Development, the minimum transaction amount for mixed credits is Gld 50 million, which at the same time is the maximum ODA–loan amount under this programme. As a result, the maximum transaction amount under this program was about Gld 67.5 million at the beginning of 1989.

4.1.3   *Resulting terms and interest rates*

For a mixed credits consisting of an ODA loan and a commercial loan, the ODA part has an interest rate of 2.5 % and a maturity of 30 years, of which 7 years are a grace period (both calculated from the commitment date *i.e.*, the DAC starting point of the ODA credit). The volume of both the commercial loan and the ODA loan depend on the Differentiated Discount Rate (DDR) in force at the time of notification and on the transaction amount because the concessionality level must be at least 35 % to conform to the Arrangement. Where the mixed credit consists of an ODA grant from the Export Financing Facility and a commercial loan, the concessionality level may be under 35 %, but this level and the volume of the grant will depend on the transaction amount and the concessionality level that is offered by the foreign competitor being matched (see 3.3.1).

4.2   Integrated credits

4.2.1   *Funds available*

Under the Programme for Export Transactions Relevant to Development (see also 4.1), transactions up to Gld 50 million are financed with integrated ODA loans.

Since 1988, Gld 220 million has been available on a yearly basis, out of a total of Fld 4.2 billion available for all the Netherlands development aid in 1988.

4.2.2   *Eligibility*

The eligibility is the same as for associated (mixed credits) financing under this programme (see 4.1.2), with exception of the transaction amount.

4.2.3   *Resulting terms and interest rates*

The terms of the transactions that are financed under the Programme for Export Transactions Relevant to Development are the following:

a) 25 years' maturity of which 7 years grace and 3.5 % interest;
b) 20 years' maturity of which 7 years grace and 3.0 % interest;
c) 15 years' maturity of which 7 years grace and 2.5 % interest.

(*N.B.* The number of years are counted from the DAC starting point of these ODA credits *i.e.*, the commitment date).

The terms offered depend on the economic life of the goods delivered and the repayment capacity of the development country involved.

4.3   Other tied or partially untied aid

A large part of all ODA given by the Netherlands on a bilateral basis is partially untied aid.

This aid consists of grants with a concessionality level of 100 %, and of loans which had the following standard terms: 30 years' maturity of which 7 years grace and 2.5 % interest. Since 1988, the Netherlands has tried to reduce the concessionality level of these loans where possible.

Chapter 11

PORTUGAL

1. ORGANISATION AND STRUCTURE

1.1 Insurance and Guarantees

1.1.1 *Representative Organisation*

Companhia de Seguro de Créditos EP
Avenida da Républica 58
1094 Lisbon Codex

Telephone: (351 1) 760131/766051
Telex: COSEC P 12885
Telefax: (351 1) 734614 (m)

1.1.1.1 *Function*

In 1965, the general basis of a scheme for export credits and credit insurance was first laid down in Portugal. The aims were, among others, to make it possible for the prefinancing of exports to become the general practice and to open up new projects for medium and long term financing. It was only in 1969, however, that the scheme took concrete shape when requisite adjustments were made to existing government structures and new institutions necessary to operate the scheme were set up.

The "Companhia de Seguro de Créditos" (COSEC) began operating in 1969 as a limited liability company with the government as a major shareholder. It was nationalised in March 1975 and then converted into a public sector company (27th January 1976). COSEC has administrative and financial autonomy but must submit its annual report and accounts to the Ministry of Finance through the Secretary of State for the Treasury.

Following a decision made by the Council of Ministers on 24 November 1988, COSEC is to be converted into a mixed capital joint stock company.

Besides providing credit insurance to Portuguese exports and domestic credit insurance, COSEC can also cover financial credit bonds, factoring leasing contracts and Portuguese investments abroad. COSEC provides commercial risk cover for its own account being responsible for the management of state guarantees to political and extraordinary (public buyer) risks.

1.1.1.2 *Summary of organisation*

COSEC has one branch office in Oporto and it is represented in the Autonomous Regions of the Madeira Islands (Funchal) and of the Azores.

COSEC is organised in eleven divisions and two departments:

— General Secretariat,
— Claims,
— Recoveries,
— Export Credit U/W,
— Domestic Credit U/W,
— Bond Insurance U/W,
— Personnel,
— Electronic Data Processing,
— Economics and International Relations,
— Sales and Marketing (where the applications are received),
— Finance and Accounts,
— Reinsurance Department.
— Planning and Audit Department.

1.1.1.3 *Resources*

COSEC covers commercial risks by means of its own capital (at present Esc 250 million) and its technical reserves. It also maintains agreements with reinsurers, particularly with foreign reinsurance companies.

As at 31st December 1988 technical reserves (guarantee reserve, claims reserve and contingency reserve) for COSEC's own operations amounted to Esc 3 077.4 million. As far as operations with the state guarantee are concerned, claims reserves amounted to Esc 1 959 million.

COSEC is empowered by the government to provide extraordinary risk cover on behalf and in the name of the Portuguese state for individual medium and long term transactions up to Esc 50 million, and for short term transactions up to Esc. 35 million, with an annual and global liability ceiling of Esc 1000 million.

1.1.1.4 *Other organisations involved*

The COSEC bodies are i) the Board of Management comprised of three to five members, including the Chairman, appointed by the government under proposal of the Minister of Finance and ii) the Auditors' Commission comprised of three members, two of whom are appointed by the Minister of Finance and the other by COSEC's employees.

The main functions of the Auditor's Commission are:

— To see that all rules and regulations governing the company's activity are complied with;
— To audit and accompany all current managerial actions;
— To assist the carrying out of the company's activity and financial plans;
— To check over the company's accounting and give its auditing opinion on the annual report and accounts.

1.1.1.5   *Relations with the state*

Extraordinary risks of a political, economic, monetary or catastrophic nature, if they are to be covered by COSEC, must be previously submitted for decision to CNGC (see 1.1.2.) except for foreign investment insurance operations for which only the advice of CNGC is required. This Commission assumes risk on behalf of and for the account of the state and can, on COSEC's request, guarantee other risks in whole or part.

1.1.1.6   *Relations with the private sector*

With the publication of the Decree Law n° 183/88 COSEC has no longer the monopoly of credit insurance, except for export credit risks with the state guarantee. As a result, export credit insurance of commercial risks may be provided by other authorized insurers.

1.1.2   *CNGC*

Comissao Nacional das Garantias de Créditos (CNGC)
(National Committee on Credit Guarantees)
Avenida da Republica, 58–13°
P–1000 Lisbon

Telephone: (351 1) 775140
Telex: 15075 CNGC P
Telefax: (351 1) 734614

1.1.2.1   *Function*

CNGC created by Decree Law n° 372/82, of 10th September 1982 and replaces the former "Comissao de Créditos e Garantias de Créditos" (Commission for Credit and Credit Guarantees). It is a specialized collegiale State body working closely with the Management Board of COSEC. Its Chairman is appointed by the Minister of Finance and the Minister of Trade and Tourism. The other members are representatives of the Ministry of Finance, Ministry of Trade and Tourism, the Portuguese Foreign Trade Institute (ICEP), the Institute for Economic Cooperation (ICE), the Bank of Portugal, COSEC, the credit institutions and the trade organisations for the support of export activities.

Besides providing credit insurance against political and extraordinary risks in the name of the State and, in exceptional cases, reinsurance of certain commercial risks of export credit insurance underwritten by COSEC, the CNGC also gives advice on investment insurance operations and makes decisions concerning state guarantees for export financing and reinsurance of domestic credit insurance transactions that may exceptionally be proposed to it by COSEC (see 1.1.1.5).

1.1.2.2   *Organisation*

See 1.1.2.1.

1.1.2.3   *Resources*

For the risks assumed by the state, an annual ceiling is entered in the General Budget of the government. However, if necessary, funds may be allocated to the CNGC to meet the amounts of compensation due.

1.1.3. *FGRG*

The Fundo de Garantia de Riscos Cambiais — FGRC — (Exchange Risk Guarantee Fund) was established by Decree Law 75–D/77, with the object of covering risks resulting from the fixing of exchange rates in certain foreign credit operations, involving both imports and exports.

The FGRC is a collective entity of public law, with juridical personality and financial autonomy. It is managed by the Bank of Portugal, which is also empowered to carry out, in its name and on behalf of the Fund, all operations pertaining to its object.

The net results, whenever positive, are regarded as income for the state; in case of negative results, they are first covered by calling up the reserve fund and then by specific budgetary allocations.

1.2   Export Finance

There is no agency or any other official institution in Portugal which directly finance export credits. Export financing is provided by the commercial banks. Commercial banks and credit institutions fund themselves with financial backing from the Bank of Portugal, which refinances the credit institutions.

According to current legislation, if the cost, nature or amount of resources used is not in line with normal export credit terms, the central bank may request the Ministry of Finance for additional funds on a case by case basis.

2.   INSURANCE AND GUARANTEE PROGRAMMES

2.1   Cover for Exporters

2.1.1   *Policies available*

COSEC policies are of the following types:
— *Wholeturnover policies*: For commercial risks cover on short term exports of goods undertaking the exporter generally to insure all his credit sales;
— *Specific policies*: For commercial risks cover on individual exports of goods or services, usually on medium and long term and for individual exports of goods or services to public buyers;
— *Endorsements:* For pre–shipment risks cover and for extraordinary risks in combinaison with commercial risks cover.

2.1.2   *Eligibility*

Commercial risk cover is decided in the light of the creditworthiness of the buyer and of the importing country.

Extraordinary risk cover is decided by the CNGC on the basis of a country grading table and of detailed analysis of the political and economic situation of the importing country.

When cover is given on behalf of the state for foreign content cannot exceed 40 per cent.

For the purpose of official support, credit terms must be consistent with international practice and agreements for similar transactions.

The maximum credit lengths are as follows :

Pre-shipment cover
— Consumer goods: one year;
— Capital goods or services: two years;
— Heavy capital goods of a value exceeding Esc 25 million: four years.

Post-shipment cover
— Current consumer goods: one year;
— Other consumer goods: two years;
— Light capital goods or services: five years;
— Heavy capital goods: eight and a half years.

However, the above maximum credit lengths are without prejudice to the exigencies of international competition as regulated by the relevant international rules.

2.1.3   *Cost of cover*

Insurance premiums are based on the invoiced value of the exports insured or on the cover requested. They vary according to the risks covered, the type of goods (for commercial risks only), the guarantees offered, the credit length, the nature of the importer, his creditworthiness, and the country concerned.

— Commercial risks cover

For cover of exports of consumer goods on short term credit to OECD countries (all risks included) a "flat" premium rate is charged which can vary from 0.24 per cent for cash against documents transactions to 0.48 per cent for transactions on ninety days credit. Medium term credits for exports of capital goods to OECD countries are covered at a basic "flat" premium rate which can vary from 1.094 per cent for transactions on two years credit to 1.717 per cent for transactions on five years credit.

— Extraordinary risk cover

Cover of exports for short term credits to relatively poor countries is available for a "flat" premium rate which can vary from 0.37 per cent for cash against documents transactions to 1.38 per cent for transactions on one hundred and eighty days credit. For exports to relatively poor countries a "flat" premium rate is charged which can vary from 4.02 per cent for transactions on two years credit to 7.47 per cent for transactions on seven years credit. The rates include all extraordinary risks.

2.2   **Guarantees for Banks**

2.2.1   *Policies available*

There are special policies for financial credits covering supplier credits, buyer credits and lines of credit.

Guarantees to banks are mainly given on behalf of the State. However, this cover is made on a restrictive basis.

2.2.2   *Eligibility*

For supplier credits, cover is decided taking mainly into account criteria similar to those used for credit insurance of commercial risks.

For buyer credits and lines of credit, decision for cover is made mainly on basis of criteria used for credit insurance of extraordinary risks.

In what concerns foreign content, credit terms and official support criteria referred to in 2.1.2 are also applicable.

2.2.3   Cost of cover

For supplier credits cover (firm orders), a premium of 0.6 per cent per annum is charged on the outstanding amount and on interest (if covered).

For buyer credits and lines of credit the "flat" premium rates charged for commercial risks and extraordinary risks (public buyers) are applicable respectively to private and public borrowers with a reduction of between 10 per cent and 30 per cent.

Depending on the terms and conditions of the credit, premium rates for financial guarantees can vary by plus or minus 20 per cent.

2.3   Other Insurance Programmes

2.3.1   Foreign exchange risk insurance

COSEC provides cover against exchange risk fluctuations with the prior guarantee of the State.

Only exchange losses exceeding a limit (e.g. 3%) are indemnified and, on a reciprocal basis, exchange profits exceeding that limit are repayable by the exporter. A ceiling on foreign exchange fluctuations can also be established.

Cover is available separately or in combination with export credit cover. In principle, all the currencies officially quoted by Portuguese Central Bank are eligible for cover.

There is little experience with this scheme.

2.3.2   Bond insurance

Bond insurance policies, covering the Portuguese exporter's failure to fulfil contract obligations under the bonds (Bid, Advance payment, Retention Payment, Performance) are provided.

For operations involving medium sized risks on construction/supply bonds, premium rates vary from 0.6 per cent per annum for bid bonds to 2.5 per cent per annum for infrastructural works.

The unjustified calling of the bonds can also be covered on behalf of the State.

2.3.3   Cost escalation and foreign exchange risk insurance

Decree Law n° 183/88 authorises COSEC to guarantee against losses arising from abnormal and unforeseeable increases in production costs, because of changed economic conditions, which affect the execution of export contracts.

Such cover must have the prior guarantee of the state. A basic "flat" rate of 2 per cent is charged on the outstanding amount. A franchise can also be established, case by case.

There has been practically no experience with this scheme.

2.3.4   Other export financing programmes cover

As regards the cover of financing of working capital for export programmes, a premium of 1 per cent per annum is charged on the outstanding amount. Insurance for financing of export promotion and market research programmes is available at a premium of 1.3 per cent per annum on the outstanding amount. According to the terms and conditions, premium rates can vary by plus or minus 20 per cent. Interest can also be covered.

Cover can also be provided on construction or purchase of the entrepots and the establishment of commercial networks abroad.

There has been practically no experience with these programmes.

2.3.5   Foreign investment insurance

Investment insurance scheme was established under Decree Law n° 273/86 and it is intended to provide a relevant contribution to the establishment and strenghthening of the economic relations between Portugal and the host country.

The cover is applicable to the following types of Portuguese investments abroad: equity contributions (in cash, kind or services) made to an overseas new or existing enterprise, purchase of existing shares, constitution or development of branches, medium and long term loans. Earnings to be reinvested or repatriated may also be covered up to a ceiling, provided that the application is made before the date of the insurance contract.

The risks covered are requisition, confiscation, transfer, general moratorium and alterations to the foreign investment law in the host country which may, in any way, reduce the investor's rights and guarantees.

To qualify for insurance the investment must be new, be made in strict observance of the legal and foreign exchange regulations in force both in Portugal and in the host country, be previously approved and enjoy adequate legal protection in the host country.

The maximum percentage of cover is of 90 per cent and basic premium rates vary from 1 per cent to 1.3 per cent per annum depending on the host country grading.

2.3.6   Exchange risk guarantee

All medium and long term export credits granted by Portuguese exporters to foreign buyers, if financed by a bank in Portugal, must be covered by a contract with FGRC. This contract provides as follows:

— FGRC will pay any loss, or receive any gain, from the difference between the interest rate on the export credit and that on the internal financing at market rates;

— FGRC will pay any loss, or receive any gain, from the difference between the exchange rate fixed in the contract and that at which actual principal and interest payments are converted into escudos.

The premium for the exchange risk guarantee, payable by the exporter, is 0.1 per cent per year on the escudo equivalent value of the amount guaranteed, at the fixed exchange rate. The exchange risk cover is available for all currencies quoted by the Bank of Portugal, and is mainly used for transactions in US dollars, deutschemarks, French francs and Swiss francs.

3.   EXPORT FINANCE PROGRAMMES

3.1   Direct Credits

Not available.

3.2   Refinancing

There are no special facilities in Portugal for refinancing export operations. Portuguese banks and other credit institutions (Banco de Fomento Nacional et Caixa General de Depositos) can, however, refinance export credits with the Bank of Portugal. The interest rate applied by the Bank of Portugal for such refinancing is not subject to any subsidy.

3.3   Interest Subsidies

Financing to the exporter is given by the banks in escudos; the amount and the period of this credit may not exceed the period and the exchange value of the credit given to the buyer, expressed in foreign currency. The applicable rate of interest is the one in force in the domestic market for operations involving the same period of credit. The exporter is required to request simultaneously that the FGRC (Exchange Risk Guarantee Fund) agree on the exchange risk for this credit in proportion to the financing received. Thus, he may collect from the Fund the balance between the interest payable on the domestic financing and the interest to be received on the external order, calculated at the rates previously authorised by the Bank of Portugal, according to the respective currency and period of credit.

The direct financing is always expressed in foreign currency. The exchange value in Escudos is disbursed to the exporter under the terms of the supply contract by the credit institution. The credit institution may request the FGRC to cover the exchange risk for its credit in terms similar to those previously referred to for financing the exporter. As for future developments, it is envisaged that Banco de Fomento Nacional will be empowered with specific functions in the field of export finance support. Technical studies are presently under preparation on terms and scheme of intervention.

3.3.1   *Types of contracts available*

Decree Law 481/80 authorisies Portuguese banks to provide financing for a wide range of activities associated with export production and marketing:

a) For *market studies and surveys,* up to 50 per cent of the costs may be financed, with repayment up to three years, or in exceptional cases, four years. For specific programmes of market promotion that may result from such studies, the same financing conditions apply.

b) *Financing of working capital* needed to carry out export programmes for acquiring raw materials and other products in Portugal or abroad may be provided at short term (with exceptional extensions) in an amount not more than 70 per cent of the cost of the finished goods.

c) *Financing for the preparation and execution of firm orders* from abroad may be obtained, with the following conditions:

— Consumer goods: one year, 90 per cent of the order;

— Equipment and services: two years, 90 per cent of the order;
— Studies and projects: three years, 95 per cent of the order;
— Heavy equipment, worth over Esc 25 million: four years, 95 per cent of the order.

d) Supplier credits for a short term export contract may be financed up to the value of the credit, or 85 per cent of the contract value at medium or long term, according to the following schedule:

— One year for current consumer goods;
— Two years for other consumer goods;
— Five years for light equipment and services;
— Eight and a half years for heavy equipment.

e) Alternatively, *buyer credits* may be provided directly to the importer for certain operations so that the exporter receives his payment immediately. This procedure may be used for individual export contracts where a 15 per cent downpayment is required. The credit may cover 85 per cent of the contract value, with a maximum term (in principle) of ten years. Prior authorisation from the Ministry of Finance is necessary for export credit with a term of more than ten years and for extension of such credits beyond ten years. Programmes for the purchase of Portuguese products may be financed by buyer credits with similar conditions except that the maturity is short term for consumer goods and medium term for other goods.

Buyer credit is provided for local costs in the importer's country, encompassing goods and services directly related to the export transaction. The terms of such financing may not be more favourable that those applied to the export itself.

f) Financing provided for certain *ancillary activities*:

— Construction or purchase by Portuguese firms of entrepots or warehouses abroad, with financing of up to 50 per cent of the value and maximum term of five years;
— Establishment of or participation in firms to exploit commercial networks abroad or to promote the sale of Portuguese goods, with financing of up to 50 per cent of the capital subscribed and paid in and a maximum term of five years.

Prior authorisation from the Bank of Portugal is necessary for financing beyond the maximum terms given above and for extension of repayment terms beyond those limits.

3.3.2   Eligibility

See 3.3.1.

3.3.3   Resulting interest rates

The indicative levels that banks charge on the domestic financing to exports (in Escudos) are, according to the respective credit period, the following:

— 18 per cent — operations exceeding ninety days but not exceeding one hundred and eighty days;
— 20.5 per cent — operations exceeding two years and up to five years;
— 21.5 per cent — operations exceeding five years.

Current commercial interest reference rates (CIRRs) for supplier credits and for direct financing to foreign buyers domiciled outside the EEC area observe the OECD Arrangement.

3.4   Other Credit Operations

Foreign currency transactions

Current monetary guidelines provide that suppliers' credits and financing given directly by the credit institutions to the buyers for export operations must be expressed in the foreign currency specified by the Bank of Portugal. Official support can only be granted subject to the following conditions: the intermediation of the FGRC in the terms referred to under 2.3.6 — which allows the reconciliation between the cost of the domestic bank financing in escudos, or of the mobilisation of the respective capital by the banks (also in escudos), and the externally established terms of credit, in terms of exchange and interest rates.

4. AID FINANCE PROGRAMMES

Portugal has no programme for associated financing.

Chapter 12

SPAIN

1. ORGANISATION AND STRUCTURE

1.1 Insurance and Guarantees

1.1.1 *Representative organisation*

Compania Espanola de Seguros de Crédito a la Exportacion, S.A.
(CESCE)
c/Velazquez 74
28001 Madrid

Telephone: (34 1) 401 70 00, 401 30 62
Telex: CESCE E 23577, 45369 and 45344
Telefax: 435 61 75

1.1.1.1 *Function*

The Spanish Export Credit Insurance Company (CESCE) was set up as a joint stock company in 1970. Its supports Spanish exporters by means of a system of insurance policies designed to cover both commercial risks and political and extraordinary risks, as well as what are known as special risks.

CESCE covers commercial risks on its own account and political and extraordinary risks on behalf of the State.

1.1.1.2 *Summary of organisation*

The issuance and management of policies is the responsibility of the Sub–Directorate General for Transactions. This, in turn, is subdivided into medium, long term and short term directorates.

Compensation and recovery of claims come under the Sub–Directorate General for Financial, Legal and Technical Affairs and the Director of Claims.

1.1.1.3 *Resources*

CESCE's share capital totals Ptas 400 000 000, including a State share of 50.25 per cent. The remaining 49.75 per cent is controlled by the private sector.

Accumulated reserves total Ptas 1 420 861 462.   Capital funds therefore total Ptas 1 820 861 462. For commercial risks, resources are from premiums paid, recoveries, fees and investment income.

For political and extraordinary risks, which are managed on behalf of the state, the company relies on reserves constituted by the Consorcio de Compensacion de Seguros (CCS), i.e. premiums paid, claims recovered, and all contributions by the state to cover these specific risks.

BOARD OF DIRECTORS

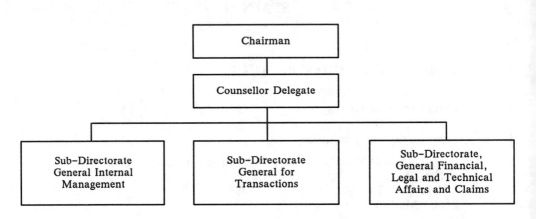

1.1.1.4 *Other organisations involved*

CESCE provides insurance for short, medium and long term operations. Decisions concerning cover are taken by an internal committee of the company. Over a specified amount, decisions are taken by the executive commissions of the Board of Directors (Commission for Political Risks and Commission for Commercial Risks), which meet every week and take their decisions on the basis of proposals put forward by the company's different services.

The payment of claims, up to a pre-established amount, must be approved by an internal committee, which meets every week. Claims exceeding this amount are submitted to the Board of Directors, which meets once a month.

1.1.1.5 *Relations with the state*

If CESCE resources should prove inadequate, the government may, on the proposal of the Ministry of Finance, authorise the opening of credit accounts with the External Bank (see 1.2.1). If the results of a financial year threaten the financial stability of the company, the funds necessary to restore the situation are provided by the CCS, an autonomous body of the Ministry of Finance.

The State budget provides the funds necessary to meet any difficulties arising from the cover of political and extraordinary risks if premiums and reserves prove inadequate.

1.1.1.6 *Relations with the private sector*

Up to 1984, CESCE had exclusive reponsibility for commercial risk insurance. Since then, private companies authorised by government may operate in this area. CESCE arranges joint insurance and co–insurance. It has concluded bilateral agreements with other export credit agencies on joint insurance.

Under the new "Ley de Ordenacion del Seguro Privado" of 2nd August 1984 (Private Insurance Act), CESCE may reinsure its risks with Spanish or foreign reinsurers and the CCS.

1.2   Export Finance

1.2.1 *Representative organisation*

Banco Exterior de Espana (BEE, External Bank of Spain)
Carrera de San Jeronimo, 36
28014 Madrid
Espagne

Telephone: (34 1) 429 44 77
Telex: 22033
Telefax: (34 1) 429 83 42

1.2.1.1 *Function*

The BEE (opened in 1928) promotes and finances Spanish exports. Also, like other credit institutions, it may undertake a range of banking transactions, subject always to the general rules governing the Spanish finance system, which includes the supervision of the Banco de Espana (Spain's Central Bank).

The Board of Directors of the External Bank is composed of representatives of the Central Administration and private sector in proportion to their respective shares in the Bank's capital. Public funds represent 65 per cent of BEE's equity capital. The remainder is held by the private sector.

Subsidised export credits accounted at the end of 1988 for 41 % of total (domestic and foreign) BEE credits and 85 % of export credits with official support extended by the overall Spanish financial system.

1.2.1.2 *Summary of organisation*

The current management of BEE's trade financing operations is run by its Foreign Trade and Export Credit Division.

1.2.1.3 *Resources*

At 31st December 1988, BEE's capital was Ptas. 26,8 billion with reserves amounting to Ptas. 50,9 billion, totalling Ptas. 77,7 billion. Besides the resources obtained from its customers' deposits and through borrowings in both domestic and international markets, BEE has an additional and exclusive access to public funds alloted for subsidized export credits. These reimbursable funds are made available to BEE by the Instituto de Credito Oficial (ICO, Institute of Official Credit)) (see 1.2.1.4).

According to the regulations governing official credit, BEE is responsible for the management of public funds put at its disposal by ICO to finance Spanish exports.

ICO lends these funds on terms that enable BEE to provide credits to exporters in conformity with the provisions of the Arrangement.

BEE sources for export credit finance depend on whether or not these operations qualify for official support. For non–subsidised transactions (where credit term is less than two years), BEE funding is limited to its own resources, customers' deposits and borrowings from domestic and international markets.

For subsidised transactions, i.e., those regulated by both the Arrangement and EEC rules on trade finance, the funding is made through:

- a percentage of BEE's total customers' deposits which must be channelled through subsidised operations and is gradually decreasing (9,5 % at the end of 1989) until its elimination on 31st December 1992. This percentage, called compulsory investment ratio on export credit, used to be as high as 32 % for BEE and was also applicable to other financial institutions (3 % for private banks and 1 % for savings banks). At present, only BEE is obliged to assign an investment ratio exclusively to finance subsidized export operations while other financial institutions maintain an obligation to apply such a decreasing ratio to the subscription of Treasury promissory notes or other public issues.
- After the above ratio has been exhausted, BEE may apply for ICO's funding to meet the exporters' needs for subsidised credits.
- Finally, like other financial institutions, BEE may also utilise its own resources and/or borrow from domestic and international markets on prevailing terms, for transactions qualifying for interest subsidisation (see 3.3).

1.2.1.4 *Other organisations involved*

ICO participates also in export credit operations. In addition to the funds provided to BEE, it also runs the management of a special fund called Fondo de Ayuda al Desarrollo (FAD, Development Aid Fund).

ICO's funding is twofold:

- funds originating from State budget appropriations for general and specific purposes (development aid, for instance)
- funds obtained from borrowings in the domestic and international capital markets. In 1988, this accounted for nearly two thirds of ICO total liability.

Since January 1st 1988, ICO has been a public holding company charged with the management, coordination and supervision of the activities of the four official banks integrating the Spanish official credit structure: Bank of Industrial Credit, Bank of Agricultural Credit, Bank of Local Credit and the Spanish Mortgage Bank (Banco Hipotecario).

The Direccion General de Politica Comercial (General Directorate of Trade Policy), a department of the Secretary of State of Commerce, also participates in decisions affecting export credit operations with official support, such as authorizations regarding the level of foreign content in goods and services, local expenses, evaluation of applications for aid funds, etc.

1.2.1.5 *Relations with the state*

In spite of its semi–public status and the fact that the majority of its capital is officially–owned, BEE works autonomously in its foreign trade transactions.

1.2.1.6 *Relations with the private sector*

Provision of financing is based on the classic relationship between banks and their clients.

1.3   Aid Finance

ICO is responsible for the management of aid finance provided in the form of soft loans extended by the Spanish Government to governments or public institutions of developing countries. Specific appropriations for these facilities are included annually in the Government's General Budget and assigned as reimbursable loans to ICO (see 4).

2.   INSURANCE AND GUARANTEE PROGRAMMES

2.1   Cover for Exporters

2.1.1 *Policies available*

As indicated above, (see 1.1.1.1) CESCE covers both political risks (on behalf of the state) and commercial risks (on its own account). In both cases, manufacturing and credit risks are covered.

Commercial risks are covered up to a maximum of 85 per cent of the loss, and up to 90 per cent if the insured exporter holds a first category exporter's card. For political risks, the limit is 90 per cent, (or 95 per cent if the exporter holds a first category exporter's card). In certain cases, for example a buyer's credit policy in foreign currency, 100 per cent cover is possible. Both policies guarantee to the exporter an indemnification for the loss he may suffer as a consequence of the contract cancellation (pre–shipment risk) or of the total or partial non–payment of the deferred value (credit risk).

Insurance may be taken out in the form of comprehensive policies (short term, bond insurance and confirmation of letters of credit) or of individual policies, whatever the nature of the operation. Whole turnover policies allow the exporter to cover the risk of non–payment of credits for all his export transactions whose repayment periods do not exceed three years. They do not include cover for possible contract cancellation (pre–shipment risk).

Payment of claims takes place within ten days following the determination of final net loss. Compensation for protracted default generally takes place six months after the notification of failure to pay. This period can however be extended to eight months or reduced to three.

2.1.2 *Eligibility*

Agreement or refusal to provide insurance cover depends on different criteria, mainly the creditworthiness of the importing country (political risks) or that of the private importer (commercial risks). Account is also taken of terms of payment, of the guarantees offered, etc.

The maximum percentage of foreign goods that may be insured is 10 per cent.

2.1.3   *Cost of cover*

Premiums are calculated according to repayment period, the country situation and the buyer's creditworthiness.

For example, the approximate premiums for a public buyer on a fourth category country are at present:

Up to one year 1.30 per cent
Up to five years 2.16 per cent

The approximate premiums for a private buyer on a first category country are at present:

Up to one year 1.60 per cent
Up to five years 3.03 per cent

2.2   Guarantees for Banks

2.2.1   *Policies available*

The following policies are available from CESCE:
— Bank guarantees policies cover a bank's losses for the non–payment of credits granted for pre–financing firm orders or defaults on credits for export transactions;
— Buyer credit policies (in pesetas and in foreign currency) cover non–payment of credits granted by a bank to a buyer);
— Confirmed letters of credit policies cover a bank's risk on letters of credit opened by foreign banks and confirmed by Spanish banks.

2.2.2   *Eligibility*

See 2.1.2.

2.2.3   *Cost of cover*

See 2.1.3.

2.3   Other Insurance Programmes

2.3.1   *Policies available*

— Unfair calling of bonds

These cover exporters and guarantors (Banks) against the unfair calling of bonds.

— Civil works

This insurance combines pre–shipment and credit risks. It insures against the impossibility of carrying out the project, work stoppage and non–payment of work certifications. It also covers confiscation of machinery and installations, unjust calling or withholding of bonds and impossibility of transferring guarantee bonds, provided that the insured has fulfilled his contractual obligations.

— Foreign investment

This covers the risks of expropriation and/or the impossibility of transferring profits of Spanish investors in foreign countries.

— Exchange risk

This covers the risks of devaluation of the export contract currency.

— Trade fairs

This covers the risks of re-exportation of Spanish goods exhibited at commercial fairs in foreign countries.

The last three policies are used on very rare occasions, either because they involve an excessive risk or due to little interest from exporters.

3.   EXPORT FINANCE PROGRAMMES

3.1   **Direct Credits**

Direct credits are granted by BEE and other financial institutions to both Spanish exporters and foreign buyers (including credit lines to financial or development institutions for the latter).

3.2   **Refinancing**

As mentioned in 1.2.1.3, ICO provides funds exclusively to BEE to finance officially supported export transactions. It also grants subsidies to the interest rates applied by any financial institution to operations of the same nature (See 3.3 below).

3.3   **Interest Subsidies**

3.3.1   *Types of contract available*

Since 1984, a source of funds to finance exports has been ICO's Convenio de Ajuste Reciproco de Intereses (CARI, Agreement on Reciprocal Adjustment of Interest Rates), under which the cost of resources is subsidised. This new scheme may be used by private banks and savings banks, BEE and foreign banks, both resident and non-resident. It subsidises the difference between the cost of funds on the market plus a profit margin and the rate of interest applied to medium and long term buyer and supplier credits granted by the bank. This rate of interest is fixed throughout the life of the credit in accordance with the rules of the Arrangement. The subsidy may be negative if the rate of interest on the market plus the profit margin is lower than the rate of interest on export credits. ICO pays the subsidy or receives it (in the case of a negative subsidy).

The CARI scheme is also applicable to discount operations in trade finance, whether or not with recourse, such as factoring and forfaiting.

3.3.2   *Eligibility*

Only medium and long term (with a credit period of two years or over) supplier and buyer credits that are granted to countries within categories II and III of the Arrangement qualify for subsidised interest.

When the CARI scheme supports these credits, they are not taken into account for the purposes of calculating the investment ratio imposed on BEE.

Because the CARI scheme eliminates the foreign exchange risk and includes a margin for the financing institutions, it stimulates an increase in the funding resources available for this type of financing.

Medium and long term buyer and supplier credits must be denominated in pesetas or in any foreign currency quoted officially on the Madrid market. Subsidies for export credit denominated in a foreign currency are paid in the same currency as the credit. The United States dollar is the foreign currency most commonly used in export financing operations. However, other European currencies such as the French franc, the pound sterling or the Deutschemark, are also used.

3.3.3   *Resulting interest rates*

Since 1977, Spain has been applying the rules of the Arrangement.

3.4   **Other Credit Operations**

Up to 1984, export credits could be insured only in pesetas, and the exchange rate risk could be covered either on the Madrid foreign currency futures market or by using the exchange rate risk guarantee scheme managed by CESCE. Since 1984, it has been possible to cover medium and long term supplier and buyer credits in a foreign currency officially quoted on the Madrid market. Thus, if a claim cannot be recovered, the insured bank is compensated in the currency in which the insured credit was denominated.

4.   AID FINANCE PROGRAMMES

The Spanish Government may grant public aid funds to other governments, either as soft-loan programmes or in combination with export credit transactions complying with the Arrangement rules.

These aid credits, called FAD credits (see 1.2.1.4), are submitted for appraisal and evaluation to the General Directorate of Trade Policy. The proposals of the latter must be approved by the Council of Ministers after being examined and authorized by an Inter-Ministerial Committee. ICO has then the responsability for the negotiation of the specific terms of the aid credit and for its management.

Chapter 13

UNITED KINGDOM

1. ORGANISATION AND STRUCTURE

1.1 Insurance and Guarantees

1.1.1 *Representative Organisation*

Export Credits Guarantee Department
P.O. Box 272
Export House
50 Ludgate Hill
London EC4M 7AY

Telephone: (44 1) 382 7811
Telex: 883601 ECGDHQ
Telefax: (44 1) 382 7649

1.1.1.1 *Function*

ECGD's main objectives are:

— To encourage UK exports by providing insurance and guarantees to UK exporters against the risks of non–payment by overseas buyers and to banks against non–payment of the finance that they advance to UK exporters and to overseas borrowers for goods sold on credit terms overseas.

ECGD currently derives its statutory powers for this task from the Export Guarantees and Overseas Investment Act 1978. Guarantees are given under Section 1 or Section 2 of that Act, according to whether they relate to business that can be accepted as involving commercial levels of risk (Section 1) or are to be given in the national interest (Section 2). Investment insurance is provided under Section 11 of the same Act.

— To trade at no net cost to public funds. This objective has been reaffirmed by successive governments for over fifty years.

ECGD carries out all the administrative work necessary to meet these objectives. This includes processing applications for cover from initial receipt to issuing guarantee documents and the supporting tasks of: obtaining relevant commercial and economic information about buyers, borrowers and countries; determining premium rates and methods of risk control, collecting premia; handling and paying claims; keeping accounts of income, expenditure and reserves; and maintaining relations with similar institutions in other countries. About 20 per cent of total UK non–oil visible exports were insured with ECGD in the Financial Year 1988/89.

1.1.1.2   Summary of organisation

See below.

1.1.1.3   Resources

ECGD derives its income primarily from premium charges for its policies. It invests its cash surpluses in or, as the case may be, funds its cash deficit from, the UK Consolidated Fund. Interest payments are credited or debited, respectively, to ECGD's accounts. Recoveries of claims payments, interest on Consolidated Fund balances, when in credit, and interest receivable under international debt rescheduling agreements, are the main sources of secondary income. There are currently statutory liability ceilings on commitments of £35 000 million for sterling business and SDR 25 000 million for foreign currency business. The sterling ceiling may be raised to £40 000 million by Statutory Instrument.

Interest rate support is provided from public funds, but while it is not limited to an annual ceiling, it is subject to overall public expenditure control. For the Financial Year 1988/89, the total net cost to public funds of interest support for fixed rate export finance amounted to £136 million.

1.1.1.4   Other organisations involved

The Export Guarantees Advisory Council (EGAC) is a statutory body that ECGD is obliged to consult before giving guarantees under Section 1 of the Export Guarantees and Overseas Investment Act 1978. Its advice, although not binding on ECGD, is generally followed. The Chairman and other members of the EGAC are leading bankers or businessmen and are appointed by the Secretary of State. ECGD provides a small Secretariat service out of its own resources.

1.1.1.5   Relations with the state

ECGD is a government department responsible to the Secretary of State for Trade and Industry.

ECGD's enabling legislation, currently the Export Guarantees and Overseas Investment Act 1978, requires ECGD to obtain the consent of HM Treasury for every guarantee it gives. In practice, however, the Treasury has delegated authority to ECGD to transact a wide range of business that is routine and that does not involve decisions about large or unusual risks. When considering particular transactions that fall outside these authorities, ECGD consults the Treasury and other UK government departments that might have an interest.

1.1.1.6   Relations with the private sector

Commercial banks in the UK do not themselves provide export credit insurance. There are private sector export credit insurance organisations which operate in the UK, but ECGD has not yet collaborated with them in the sharing of risk. However, this is an area which is currently under review.

Chief Executive

Chief Executive's Division:

Support services to Chief Executive. Secretariat to Management Board and Export Guarantees Advisory Council. Strategic and Business Planning. Legislation and Parliamentary Relations. International Policy and Relations. Press and Publicity.

Director, Insurance Services Group

Responsabilities:

Providing and developing credit insurance and related services for export business on short terms of payment. This translates into the following Group functions: strategic/business planning and financial management, underwriting, marketing, customer service via a nine office regional network and examination, payment and recovery of claims.

Director, Project Group (a)

Responsabilities:

(a) Underwriting of projects and Country Policy: Europe, Middle East, Africa, Defence Business, Bank Guarantees.

Director, Project Group (b)

Responsabilities:

(b) Project Group Development and Policy; underwriting of Projects and Country Policy: Asia, Australia, Americas, Aircraft, Ships, Services, Project Group Claims Work.

Director, Resource Management Group

Responsabilities:

Personnel management and financial management. Negotiation of International Debt Agreements.

Director, Information and Risk Management Group

Responsabilities:

Information Technology and Management services.

1.2   Export Finance

There is no official institution in the United Kingdom for export credit financing or refinancing. See section 3.

1.3   Aid finance

1.3.1   *Representative organisation*

The British aid programme is administered by the Overseas Development Administration (ODA), which is part of the Foreign and Commonwealth Office. This programme includes the "Aid and Trade Provision" (ATP), established in 1977 and the "single integrated loan facility", introduced in the ATP in 1985 (see section 4).

2.   INSURANCE AND GUARANTEE PROGRAMMES

2.1.   Cover for Exporters

2.1.1   *Policies available*

Comprehensive Short Term (CST) policies are designed for all types of export businesses who sell on short credit up to 180 days. Although ECGD has a flexible approach and tailor–makes policies to suit individual customers' needs, many customers prefer to cover all the buyers to whom they export. The guarantees are normally issued for one year and may be renewed annually. The risks covered include insolvency, default by the buyer, or the buyer's refusal to accept the goods after shipment and a range of political risks which include currency transfer delay. Cover is also given against the failure or refusal of a public buyer to perform the contract. The customer has the option to extend his policy to provide cover during the pre–shipment period. The policy may also be extended by a supplemental policy to insure regular business in capital or engineering goods on longer credit terms and contracts with pre–shipment periods in excess of 12 months.

Under its CST policies, ECGD normally covers 90 % of loss for commercial risks and 95 % for political risks. The percentage of cover on commercial risks rises to 95 % where ECGD covers unconditional loan contracts between a first class UK finance house and an overseas bank or borrower of similar standing and where payment is to be made irrespective of the performance of the supply contract.

ECGD does not normally cover political or commercial risks separately under its CST policies. Customers are offered post–shipment cover for both risks and may opt for pre–shipment cover as well. Where sales to associate or subsidiary companies are involved, cover for the commercial risks is excluded. As well as cover for the sale of goods from the UK and services rendered, short term cover is available to UK merchants and manufacturers selling goods from one foreign country to another, or a mix of UK and foreign goods.

Specific guarantees are available for single contracts for capital goods or projects that cannot be accommodated in the comprehensive pattern. The dates of commencement of cover and the causes of loss are similar to those for comprehensive guarantees, but the percentage of loss covered is 90 per cent for all risks. ECGD can consider separate cover for political risks only under its specific guarantees and buyer credit guarantees (see 2.2.1) if the commercial risks are unacceptable to it.

In cases where the credit period is three years or more, ECGD may raise the percentage of its cover on a contract to 100 per cent, without extra charge, after a satisfactory period of trouble free operation.

2.1.2   *Eligibility*

ECGD will tailor CST policies to suit an individual customer's needs. However, customers who offer a good spread of business would normally see this reflected in more favourable premium rates. The CST gives the customer some discretion to take on small contracts without ECGD's approving a formal credit limit but for all other business (i.e. larger contracts; terms in excess of 180 days; specifically insured; or covered by a buyer credit guarantee) ECGD makes an individual assessment of the risk it is prepared to take on the buyer or borrower and, where necessary, investigates the soundness of the project. In some cases, additional security in the form of a third party guarantee — often a bank letter of credit and occasionally even a government guarantee — may be required.

ECGD reviews the economic and financial standing and prospects of all overseas markets on a continuous basis. For some countries it sets limits on the total amount it will insure and may introduce other market restrictions, such as stipulations about methods and timing of payment.

Payments on delivery are invariably required where credit exceeds twelve months. These will normally be 15 to 20 per cent, of which at least 5 per cent is usually required on signature of contract. Repayment and interest rate terms and conditions must normally be in accordance with the Arrangement.

There is no limitation on the proportion of foreign and local costs that can be considered for inclusion in credit insurance where the post–shipment credit period is six months or less.

Where post–shipment credit is more than six months, foreign and local costs may be included in credit insurance and in guaranteed financings up to the level of payments due at or by the appropriate starting point of credit.

Under bilateral agreements with Austria, Norway, Sweden and Switzerland, sub-contracts in these countries may be included in credit insurance and in guaranteed financings up to 30 per cent of contract value. Under reciprocal arrangements between EC member states, Community subcontracts may be included in credit insurance and in guaranteed financings up to 30 or 40 per cent of contract value whether or not interest rate support is involved.

2.1.3   *Cost of Cover*

Premium rates for CST cover are based on three main elements. There is an annual premium calculated according to export turnover and the use made of the credit limit service by the policyholder. There is also an ad valorem premium, at a rate set for each policy, payable monthly on the value of the export business declared and Market Rate Additions are added to these basic rates for markets where the political risk is perceived to be significant. In 1988/89 the average premium rate was £ 0.58 per cent £ 100 of business declared.

Premium rates for the supplemental extended terms policy are assessed on an individual transaction basis. Typical charges for buyer credit guarantees and specific guarantees (2 years pre–credit, 5 years credit) vary between 2 and 8 per cent, according to the category of the market and the overall horizon of risk.

2.2   Guarantees for Banks

2.2.1   *Policies available*

Supplier credit

To facilitate the provision of finance for those supplier credit transactions that are insured with ECGD, 100 per cent guarantees for the credit amount may be given to financing banks. ECGD retains a right of recourse to the exporter for any sums paid to the bank in excess of those covered by the credit insurance guarantee. These guarantees are only available for business on credit of longer than two years.

ECGD also encourages the provision of export finance by financial intermediaries, by giving the latter its normal credit insurance guarantees. Exporters can choose to use these intermediaries instead of insuring their business directly with ECGD.

Buyer credit

ECGD guarantees the lending bank the repayment of a loan made to an overseas borrower for the purchase of major UK capital goods with a contract value of £1 million or more. The guarantees are normally for 100 per cent of the principal and interest. In rare instances, risk sharing may result in a lower percentage of guaranteed principal or interest. ECGD retains a right of recourse to the exporter for amounts it may have paid under the guarantee to the bank at a time when the exporter is in default under the terms of his contract.

For project loans of at least £20m (UK export credit loan value) where cover is given on a *Project Financing basis* – (i.e. where repayment will not be secured by guarantees from project sponsors or third parties but will depend on the revenue earning capacity of the project), ECGD provides cover for defined political risks and in some cases a share of commercial risks. The basic structure is as for normal Buyer Credits but, because cover is for selected risks, the lending bank(s) may not be guaranteed for 100 per cent of principal and interest.

Lines of credit

ECGD guarantees lines of credit extended by lending banks to certain overseas borrowers to facilitate the placing of orders for British capital goods. The guarantees are for 100 per cent of the principal and interest. The loans are usually repayable over two to five years according to the value of each contract. Certain arrangements that are made by finance houses that are designed to provide for a number of supply contracts under one financing agreement may also be covered by comprehensive guarantees, but in these cases the percentage guaranteed is a maximum of 95 per cent.

2.2.2   *Eligibility*

See 2.1.2.

2.2.3   *Cost of cover*

See 2.1.3.

2.3   Other insurance programmes

2.3.1   *Bond risk cover*

ECGD can insure exporters against the calling of bonds that is not the consequence of any fault of the exporter. The cover (100 per cent) is available as an optional extra to all the normal credit insurance guarantees and is for bonds obtained against the exporter's own resources. It is normally available only for business with public buyers. The charge for this cover is 0.5 per cent per annum of the bond value where given under specific guarantees or buyer credit guarantees.

2.3.2   *Investment insurance*

ECGD's investment insurance scheme insures UK companies that invest directly by equity or loan in overseas enterprises. Cover is provided against the risks of war, expropriation and restrictions on remittances. The normal maximum period of cover is fifteen years, and a premium of between 0.7 and 1 per cent is charged annually on the current insured amount. In addition, a commitment premium is charged on any difference between this amount and the maximum insured amount determined at the outset of the cover.

2.3.3   *Cover to supplement commercial forward foreign exchange facilities*

ECGD operates three forms of cover to supplement UK exporters' use of the commercial forward foreign exchange market. These:
— Protect exporters in cases where an insured loss has arisen and the amount of that loss is increased through currency fluctuations;
— Give a measure of protection against adverse exchange rate movements in the period between the date of tender and signature of contract to exporters quoting for major capital goods contracts denominated in US dollars, Deutschemark, Japanese yen, Swiss francs or Canadian dollars ('tender to contract' cover); and
— Provide a similar measure of protection against adverse exchange rate movements should an exporter be unable, initially to sell forward in the commercial exchange markets, sums receivable under a major capital goods contract. This facility, which is available in conjunction with the 'tender to contract' cover described above or as a separate facility, may be applied to contracts denominated in the currencies eligible for tender to contract cover.

The charge for the protection mentioned in the first paragraph of this section is 15 per cent of the credit insurance premium payable where the cover is given under a CST. Where the cover is given under a supplemental extended terms guarantee or a specific guarantee, the exporter may select the margin of additional cover he requires. Credit insurance premium is then charged on the amount of ECGD's increased liability.

The major part of premium for Tender to Contract and Forward Exchange Supplement (TTC/FES) cover is only paid if a tender results in a foreign currency contract. It is then based on the tender to contract period. The average tender period covered by ECGD has been between seven and eight months, for which the premium charge is 3.75 per cent of the sterling value covered.

In view of the length and depth of forward exchange markets in major currencies against sterling, there is virtually no demand for Forward Exchange Supplement cover. (It has been used once only since its introduction in 1982.) It should be possible for exporters to arrange all necessary forward contracts, with ECGD being called upon only rarely to cover residual amounts for short periods until forward contracts can be put in place. Since ECGD would benefit from favourable exchange rate movements in such periods, a flat charge of £5 000 only is made if such cover proves necessary.

2.3.6   *Pre-shipment cover*

The exporter has the option of cover during the pre-shipment period, ie from date of contract to shipment, at a small additional premium charge. Cover is given against non-performance of contract due either to the buyer's insolvency or to any of the range of political causes of loss. Claims are assessed in terms of the exporter's costs incurred in design, manufacture or supply of the goods.

3.   EXPORT FINANCE PROGRAMMES

3.1   Direct Credits

ECGD does not provide a direct lending facility.

3.2   Refinancing

ECGD does not provide refinancing for banks (but see 3.3.1).

3.3   Interest subsidies

3.3.1   *Subsidies available*

For exports on credit terms of two years or more, exporters and overseas borrowers have access to bank finance at fixed rates of interest, determined in accordance with the Arrangement guidelines. The banks receive guarantees from ECGD that their lending will be repaid, and interest support, which assures them of a commercial rate of return on both sterling and foreign currency lending. The cost is borne by Her Majesty's government.

In order to reduce the cost of interest support, a small proportion of existing bank finance has been refinanced by a privately owned company using funds raised in the capital market under ECGD's guarantee. In addition, in order to hedge part of its open-ended exposure to interest rate changes, ECGD entered into a series of US dollar interest rate swap agreements during the second half of 1986/87. The result of this action is that at 31 March 1989 some 72 % of ECGD's US dollar loan portfolio was hedged against future adverse movements in commercial interest rates.

3.3.2   Eligibility

All banks registered under the 1987 Banking Act are eligible in principle as sole lenders or to participate in syndicates as lenders or leaders. Other financial institutions are also eligible in principle to participate as members of lending syndicates. ECGD, however, has the right to determine the role played by any individual bank, or to refuse or to modify its support either generally or in particular cases.

Banks or other lenders participating in officially supported export credit financing in the United Kingdom receive an agreed rate of return for their sterling or foreign currency lending. For sterling, this is based on the three months' London Inter–Bank Offered Rate (LIBOR), plus an agreed margin. If the agreed rate is lower than the underlying fixed rate, the banks pay the difference to ECGD.

3.3.3   Resulting interest rates

Pre–shipment financing

This is normally restricted to buyer credit financing where the supply contract provides for progress payments. Drawings may be made from the ECGD guaranteed loan to finance these payments at fixed rates of interest in accordance with the Arrangement.

Post–shipment financing

The fixed rates of interest charged for this type of finance are determined by ECGD in accordance with the minimum interest rates set out in the Arrangement or at Commercial Interest Reference Rates (CIRRs). In the case of Category 1 countries only the latter is available. Those transactions which benefit from interest rate support have to carry an ECGD risk insurance or guarantee covering non–payment. In addition, the banks normally charge commitment fees on undrawn balances and other flat commissions on the maximum loan value. The level of these charges is decided by the banks and will normally depend on the size of the loan.

3.4   Other Credit Operations

Foreign currency transactions

ECGD support for fixed rate finance for both buyer and supplier credit is available in a wide range of currencies: Australian dollar, Canadian dollar, Danish Kroner, Deutschemark, Dutch florin, European Currency Unit (ECU), Finnish Markka, French franc, Hong Kong dollar, Italian lira, Japanese yen, Norwegian krone, Spanish peseta, Swiss franc, Sterling and US dollars. ECGD is also prepared to consider, on a case by case basis, support for finance in the Austrian schilling, Belgian franc, Greek drachma, Irish punt, Malaysian ringgit, New Zealand dollar, Portugese escudo, Singapore dollar, South African rand and Swedish krona.

The agreed rate of return for US dollars and Deutschemark is normally based on 6 months LIBOR. For most other currencies, the requirement is that the source of funding should be the domestic market although in some instances the euro-market can be used.

Of ECGD's total fixed rate amounts outstanding as at 31 March 1989 about 30 per cent related to financing in foreign currencies. Of the latter 84 per cent was denominated in US dollars.   Other currencies being supported included Deutschemarks, Hong Kong dollars, Canadian dollars, Australian dollars, New Zealand dollars and ECUs.

4.   AID FINANCE PROGRAMMES

4.1   Associated Financing (mixed credits)

The Aid and Trade Provision (ATP) was established in 1977 and is a separate allocation within the UK's Bilateral Aid Programme.   Such funds are traditionally deployed in the form of an aid grant in conjunction with an export credit on normal Consensus Terms (under two separate financial contracts) ("mixed credits").   The ATP is jointly administered by the Department of Trade and Industry (DTI), and the Overseas Development Administration (ODA), in close collaboration with ECGD.

4.1.1   *Funds available*

The 1989/90 total ATP budget (which includes the soft loan facility) was £86m, of which £66m was allocated to grants for "mixed credits".   This allocation is expected to remain unchanged for 1990/91.

4.1.2   *Eligibility*

Projects to be supported under ATP must meet certain industrial and commercial criteria and satisfy developmental criteria as laid down in the DAC Guiding Principles. The ATP grant is generally tied to UK goods and services.   Where the project includes EC goods and services falling within the EC Reciprocal Arrangements, the aid grant will be calculated on the aggregate figure.   The "mixed credit" type facility is generally only extended to individual cases.

All UK firms, e.g., manufacturers, contractors or consultants may apply for ATP support for their eligible UK and EC goods and services.   Projects to be supported are initially assessed by the DTI against industrial and commercial criteria of relevance to the UK and then by ODA against developmental criteria.   Assistance under ATP is normally only available to support projects and orders in developing countries that have a GNP per capita below $3 000.   Exceptionally ATP may be available to support projects in developing countries with a GNP above this level.

4.1.3   *Resulting terms and interest rates*

Under the "mixed credit" facility the export credit component is financed by a buyer or supplier credit on appropriate Consensus terms.   The level of support is based on an assessment of the country and buyer risk and on the type of project.   The level of the grant will normally meet the minimum aid input required under the OECD Consensus Arrangement unless matching a competitor's offer.

4.2.   Integrated credits

In 1985, a "soft loan facility" was introduced under the ATP.   Under this facility, long term loans at concessional rates of interest are extended (under one loan contract) to finance projects mutually agreed between the donor and recipient governments. The loans are funded by commercial banks with repayment guaranteed by ECGD, and interest support made available by ODA from the ATP. Lines of credit, on a soft loan basis, have been extended to Indonesia and China and more recently to Thailand. Soft loans for individual contracts have been extended to other countries but only where it is clear that their use will be more effective than an aid grant and export credit, i.e., to meet a buyer's preference or more effectively to match the practice of other OECD countries. Such cases are required to meet the same industrial, commercial and developmental criteria as for "mixed credit" cases.

4.3   Other tied or partially untied aid

The aid budget may also be used to support a company's bid for a project which relates to technical co–operation such as a feasibility study, a consultancy or training. The level of ATP/TC is determined on the merits of a case but will conform to the OECD minimum concessionality requirements. The UK does not have any partially untied aid allocation.

Chapter 14

AUSTRIA

1. ORGANISATION AND STRUCTURE

1.1 Insurance and Guarantees

1.1.1 *Representative organisations*

Bundesministerium für Finanzen
(Federal Ministry of Finance)
Gruppe V/C
Himmelpfortgasse 4–8
A – 1010 Wien

Telephone: (43–1) 51433–0
Telex: 13 – 6214 bmffa
Telefax: (43–1) 51433–1777

Oesterreichische Kontrollbank AG
Abteilung Exportgarantien
Postfach 70
A–1011 Wien

Telephone: (43–1) 53127–0
Telex: 13 2785 oekbe
Telefax: (43–1) 53127/693

1.1.1.1 *Function*

The Republic of Austria (the "Republic"), represented by the Federal Ministry of Finance, provides an elaborate export and investment insurance system that has been developed since 1950 and is now based on the Export Promotion Act of 1981, as amended from time to time.

The Federal Minister of Finance, acting on behalf of the Republic, is authorised to issue guarantees on behalf of the Republic for the due performance of contracts by the foreign contracting parties as well as for the integrity of rights of export enterprises that serve directly or indirectly the improvement of the balance of current transactions in goods and services.

The Oesterreichische Kontrollbank Aktiengesellschaft (OKB) was founded in 1946 to provide services not normally available from commercial banks. It has administered the official Austrian Export Credit Guarantee Scheme on behalf of the Federal Ministry of Finance since 1950. OKB acts as the sole agent for the Republic for the administration of the guarantees — including the collection of premiums and the payment of claims — issued by the Republic to facilitate Austrian exports. Legal provisions related to the present programme are enunciated in the Export Promotion Act 1981. OKB's shareholders are exclusively Austrian commercial banks.

1.1.1.2 *Summary of organisation*

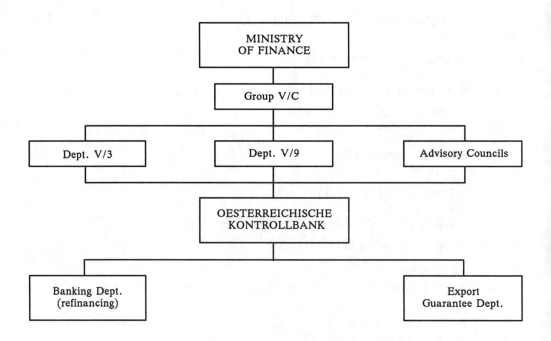

1.1.1.3 *Resources*

A guarantee ceiling of ATS 290 billion is presently set by the Export Promotion Act of 1981, published in the Federal Legislation Gazette no. 216. As of 31st December 1988, the total cover of export contracts amounted to ATS 243,5 billion. The insurance scheme is administered on account of the Republic and is conceived to operate on a self–supporting basis.

OKB funds its refinancing operations by borrowing in national and international capital and money markets. Total borrowings, mainly from international sources, expanded rapidly in the 1970s but have declined somewhat since 1981.

Total net borrowings reached their peak in 1981 with ATS 30.1 billion and had declined to ATS 2.6 billion in 1988. Over the longer period from 1960 to 1988, the share of net domestic borrowing amounted, on average, to a quarter of total net funds raised by OKB.

	1980	1981	1982	1983	1984	1985	1986	1987	1988
				in ATS bn					
Net domestic borrowings	11.6	0.2	5.8	8.8	−3.3	0.9	−6.5	0.3	−3.4
Net foreign borrowings	17.7	29.9	−0.7	0.7	17.0	−0.4	−0.4	3.7	6.0
Total net borrowings	29.3	30.1	5.1	9.5	13.7	0.5	−6.9	4.0	2.6
Total borrowings outstanding	91.1	121.2	126.3	135.8	149.5	150.0	143.1	147.1	149.6

OKB has relied heavily on foreign capital markets for its funds since the mid–1970s because its requirements were too large to be accommodated in the relatively small Austrian domestic market.

Funds are borrowed when and as required to meet disbursement schedules, and OKB frequently arranges "stand–by" credits to be drawn down when needed. Most of OKB's foreign borrowings are through medium and long term bonds, (public issues and private placements), and loans ("Schuldscheindarlehen" and bank–to–bank credits). OKB is represented in the Euro–CP and US–Domestic CP market and also uses the Eurocurrency market for short term funding requirements. In general, OKB makes a practice of matching average maturities on its assets and liabilities.

The Export Financing Promotion Act of 1981, as amended from time to time, authorises the Minister of Finance to issue unconditional guarantees of the Republic for the payment of principal and interest on borrowings incurred by OKB for the purpose of financing export transactions, including export loans. It is standard policy not to issue repayment guarantees for domestic borrowings. In addition, the Republic is authorised to guarantee, in the case of foreign currency borrowings, that OKB shall not have to pay more principal and interest expressed in Schillings than contemplated at the time of the borrowing on the basis of then prevailing exchange rates. The Export Financing Promotion Act provides that the Republic's guarantees may only be issued if, after giving effect to such issuance, the total of all liabilities of the Republic under all guarantees under the Export Financing Promotion Act in effect does not exceed ATS 190 billion. This ceiling of liability relates to the principal amounts guaranteed without interest and cost; a supplemental amount of 10 per cent is to be added for exchange risk.

Whereas most of OKB's foreign borrowings carry an Exchange Risk Guarantee, OKB has pursued the aim of a balanced performance of exchange rate gains and losses.

1.1.1.4 *Other organisations involved*

Advisory Council

The examination of applications from the point of view of the economy in general and the conditions of guarantee contracts in the case of guarantee applications not exceeding ATS 10 million is entrusted to an advisory council at the Federal Ministry of Finance. Members of the advisory council are a representative of the Federal Ministry of Finance as Chairman and a representative each of the Federal Ministry for Public Economy and Transport and of the Federal Ministry for Commerce, Trade and Industry, a representative of the Federal Economic Chamber, a representative of the Austrian Chamber of Labour and a non–voting representative of Oesterreichische Kontrollbank Aktiengesellschaft.

Enlarged Advisory Council

An enlarged advisory council is competent for amounts exceeding ATS 10 million. This body comprises further representatives from the Federal Ministries of Social Affairs, of Agriculture and Forestry and of Foreign Affairs, a representative each of the Conference of Presidents of the Austrian Chambers of Agriculture and of the Austrian Trade Union Federation and a representative of Oesterreichische Nationalbank (Central Bank).

1.1.1.5 *Relations with the state*

The government sets premiums. In case the claims to be paid exceed the collected premiums and recoveries, the Federal Ministry of Finance would be obliged to back OKB by paying the difference.

1.1.1.6 *Relations with the private sector*

Private export credit insurers operate in Austria and may co–insure risks with OKB.

1.2   **Export Finance**

See 1.1.

1.3   **Aid Finance**

See 4.

2.   INSURANCE AND GUARANTEE PROGRAMMES

2.1   Cover for Exporters

2.1.1   *Policies available*

Cover is generally extended for combined commercial and political risks and ranges up to 100 per cent. Pre–shipment risks may be included. Moreover, for exports to some countries an extended waiting period of up to twenty four months is imposed. Most guarantees are for individual contracts, although comprehensive guarantees are also available.

Eligible for cover are purchase, lease and work contracts, licence agreements and agreements on the exploitation of patents, on know–how or on copy–rights, export bills of exchange and credit agreements. Furthermore, political risk cover for cash deposits and bid bonds, for the integrity of stocks on commission or for the integrity of machinery and equipment used for the purpose of performing export transactions abroad as well as for investments in enterprises domiciled abroad is possible. Under the investment insurance scheme commercial cover is available in exceptional cases.

2.1.2   *Eligibility*

Criteria for accepting cover

A satisfactory creditworthiness assessment is required on the basis of exporters' reports and OKB's investigation, satisfactory country assessment by means of the International Monetary Fund's and the World Bank's reports as well as on information from diplomatic missions and satisfactory buyer assessment.

The criteria for accepting cover are in accordance with the Arrangement subject to acceptable country risk and satisfactory buyer's assessment.

In general, the repayment period will increase in accordance with the nature of the product and services to be exported and the size of the order. The shortest repayment period is required in respect of the first group of products shown in the table below and increases for subsequent groups:

— Consumer goods, raw materials;
— Mass produced light investment goods (small orders);
— Mass produced light investment goods (large orders);
— Heavy investment goods (small orders);
— Heavy investment goods (large orders);
— Plants.

Local costs may be included on a case by case basis with a maximum of 15 per cent of the total of the contract value or in the amount of a higher down payment.

Although the currency of the credit is usually Austrian Schillings, other currencies are admitted.

Nationality requirements

Guarantees are available for:
— Enterprises domiciled in Austria or abroad exporting products of Austrian origin (supplier credits) or investing abroad;

— Credit institutions domiciled in Austria or abroad, provided that the contracts serve to finance Austrian exports (buyer credits or acquisition of export receivables).

Decisions on foreign content up to 25 per cent are made on a case to case basis. Where there are reciprocal agreements, reinsurance of foreign export credit insurance institutions can be granted for their cover of the Austrian part of export contracts.

2.1.3   *Cost of cover*

A fee for handling the application of 0.1 per cent (ATS 50 as a minimum and ATS 3 000 as a maximum) is payable and premiums of one eighth of 1 per cent are charged for each commenced quarter of the lifetime of the guarantee. The computation is to be based on the required cover for the respective quarter calendar year.

Premium rates do not vary by value of contract or creditworthiness of buyer and/ or country. However, the extent of cover may vary from case to case.

2.2   Guarantees for Banks

Guarantees for banks are available in the form of guarantees for tied financial credits and guarantees for the acquisition of accounts receivable from export transactions by domestic or foreign credit institutions.

2.3   Other Insurance Programmes

2.3.1   *Foreign exchange risk insurance*

According to the Export Promotion Act, a foreign exchange risk guarantee may be issued by the Republic of Austria. At present no cover is accepted under this scheme.

2.3.2   *Bond insurance*

Bond insurance has been available since 1975. The guarantee covers the integrity of rights of export enterprises arising from their advances made abroad in the context of export transactions (bid and performance bonds). Indemnification takes place in case of unjustified calling of the bonds.

3.   EXPORT FINANCE PROGRAMMES

3.1   Direct Credits

N.A.

3.2   Refinancing

Commercial banks may be refinanced by OKB up to the insured portion on the basis of guarantees according to the Export Promotion Act. OKB provides refinancing to commercial banks via the "Statutory Export Financing Scheme".

3.2.1 *Types of contract available*

OKB primarily provides refinancing of medium and long term supplier and buyer export credits related to the sale of Austrian goods and services with special emphasis on the export of capital goods.

3.2.2 *Eligibility*

Provided that an export credit is guaranteed by the Republic of Austria according to the Export Promotion Act 1981, Austrian exporters and banks have access to the refinancing facilities.

In general, up to 85 per cent of the total contract price of the export project is eligible for financing. Down and progress payments are required amounting to a minimum of generally 15 per cent of the total contract price.

3.2.3 *Resulting interest rates*

OKB charges both fixed and floating interest rates on its refinancing credits at rates sufficient to earn a positive spread over the cost of funds. These rates are not subject to Arrangement guidelines.

Each credit is made available in two tranches. The relative size of each tranche depends on the length of the repayment period. Interest at a floating rate is payable in arrears on tranche A on the last day of each quarter at the quarterly export finance rate as determined by OKB and published in the Viennese Gazette. Fixed rate interest is payable on tranche B quarterly in arrears.

In order to reduce the interest risk, repayments of principal are applied in full first in repayment of tranche A and thereafter in repayment of tranche B.

The following table shows the prevailing floating and fixed interest rates and the relative sizes of tranches A and B depending on the repayment period. Given the floating rate feature of the Austrian system, the actual interest rate for a given contract may only be determined after a credit has been fully repaid. Historically, the floating rate has been as high as 11.25 per cent per annum and as low as 6.75 per cent per annum. In any event, the floating rate feature ensures that the effective interest rates of the Austrian scheme are adapted to market conditions over time.

Interest Rates
(as of 1st July 1989)

Repayment Period of the Loan	Tranche A of the Loan (Floating Rate Portion) %	Quarterly OKB Export Finance Rate (current) p.a. %	Tranche B of the Loan (Fixed Rate Portion) %	Prevailing Fixed Interest (Rate p.a. %
Less than 2 years	50	7	50	6.125
2 years or more but less than 5 years	50	7	50	6.250
5 years or more but less than 8 years	20	7	80	6.500
8 years or more	10	7	90	6.625

Short term financing is also available either from the Austrian National Bank (up to 10 per cent of export turnover) or from Österreichischer Exportfonds GmbH (up to 20 per cent of export turnover).

The cost for rediscounting with Österreichische Exportsfond Gmbh is 6.25 per cent including a commercial bank margin of 0.5 per cent. The cost of the rediscount facility with the Austrian National Bank is the discount rate plus bank charges of 0.5 per cent, plus an "aval" fee of 0.5 per cent per annum.

3.3   Interest Subsidies

N.A. (but see 4.2.2).

3.4   Other Credit Operations

N.A.

4.   AID FINANCE PROGRAMMES

4.1   Associated Financing

Available in principle; however presently not used.

4.2   Integrated Credits

4.2.1   *Funds available*

Integrated single transactions ("Concessional export credits" drawn from special funds) are extended by OKB as part of the official export credit scheme.

4.2.2   *Eligibility*

An interest rate subsidy from the Federal budget enables OKB to extend the credits at below market rates. Projects to be financed by these concessional export credits are appraised by the Export Financing Committee, chaired by the Ministry of Finance, and at which the Ministry for Foreign Affairs is represented among other Ministries and institutions. The assessment of the ODA quality of a single transaction lies in the responsibility of the Ministry for Foreign Affairs.

4.2.3   *Resulting terms and interest rates*

These are in accordance with Arrangement guidelines.

Chapter 15

FINLAND

1. ORGANISATION AND STRUCTURE

1.1 Insurance and Guarantees

1.1.1 *Representative organisation*

Valtiontakuukeskus (Finnish Guarantee Board, FGB)
P.O. Box 1010
SF–00101 Helsinki

Telephone: (358 0) 134 111
Telex: 121778 VTL SF
Telefax: (358 0) 651 181

1.1.1.1 *Function*

Export credit insurance and guarantees are granted by FGB instituted by the Act on the Finnish Guarantee Board of 1989 as a government agency under the Ministry of Trade and Industry. FGB which succeeds Vientitakuulaitos (VTL, Export Guarantee Board) set up in 1963 and Valtiontakauslaitos (State Guarantee Office) started its operations on September 1, 1989. It continues its predecessors' operations in all respects.

Export guarantee operations are based on the Export Guarantee Act and the Export Guarantee Statute.

According to the Act on the Finnish Guarantee Board FGB is governed by a Supervisory Board, a Board of Directors which has separate sections for export guarantee operations and for State guarantee operations, and a Managing Director (see 1.1.1.4). The day to day operations of FGB are conducted by the Managing Director. Some of the powers of the Board of Directors, especially those concerning the underwriting of risks, have been delegated to the Managing Director and senior officers of FGB.

1.1.1.2 *Summary of organisation*

(Not supplied)

1.1.1.3   *Resources*

FGB operates under a government guarantee but without capital dotation on a self supporting basis, i.e. accumulated premium income is intended to cover payment of claims and administrative expenses in the long run. Surpluses on its operations are paid to the Export Guarantee Fund managed by FGB.

The maximum liability of export guarantee operations of FGB set by Parliament amounts to 25 billion Finnish markkaa (FIM) (September 1989). Offers of cover are deducted from the liability ceiling to one half of the amount of the proposed guarantee.

The Supervisory Board is appointed by the government. It shall have representatives from the Ministry of Foreign Affairs, the Ministry of Trade and Industry, the Ministry of Labour, and the Bank of Finland, and four representatives of industry and commerce, two of whom shall represent small and medium–sized companies. The Board is responsible for the general policy of FGB.

Decisions concerning the underwriting of risks and payment of claims rest with the Board of Directors, which is appointed by the Supervisory Board. It consists of members representing the same ministries, institutions and organisations as the Supervisory Board and the Managing Director of FGB.

1.1.1.4   *Relations with the state*

Claims that may result from the export guarantee operations of FGB and for which the means of the Export Guarantee Fund are insufficient are reimbursed from the national budget.

1.2   **Export Finance**

1.2.1   *Representative organisation*

Finnish Export Credit Ltd (FEC)
P.O. Box 123
SF–00131 Helsinki

Telephone: (358 0) 131 171
Telex: 121893 excre sf
Telefax: (358 0) 174 819

1.2.1.1   *Function*

Finnish Export Credit was established in 1956 by the major commercial banks and certain industrial companies. The Government became the major shareholder in 1963. The Government is the biggest shareholder (55 per cent); the other shareholders are major banks (35 per cent) and several enterprises engaged in capital goods manufacturing (10 per cent). Irrespective of the government's role as the majority shareholder, FEC operates on commercial business principles. FEC is governed by the Supervisory Board and the Board of Directors.

1.2.1.2   *Summary of organisation*

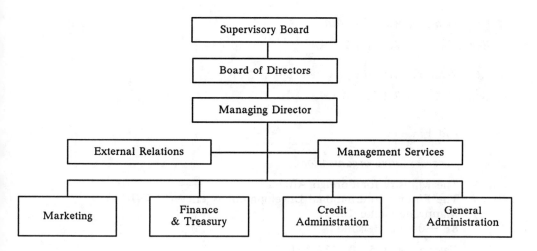

1.2.1.3   *Resources*

The share capital of FEC is FIM 108 million. FEC has regularly paid its shareholders the maximum statutory rate of dividends, i.e. 8 per cent.

Until the early 1980s, the principal source of funds for the Company's operations
was issuing long term subordinated debentures to the Republic of Finland and to the
shareholder banks. In order to meet the Company's funding requirements in foreign
currencies, domestic funding was increasingly replaced by borrowing from foreign capital markets during the 1980s. At the same time, the Finnish government substituted
its participation in the subsequent debenture programme with an interest rate subsidy
scheme. Moreover, FEC has been exempted from income and wealth tax from the
beginning of 1983.

The Company has established its standing in the international capital markets by
issuing short and long term loans without a government guarantee. FEC's foreign short
term financing operations include inter alia a borrowing programme in the US dollar
commercial paper market. The Company's foreign borrowings have received top ratings from the major rating agencies in the US.

Annual interest subsidies amounted to FIM between 22.5 million and 38.7 million in the years 1984–1988.

1.2.1.4   *Other organisations involved*

The Supervisory Board is appointed by the General Meeting of Shareholders. Its
twelve members include representatives of the Ministry for Foreign Affairs, the Ministry of Finance, the Ministry of Trade and Industry, the Bank of Finland, the shareholder banks and the industrial companies.

The Board of Directors is appointed by the Supervisory Board and its eight members include representatives of the Ministry for Foreign Affairs, the Ministry of Trade

and Industry, the Bank of Finland, the shareholder banks, the Finnish Foreign Trade Association and the Managing Director of FEC.

1.2.1.5   *Relations with the state*

See 1.2.1.1, 1.2.1.3, 1.2.1.4.

1.2.1.6   *Relations with the private sector*

See 1.2.1.1, 1.2.1.3, 1.2.1.4.

1.3   Aid Finance

1.3.1   *Representative organisation*

The Ministry for Foreign Affairs/
The Finnish International Development Agency (FINNIDA)
Mannerheimintie 15 C
SF – 00260 Helsinki

Telephone: (358 0) 134 161
Telex: 124636 umin sf
Telefax: (358 0) 440 257

1.3.1.1   *Function*

FINNIDA together with FEC administers the premixed concessional credit scheme of Finland described in Section 4. The scheme became effective from the beginning of 1987.

The main objective of the scheme is to increase financial flows from Finland to developing countries and particularly into projects with high developmental effects by combining ODA funds with export credit funds in financing projects, for which ODA funds alone would not be sufficient.

The OECD guiding principles for associated financing are followed. The credits are not intented to be used for matching.

1.3.1.2   *Summary of organisation*

The credits are extended by FEC and guaranteed by FGB. The interest subsidy is paid by FINNIDA.

1.3.1.3   *Resources*

Funds borrowed by FEC from domestic and international capital markets and interest subsidy provided by FINNIDA from the development assistance budget of the government (see Section 4.2.1).

1.3.1.4   *Other organisations involved*

After preliminary examinations by FEC and positive tentative assessments by FIN-NIDA of the possible developmental impacts, requests are submitted to an Associated Financing Group set up by the Ministry for Foreign Affairs for this purpose. The

Group is chaired by the Director General of FINNIDA and comprises representatives from the Ministry for Foreign Affairs, the Ministry of Finance, the Ministry of Trade and Industry, FGB and FEC.

2.   INSURANCE AND GUARANTEE PROGRAMMES

2.1   Cover for Exporters

2.1.1   *Policies available*

Supplier credits

FGB's L–guarantee programme provides export credit insurance cover against political and/or commercial risks in supplier credit transactions. There are separate schemes for exports of goods and exports of construction works and of services.

For post–shipment or combined pre– and post–shipment periods, cover is normally provided on a specific policy basis. Comprehensive policies are also available but only for short term business.

Maximum coverage is 95 per cent for political and 85 per cent for commercial risks. The exporter is required to assume the remaining 5 – 15 per cent.

Local cost financing may be covered within the limits of the Arrangement.

2.1.2   *Eligibility*

Criteria for accepting cover

The main criteria are satisfactory creditworthiness of the buyer and the country of destination. In some cases public guarantees in the importing country may be required.

Insurance is granted by FGB provided that the terms are consistent with those normally accepted by conventional international practice:

Maximum credit lengths:

— Raw materials, semi–manufactures and consumer goods: up to six months;
— Consumer durables: up to two years, exceptionally longer;
— Quasi–capital goods: up to five years;
— Capital goods: up to five years for relatively rich countries, eight and a half years for intermediate countries and ten years for relatively poor countries in accordance with the Arrangement.

Downpayment: minimum 15 per cent.

Repayment: without grace period normally in equal semi–annual instalments.

Nationality requirements

FGB has bilateral agreements with Switzerland (foreign content up to 30 per cent) and with the Nordic countries [foreign content up to 40 per cent (Denmark up to 30 per cent only because of EC's internal restrictions)]. For other countries foreign content up to 40 per cent is normally permitted.

2.1.3   *Cost of cover*

Premia for L–guarantees depend on risks covered, creditworthiness of the buyer, country of destination, terms of payment and length of risk period.

2.2   Guarantees for Banks

2.2.1   *Policies available*

Bank guarantees related to supplier credits

Direct bank guarantees (R–guarantees) are guarantees to banks and other credit institutions for credits made available to Finnish exporters. Guarantees are issued both for pre– and post–shipment credits. R–guarantees are issued with full recourse to the exporter. No counter–guarantees in the form of hard security are, however, required. R–guarantees thus leave the exporter's borrowing capacity unaffected.

R–guarantees cover 100% of the credit. The items eligible for cover are the following:
— Principal amount of the credit;
— Interest, including interest on overdue amounts;
— Management and commitment fees;
— Reasonable collection costs and certain legal fees.

Buyer credit

FGB's F–guarantees are export credit guarantees issued as security to lenders financing purchases of Finnish exports. An F–guarantee provides the lender with cover against non–payment by the foreign borrower. Both commercial and political risks are covered. F–guarantees covering political risks only are also issued. An F–guarantee can be used in connection with various financing arrangements structured on a buyer credit basis, e.g. direct buyer credits, bank to bank credits, or general purpose or project lines of credit.

F–guarantees cover 100% of the credit. The items eligible for cover are the following:
— Principal amount of the credit;
— Interest, including interest on overdue amounts;
— Management and commitment fees;
— Reasonable collection costs and certain legal fees.

For safeguarding the supply of basic raw materials, FGB can grant M–guarantees for credits that Finnish firms have to arrange in order to assure themselves of imports of raw materials by means of long term supply contracts. The cover can be 100 per cent for political and commercial risks relating to the repayment of credits. Decisions in principle about granting the guarantees are made by the government.

Political risk guarantees

In 1984, D–guarantees were introduced. These provide cover to Finnish banks for political risks connected with confirming of documentary letters of credit. Coverage is 85 – 95 per cent depending on the country of the opening bank.

2.2.2   *Eligibility*

See 2.1.2.

2.2.3   *Cost of cover*

The guarantee premium for buyer credit guarantees (F–guarantees) is charged as a flat fee calculated on the principal amount. The premium is usually charged to the lender in connection with disbursements of the credit funds.

Premia for direct bank guarantees (R–guarantees) depend on the exporter's recourseworthiness and are 0.1–1.0 per cent per annum for pre–shipment guarantees and 0.1–0.4 per cent per annum for post–shipment guarantees calculated on the outstanding amount of principal.

Premia for political risk guarantees (D–guarantees) depend on risks covered, creditworthiness of the buyer, country of destination, terms of payment and length of risk period.

2.3   Other Schemes Available

2.3.1   *Bond insurance*

Bond support is made available under FGB's B–guarantee scheme in three ways: first, as an insurance to the exporter against the risk of unfair calling of bonds, second, as a back–up guarantee in favour of the bond giver with full recourse to the exporter and third, as a back–up guarantee in favour of the bond giver combined with an insurance against the risk of unfair calling in the form of a limited recourse to the exporter.

The scheme covers bid, advance payment, performance, progress payment, retention and maintenance period bonds. The bond giver may be either a Finnish or foreign institution, a bank or an insurance entity.

The cost of bond support varies according to risks covered and ranges from 0.2 per cent to 1.4 per cent per annum payable quarterly in advance on the respective value of the bond from time to time.

2.3.2   *Investment risks insurance*

The Finnish investment insurance scheme (I–guarantees), which came into operation in February 1981, is administered by FGB. The scheme is in principle available for investments in all countries. It provides a guarantee against the three main categories of political risks: expropriation, war and restrictions on remittances.

All companies and institutions based in Finland are eligible for investment guarantees provided that they can be expected to carry out the investment successfully. The investment may be in the form of equity participation in a foreign enterprise or of loans or guarantees of loans to such an enterprise. Reinvested earnings may be also insured to the extent that such earnings at the time of reinvestment are freely transferable to Finland. Coverage can also be given for remitted earnings up to 8 per cent per annum. The maximum period of coverage is twenty years.

To qualify for insurance, the investor must intend to keep his investment for at least three years. The investor is also required to demonstrate that his project will provide economic benefits to both Finland and the host country. The investment must always receive the approval of the local government.

Coverage will be provided only for projects that represent new investments or considerable expansions, modernisations or improvements of existing investments. The policy always covers all three risk categories, the annual premium for capital investment being 0.5 per cent and for insured earnings 0.7 per cent. The maximum percentage of cover is 90 per cent. FGB's liability ceiling for the investment guarantee scheme is FIM 400 million (May 1989).

2.3.3   Cost escalation insurance

The Finnish cost escalation insurance scheme (K–guarantees) is operated by FGB. Mainly exports of ships, forest industry machinery and other heavy metal machinery and engineering products are eligible for cover for risks caused by unforeseen high increases in production costs due to domestic inflation during the delivery period.

The effective annual cost increases over the life of the insurance contract are calculated on the basis of a special cost index calculated by the Central Statistical Office. The exporter is required to bear a certain initial annual increase of costs — at present (May 1989) 7 per cent. The percentage is to be reviewed occasionally by the government; however, the same percentage remains valid for a policy throughout its life.

The indemnity is limited to the maximum of 25 per cent of the eligible value (the contract price less the value of foreign sub–deliveries). Due to the method of calculation of the indemnity, the exporter is required to carry from 15 to 50 per cent of the increase in costs beyond the threshold confirmed by the government. The premium is 0.04 per cent for each month of the guarantee period calculated from the basic price insured.

Due primarily to the slowing rate of inflation in Finland no applications have been received since 1986. The K–guarantee scheme has produced net income totaling FIM 45.5 million in 1983–1988.

3.   EXPORT FINANCE PROGRAMMES

3.1   Direct Credits

3.1.1   Types of contract available

Financing is provided on a supplier credit basis and on a buyer credit basis. Also credit lines to foreign financial institutions are available.

FEC financing is available for the export of capital goods, construction and of consulting services including project exports in the form of medium and long term credits.

3.1.2   Eligibility

A minimum 15 per cent cash payment must be made by the buyer before delivery. FEC provides finance to a maximum of 85 per cent of the export contract value. However, the size of the loan depends on the domestic value added of the contract. In general the loans are disbursed on delivery, but advances up to 100 per cent of the loan can be disbursed under the predelivery financing schemes at market rate.

FEC also provides unsubsidised post delivery market rate lending.

Export credits must be secured by adequate collateral, e.g. by guarantees of FGB or by first class commercial banks or by security such as pledges of notes of the foreign buyer, or bills of exchange accepted by the buyer, both of which are generally guaranteed by the buyer's bank.

3.1.3   *Resulting interest rates*

The terms and conditions of the credits extended are in conformity with the guidelines of the Arrangement and of the Understanding on Export Credits for Ships.

The interest rate for post delivery loans granted by FEC depends on the recipient country, repayment term and the currency concerned. The rate is confirmed at the very latest on the signing of the commercial contract and is fixed over the whole repayment term. The interest rate charged by FEC for the predelivery financing is determined in accordance with the market rate of interest.

For the undisbursed loan commitments FEC charges a commitment fee of 0.25 per cent per annum which is applied from the date of the signing of the contract. As far as the buyer credit is concerned, FEC charges a management fee of 0.125 per cent flat on the loan and, in addition, charges for any further legal or other expenses.

FGB's premiums for supplier credits as at May 22nd 1989

	Short-term[1] flat	Medium term[2] per cent per annum
Minimum[3]		
Combined pre-shipment and pos-shipment[4]	0.13	0.15
Post-shipment	0.08	0.14
Maximum[5]		
Combined pre-shipment and post-shipment[4]	1.06	1.50
Post-shipment	0.71	1.40

1. Six months.
2. Five years.
3. Best public buyer risk.
4. Manufacturing period of six months.
5. Worst combined political and average commercial risk for a private buyer.

Premiums for buyer credits are approximately 20 per cent higher. For a guarantee offer for a buyer credit a flat fee corresponding to FIM 5 000–10 000 is charged. This fee will be credited toward payment of the guarantee premium.

In respect of guarantees issued after May 15th 1989 FGB no longer charges premium for cumulative interest.

3.2   Refinancing

Not available.

3.3   Interest Subsidies

Not available.

3.4   Other Credit Operations

FEC has operated since December 1984 a facility for market rate lending in foreign currencies. This supplementary facility operates on a purely commercial basis and does not require official support. The terms and conditions of each individual loan transaction from the facility will be based on the actual cost to FEC of market borrowing.

On 31st December 1988, FEC's lending in foreign currencies accounted for 69 per cent of the outstanding loans. The main foreign currency is the US dollar.

4.   AID FINANCE PROGRAMMES

4.1   Associated Financing

At present Finland extends only premixed credits.

4.2   Integrated Credits

4.2.1   *Policies available*

Neither country frames nor credit lines have been established by FINNIDA or FEC. The decisions are made on a case by case basis applying the criteria described in Section 4.2.2. FEC has, however, signed frame agreements concerning general procedures with China, Malaysia, and Thailand.

The amount of credits to be extended between 1987–1990 has been limited to FIM 2 billion in the state budget. If this level is reached, the estimated yearly interest subsidy payments will reach the level of approximately FIM 200 million, which equals about 15 % of total bilateral aid disbursements. It has been estimated that the interest subsidy payments will reach the level of FIM 15 million in 1989.

4.2.2   *Eligibility*

FEC, acting on behalf of FINNIDA, is responsible for the administration of the credits. Applications by exporters are sent to FEC. After preliminary examination it submits the credit application and its review report to FINNIDA, which makes a tentative assessment of the possible developmental impact of the project. If the conclusion is positive the request is submitted to an Associated Financing Group (see Section 1.3.1.4). If the Group concludes that the application meets with the criteria established for ODA transactions, FINNIDA will then appraise the feasibility, priority and developmental effects of the project applying the same criteria as in Finnish development projects in general. If the appraisal is positive, Government grants the interest subsidy for the credit. Before the subsidy is paid, the competent authority in the recipient country has to approve the development assistance to be used for this purpose. The credit agreement is concluded between the borrower and FEC. The progress of the projects is supervised jointly by FEC and FINNIDA. The required amount of interest subsidy will be transfered by FINNIDA to FEC when the payments of interest are due. Eventual claims are paid by FGB from Export Guarantee Fund.

The priority sectors to be financed are agriculture, forestry, infrastructure, construction and industry.

The projects financed from the scheme should contribute to economic development in the recipient country. They should also have a priority status in the development plans of the recipient country. The projects should be clearly identified and technically and economically feasible. The credits are not to be used for the procurement of recurrent goods or equipment.

Usually the amount of the credit should not exceed 85% of the total costs of the contract price.

80 per cent of a concessional credit is tied to procurement from Finland, but whenever possible, international competitive bidding is to be organised to ensure that Finnish suppliers are competitive. Eligible recipients are low — and middle — income countries, as classified by the World Bank, provided they are creditworthy to receive export credits and guarantees. Primarily, concessional credits are to be extended to countries with a GNP per capita below $2 000, but only exceptionally to least developed countries. If a project is deemed to have a particularly high development impact, a concessional credit may be extended also to a richer country, the upper GNP per capita limit being $ 3 000.

4.2.3   Resulting terms and interest rates

These are in accordance with Arrangement guidelines and with the DAC Guiding Principles.

Chapter 16

NORWAY

1. ORGANISATION AND STRUCTURE

1.1 Insurance and Guarantees

1.1.1 *Representative organisation*

Garanti–Instituttet for Eksportkredit
Postboks 1763 Vika
0122 Oslo 1

Telephone: (47 2) 205140
Telex: GIEK N 76783
Telefax: (47 2) 426855

1.1.1.1 *Function*

The Guarantee Institute for Export Credits (GIEK) is a State agency responsible to the Ministry of Trade and Shipping. GIEK was re–organised in 1960 in continuation of Statens Eksportkredittkommisjon and set up under its present name.

1.1.1.2 *Summary of organisation*

GIEK is organised in two departments dealing with commercial and political risks, respectively. There are also legal and administrative services. Applications regarding exports to developed countries are handled by the commercial risk department, whereas applications regarding exports to developing or state trading countries are dealt with by the political risk department.

1.1.1.3 *Resources*

The guidelines for operation of GIEK's general guarantee scheme are to cover indemnities and operating expenses. GIEK's own funds for operation of this scheme were depleted in 1981 due to heavy losses. Funding is now provided by the government according to need.

The operation of the general guarantee scheme is subject to an underwriting ceiling, which is revised annually. The present ceiling is NKr 13 billion.

The funds for operating GIEK's special scheme of guarantees for export credits to, or investments in, developing countries have also been depleted. Funding for this guarantee scheme is also provided by the government of Norway on a need basis. The underwriting ceiling for this scheme is revised annually. At present it is NKr 7 billion.

1.1.1.4   Other organisations involved

GIEK is administered by a Board of eleven members who represent inter alia the Ministries of Trade and Shipping, Foreign Affairs, Finance and Industry, the banks, the national Trade Union, the Export Council and GIEK itself by its managing Director.

An additional Board member representing the Norwegian Agency for Development Aid (NORAD) participates when cases under the special scheme for developing countries are dealt with.

1.1.1.5   Relations with the state

The state provides funds for GIEK and sets underwriting ceilings. Special provisions for cover of export credits to developing countries enable the Board of twelve members (i.e. including the representatives of NORAD) to accept risks that would otherwise be refused, if the project is approved by the Norwegian Agency for International Development.

1.1.1.6   Relations with the private sector

Private banks and insurance companies can provide some forms of cover. Risk sharing between GIEK and private banks or insurance companies is obligatory for credits over NKr 10 million.

1.2   Export Finance

1.2.1   Representative organisation

A/S Eksportfinans (Forretningsbankenes finansierings–
og eksportkredittinstitutt)
Dronning Mauds gate 15
0250 Oslo 1

Telephone: (47 2) 425960
Telex: 78213
Telefax: (47 2) 419201

1.2.1.1   Function

A/S Eksportfinans (The Financing and Export Credit Institute of the Norwegian Commercial Banks) was incorporated in Norway on 2nd May 1962 with limited liability. It is a private company owned by the commercial banks of Norway. The objective of the company is to grant medium and long term loans for export promotion and for manufacturing trade and handicraft. In addition to extending credits on commercial terms, the company is authorised to give export credit with governmental support.

The principal business of the company is the provision of medium and long term credits mainly in connection with Norwegian exports, but also in connection with the substitution of domestically produced goods for imports.

The company is required by its articles of association to operate in accordance with sound commercial principles. Like other Norwegian financing corporations, the company is governed by the companies Act of 4th June 1976 and the Financing Activities Act of 11th June 1976.

1.2.1.2 *Summary of organisation*

Not supplied.

1.2.1.3 *Resources*

The company has a share capital of NKr 82.5 million, which is subscribed by the share holding banks. The funds needed for the company's financing activities are raised by borrowing in the medium and long term domestic and international capital markets.

The company's bonds in the United States have been granted AAA rating. The company has access to all the international capital markets.

There is no government guarantee on its borrowings, and the company has no special government supported funding resources.

1.2.1.4 *Other organisations involved*

N/A.

1.2.1.5 *Relations with the state*

See 1.2.1.3.

1.2.1.6 *Relations with the private sector*

See 1.2.1.1.

1.3   Aid Finance

1.3.1   *Representative Organisation*

Royal Norwegian Ministry of Development
Cooperation (MDC)

2.   INSURANCE AND GUARANTEE PROGRAMMES

2.1   Cover for Exporters

2.1.1   *Policies available*

GIEK offers several forms of cover for both pre–shipment and post–shipment risks. The form in which insurance is given depends upon a number of variables, inter alia, credit amount, payback period, risk level, type of transaction. For short term credits, whole–turnover coverage from GIEK is available, covering both political and commercial risks. GIEK is presently also offering coverage in cooperation with a number of domestic banks, where the banks provide funding and also absorb a share of the credit risk. Cover is not available for exporters using the "cash contract scheme".

For credits tied to exports of capital goods, GIEK may cover both political and commercial risks. Insurance for credits less than NKr 10 million to foreign or domestic lenders covers 100 per cent of the credit. This applies to both suppliers' and buyers' credits, with a 10 per cent recourse to the exporter being the norm. Recourse for political risk to exporters is dropped altogether after three years provided there has been no payment default during this period. Recourse for commercial risk is dropped after eight years. For these credits, GIEK's guarantee is available without a need to share the risk.

For credits of NKr 10 million or larger, cover is only available on a risk sharing basis, i.e. a commercial bank must also be willing to undertake part of the credit risk. Cover given on this basis is unconditional and irrevocable. For insurance given on a pro rata basis, GIEK and other guarantors must have identical securities, third party guarantees, mortgages etc. GIEK's share of the commercial risk may not exceed 75 per cent of total guaranteed credit. GIEK's share of the political risk may not exceed 90 per cent of total guaranteed credit. However, if the private guarantee market totally withdraws from a market, GIEK may increase cover to 100 per cent with a 10 per cent recourse to the exporter.

2.1.2   *Eligibility*

The exporter is required to make sufficient credit information available before application for cover is processed. Securities in the form of government of central (state) bank guarantee may allow for an increased percentage of cover. GIEK provides cover for credits that are in accordance with terms normal for the trade in question. In general, the following limits are respected:
- For consumer goods/raw materials, credit period up to six months is accepted. Certain exceptions are allowed within Berne Union agreements;
- For capital goods, credit period, downpayment, repayment terms and level of local cost financing must be within the limits of the OECD Arrangement.

Up to 30 per cent of foreign components may be accepted in contracts underwritten by GIEK. For components of Swedish or Finnish origin the percentage may be increased to 40.

2.1.3   *Cost of cover*

Premiums/fees are calculated as a percentage of the direct amount of the transaction.

The premium depends upon variables such as: credit period, public or private buyer, securities available and general creditworthiness. For purposes of setting premia for political risks countries are classified in five categories.

2.2   Guarantees for Banks

GIEK may provide cover to Norwegian or first class international banks or other financial institutions.

2.3   Other Insurance Programmes

GIEK may accept liabilities in a foreign currency and pay claims in the same currency. Risk exposure can be covered either on domestic or international forward markets.

3.   EXPORT FINANCE PROGRAMMES

3.1   Direct Credits

3.1.1   Types of contract available

Only post shipment credits are extended.

The criteria for granting credits are determined by a set of detailed regulations. The main rule is to support Norwegian exporters facing officially supported credit competition. Credits may be extended either from A/S Eksportfinans' official or commercial windows.

For the export credits offered under the officially supported sector, lending terms are determined by the Arrangement and the Understanding on Export Credits for Ships. In 1985, 45 per cent of new loans paid out fell within the shipbuilding sector. The financing of foreign components is limited to 30 per cent of the contract.

For the commercial lending sector of A/S Eksportfinans, the lending terms are determined by the cost of funds plus a normal commercial margin. The rate of interest is fixed on the day of lending. Currency risk exposures, if any, are carried by the company.

3.1.3   Resulting interest rates

Medium and long term credits are financed by A/S Eksportfinans. Eksportfinans finances post shipment credits through its official window up to 85 per cent of the transaction value at the agreed Arrangement minimum rates plus a front end fee of 0.3 per cent of the financed amount. The interest rate is fixed at the time of commitment. Examples of financing cost in the beginning of 1986 were as follows:

Credit length	Three years	Eight years	Ten years
Eksportfinans	Arrangement terms	Arrangement terms	Arrangement terms
(front end fees)	0.3	0.3	0.3
GIEK fees[1]			
Maximum	1.3	0.85	0.80
Minimum	0.75	0.3	0.25

1. To be fixed case by case.

There is no government support available for short term credits. They are financed directly by exporters or refinanced with the commercial banks at market rates. The interest rate is fixed at time of disbursement.

3.2   Refinancing

N/A.

3.3   Interest subsidies

N/A.

3.4   Other credit operations

Because of the narrowness of the Norwegian capital market, foreign funding in connection with medium and long term export credit transactions has been encouraged by the government. Exporters and banks may freely extend foreign currency provided that the conditions are in conformity with normal commercial practices. Buyers' credits extended by Norwegian financial institutions require formal approval by the Bank of Norway or the Ministry of Trade and Shipping.

4.   AID FINANCE PROGRAMMES

4.1   Associated Financing (Mixed credits)

4.1.1   *Funds available*

Norway operates a mixed credit scheme administered by the Royal Norwegian Ministry of Development Corporation (MDC). The scheme is based on aid principles. The grant element may be given either in form of interest subsidies for commercial bank credits or a cash grant. In the former case, the credit will usually be in a pre-mixed form and extended either by Eksportfinans or another financial institution.

4.1.2   *Eligibility*

The purpose of the scheme is to increase the amount of finance available for investment in high priority projects of developing countries. Eligible recipients are, from July 1987 onward, low income (including LLDCs) and lower middle–income countries. The funds can be used for matching and are normally tied to procurement from Norway, but third country procurement is possible for up to 30 per cent. As far as possible, international competitive bidding is used. For the time being, the new scheme is restricted to smaller supply contracts (below NKr 50 million), in order to limit the budget funds required.

4.1.3   *Resulting terms and interest rates*

These are in accordance with Arrangement guidelines.

Chapter 17

SWEDEN

1. ORGANISATION AND STRUCTURE

1.1 Insurance and Guarantees

1.1.1 *Representative organisation*

Exportkreditnamnden–EKN (Swedish Export Credits Guarantee Board)
Box 7334
S–103 90 Stockholm

Telephone (46 8) 701 00 00
Telex EKN S 17657
Telefax (46 8) 11 81 49

1.1.1.1 *Function*

The Swedish Export Credits Guarantee Board (EKN) is an official agency established in 1933 that acts on behalf of the government. EKN covers either political risks only or, in certain cases (industrialized countries), commercial risks only or political and commercial risks incurred in exporting Swedish goods and services.

1.1.1.2 *Summary of organisation*

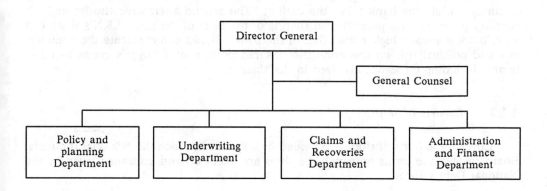

1.1.1.3   *Resources*

The Swedish Parliament has determined that, in the financial year 1988/89, EKN may have maximum liabilities of SKr 73 billion, of which SKr 32 billion is specially earmarked for insurance given in the s-/system (see 2.1.1). Separate sub-ceilings have also been set for exchange risk insurance (SKr 2 billion) and investment insurance (SKr 1 billion).

Parliament has also made available a credit line for EKN in the National Debt Office (riksgaldskontoret). The maximum amount permitted is SKr 3.7 billion. At the end of June 1988, some SKr 2.1 billion had been drawn on. In addition, EKN is entitled to borrow the equivalent of 500 million SKr in foreign currencies.

1.1.1.4   *Other organisations involved*

EKN's Board of Governors is appointed by the Swedish government. Its members include not only representatives of the Ministries concerned but also of the export industries, industrial associations, banks and trade unions. The Board decides important matters of policy and makes decisions on major applications for insurance and major settlements of claims.

1.1.1.5   *Relations with the state*

Although EKN should be self-supporting in principle, the state is responsible for EKN's guarantee commitments.

EKN administers a guarantee system for credits given under the concessionary credit scheme for which the Swedish Agency for International Technical and Economic Co-operation (BITS) is responsible.

1.1.1.6   *Relations with the private sector*

Private banks can provide political as well as commercial risk cover and share risks with EKN. EKN allows private banks to share risks in two ways. The first method (vertical risk sharing) splits the length of the credit. EKN covers the later maturities, while the bank takes the earlier. The second alternative (horizontal risk sharing) provides for a proportional sharing of the level of the risk. EKN's share can vary, but it is usually higher than that of the bank. Banks can syndicate the commercial and political risk on the non-EKN insured portion of a buyer's credit to other banks, including those not involved in the finance.

1.1.2   *Exports of ships*

Cover for exports of ships is provided by a system in which the National Industrial Board reviews the terms on which the ships are exported and insurance given by the National Debt Office.

1.2   Export Finance

1.2.1   *Representative organisation*

AB Svensk Exportkredit (SEK)
(Swedish Export Credit Corporation)
Box 16368
S–103 27 Stockholm

Telephone: (46 8) 613 80 00
Telex: 12166 SEK S
Telefax: (46 8) 20 38 94

1.2.1.1 *Function*

The Swedish Export Credit Corporation (SEK) was established in 1962 for the purpose of providing financing for exports of Swedish capital goods and services on commercial terms.

1.2.1.2 *Summary of organisation*

SEK is a joint stock company with limited liability incorporated under the laws of Sweden. The Swedish government owns 50 per cent of the share capital. The remaining 50 per cent is owned by eleven of the largest Swedish commercial banks. The government elects five members and the banks six members of SEK's Board of Directors.

1.2.1.3 *Resources*

SEK's share capital amounts to SKr 700 million. Total shareholders' equity and reserves amount to about SKr 3 000 million. SEK's access to the domestic capital market is regulated by the Central Bank (Sveriges Riksbank) and is strictly limited. SEK is rated AAA by Moody's and by Standard and Poor's.

Funding requirements for the S system are separated from SEK's funding for the M system (see 1.2.1.5 below). The main source of funding for the S system is provided by the international public capital markets. Other sources are bank loans and private placements. In the M system bank loans and private placements are most important sources of funding. Floating rate US dollars are often borrowed and swapped into fixed rate US dollars or other currencies. Lending in the M system is to a higher extent than in the S system linked to tailor made funding in order to avoid funding risks.

At year end 1988, 53 per cent of loans outstanding were granted by official guarantees, 39 per cent by Swedish banks groups and financial institutions and 5 per cent by foreign bank groups and States within OECD.

US dollars and Swedish kronor are the major currencies used for financing Swedish exports. Foreign currencies account for about 83 per cent of SEK's total lending, heavily dominated by US dollars, and Swedish kronor for about 17 per cent.

1.2.1.4 *Other organisations involved*

N/A.

1.2.1.5 *Relations with the state*

From 1962 to 1978, SEK only granted purely commercial credits. In 1978, the government entrusted SEK with the administration of an officially supported export credit system, the State Support System. From 1978, SEK's financing activities are carried out under two programmes, the Market Rate System (M system), which is a continuation of former activities, and the State Support System (S system). The accounting for the two systems is completely separated within the company.

SEK's lending activities under the S system are regulated by a government decree. The interest differential between lending rates and cost of funds as well as foreign exchange losses are reimbursed by the government on a quarterly basis in accordance with a separate agreement between the parties. There are no other government obligations or guarantees involved. A report on the S system activities is given by SEK to the government on a yearly basis. Credits under the S system are today of less importance in SEK's business.

1.3   Aid Finance

1.3.1 *Representative organisation*

The Swedish Agency for International Technical and Economic Co–operation (BITS)

1.3.1.1 *Function*

BITS administers the concessionary credit scheme (see 4.1) and is also entrusted with technical co–operation with "non–programme" countries.

1.3.2   Swedish International Development Authority (SIDA)

1.3.2.1 *Function*

SIDA is responsible for administering the bilateral aid programmes (on grant basis) for the poorer "programme" countries and cofinances some projects with BITS in those countries.

2.   INSURANCE AND GUARANTEE PROGRAMMES

2.1   Cover for Exporters

2.1.1 *Policies available*

Primarily, EKN grants cover in the form of what are called "normal guarantees". Such insurance is granted for transactions in which the risks relative to the political and economic situation in the buyer country can be reasonably well appraised.

For certain transactions that EKN does not consider eligible under the "normal guarantee" system, cover may be given through the s–/system (*i.e.,* the national interest). Risk–taking of a greater magnitude can be accommodated in this system provided that the transaction is considered to benefit the Swedish economy.

Insurance is available for political and, if requested, commercial risks. EKN can cover commercial risks only on private buyers in industrialized countries. Guarantees can be denominated in SKr, CHF, DEM, USD, JPY and ECU.

There is no minimum amount prescribed for cover of supplier credits, but the minimum premium of SKr 250 constitutes a limitation in practice. Local costs up to the amount of cash payments are usually covered provided that the terms are not more favourable than those for the exports concerned.

In the case of relay country exports, where the risks covered relate to the fulfilment of the obligations of the buyer in the country of final destination, the conditions governing the granting of cover for exports to the latter country generally apply.

Export credit insurance is normally granted as a specific policy of two general types: insurance for credit risks for exporters (F guarantee) and insurance for manufacturing and credit risks for exporters (T+F guarantee). Under a whole turnover insurance agreement concerning short term business between EKN and an exporter, the exporter may enjoy a premium discount and benefits in regard to possibilities of cover. Credit lines are covered on certain conditions, e.g. payment terms for each transaction under such a line must be acceptable for the goods in question.

2.1.2   *Eligibility*

Criteria for accepting cover

The political and economic situation of the buyer country is evaluated and, in the case of commercial risks, the creditworthiness of the buyer. For short term transactions, i.e. credit periods not exceeding 12 months, importing countries are graded into four classes according to the assessed political risks. As regards medium and long term transactions, importing countries are graded into six classes. In the case of exports to public sector debtors, i.e. debtors who enjoy public status and who cannot be declared bankrupt, the cover will always encompass both political and commercial risks.

Credit terms must not be out of step with either terms customary for the goods or for the market or with the economic life of the goods. The maximum credit lengths that EKN accepts are in accordance with those agreed in the Arrangement as well as within the Berne Union.

In the case of exports to state trading countries and many developing countries, transfer security (preferably a guarantee from the central bank or the ministry of finance or a foreign trade bank but often a guarantee from a first class bank to make payment in accordance with the contract outside the buyer country) is required for medium and long term transactions when the amount covered exceeds certain fixed amounts. Security for payment when commercial risks are covered is required on a case by case basis.

Nationality requirements

Insurance is available against non payment for exports of goods or services of Swedish origin. In accordance with reciprocal agreements with insurance institutions in a number of countries, cover may be extended to include foreign sub–deliveries of capital goods provided that these do not exceed 30 per cent — in some instances 40 per cent — of the value of the transaction.

2.1.3   Cost of cover

The following examples show normal premiums for guarantees. For short term guarantees the premiums are calculated as a percentage of the sum of the payments to be covered by the guarantee. An example of premium levels for short term guarantees is shown below:

	Political events concerning private debtor				Political and commercial events concerning private debtor				Political and commercial events concerning public debtor			
Premium class of the country of import	1	2	3	4	1	2	3	4	1	2	3	4
	0.05	0.15	0.43	0.68	0.38	0.50	0.75	1.00	0.13	0.30	0.60	0.90

The whole amount is to be paid cash on delivery or on credit not exceeding three months. For medium and long term guarantees, the premiums are, as from April 24, 1989, expressed as a per annum rate on the amount outstanding. An example of premium levels for medium and long term guarantees is shown below:

Premium grade[1]	Political events only P	Political and commercial events concerning public debtor K	Political and commercial events concerning private debtor P + K
1	0.05	0.06	0.74
2	0.32	0.36	0.96
3	0.76	0.83	1.32
4	1.30	1.43	1.77
5	1.89	2.08	2.27

1. The 6th premium grade is divided into subgrades. The premium levels are set as a surcharge on the premium level of the 5th grade. The surchage varies from 25 to 300 per cent.

2.2   Guarantees for Banks

2.2.1   Policies available

The aim of lenders' guarantees, which are granted directly to Swedish as well as foreign banks or other credit institutions for the coverage of risks on buyer credits, is to facilitate financing of major export business transactions. Cover is available in forms similar to T and T+F guarantees. Insurance for supplier credits granted to exporters can facilitate refinancing of these credits since the exporter may assign his rights under a guarantee to a credit institution.

EKN can also issue supplementary, in practice unconditional, guarantees for financiers of supplier credits. Under these guarantees, financiers may obtain cover for up to 100 per cent of the credit. However, these guarantees become effective only after delivery and usually only after the final acceptance of the goods by the buyer.

2.2.2   Eligibility

In the case of political risks, cover is extended up to 90 per cent. However, for bank to bank credits and bank to government credits, cover is normally extended to 95 per cent.

Normally, up to 85 per cent of commercial risks on private buyers (less for unfavourably rated risks) are covered, but this may be increased to a maximum of 90 per cent if a payment guarantee from either a relevant government authority or from a first class commercial bank is provided.

2.2.3   Cost of cover

The same as for guarantees for supplier credits (2.1.3).

2.3   Other insurance programmes

2.3.1   Foreign exchange risk insurance

In special circumstances, EKN may grant exchange risk cover for transactions that are not necessarily covered by export credit guarantees but are acceptable for such insurance. The preliminary period is twenty four months, during which the exporter normally covers himself on the forward market.

The exporter carries at least 3 per cent (franchise) of the exchange cost before he is indemnified. No ceiling for claims is generally laid down. For all claims, the date of reference is the day of contract or the day of binding quotation. Any exchange rate profits in excess of 3 per cent after the preliminary period must be paid to EKN. At present, the only currency covered is the US dollar. Applications under the foreign exchange risk insurance scheme have been received in only a few cases.

2.3.2   Bond insurance

Bond insurance may be issued either in favour of the exporter/bank principal or in the form of a "counter guarantee" in favour of the Swedish institution issuing the bond proper [a bank or an insurance corporation (see 2.3.3)]. Bond insurance in favour of the exporter covers losses caused by an unjustified calling of the bank, irrespective of whether the bond is payable "on demand" or not. Such an insurance covers losses caused by the calling of the bond to the extent that this is not based on a default of the exporter. EKN has the right to ask the policy–holder (exporter) for acceptable proof that such grounds do not exist. The insurance also covers the risk that a beneficiary who has admitted an obligation to return an amount paid under the bond does not effect such payment under certain conditions, including protracted default.

2.3.3   *Counter guarantee*

A counter guarantee will provide almost unconditional cover for the calling of bonds, including cover for non–performance on the part of the exporter/bond principal. It entails a closer assessment of the exporter's capability than in EKN's granting of bond insurance. It also requires the exporter to enter into certain obligations towards EKN, in particular to follow EKN's instructions for measures to minimise losses and to remunerate EKN for amounts paid to the guaranteed institution in case the bond is called because of a default by the exporter.

The bond insurance and counter guarantee schemes are principally intended for bonds to public buyers in non–industrialised countries. Hitherto, cover has been granted mainly for bonds to certain oil exporting countries.

2.3.4   *Guarantee for confirmation of L/C*

Political and commercial risks for Swedish banks confirming documentary credits in conjunction with a Swedish export transaction can be covered.

2.3.5   *Investment insurance*

Political risks involved in new investments in certain developing countries can be covered. As from October 1, 1987, EKN offers a new scheme for investment guarantees. One of the most important changes is that such guarantees may now be granted for investments in all countries.

2.3.6   *Guarantee for physical loss*

Covers the risk of confiscation of equipment abroad and damage caused by war etc. Normally only available in combination with a T+F guarantee for the transaction.

2.3.7   *Stock–keeping guarantee*

Covers the risk of confiscation of stocks and damages to stocks caused by war, etc.

3.   EXPORT FINANCE PROGRAMMES

3.1   Direct Credits

SEK's official financing support is predominantly by means of refinancing (see 3.2) and therefore only in exceptional cases does it extend credits in its own name. In certain markets, however, SEK has credit lines/financial protocols. At present such arrangements exist with the People's Republic of China, the Soviet Union, the German Democratic Republic and India for mixed credits (see 4.1).

3.2   Refinancing

3.2.1   *Types of contract available*

S–system credits are available for all types of exports including services but excluding raw materials and consumer goods within the limits of the Arrangement. Credit terms must comply with the EKN requirements to qualify for the S–system.

SEK makes most of its loans to or through commercial banks. The bank involved has the administrative responsibility for the loan during its lifetime.

3.2.2   *Eligibility*

SEK is not normally involved in negotiating the terms, preparing the documentation or assessing the credit risk and arranging security for the loan.

3.2.3   *Resulting interest rates*

Within the S system lending, terms are based on the Arrangement and the Understanding on Export Credits for Ships. When financing in foreign currencies, 0.25 per cent is added to the matrix rates and 0.75 per cent to the WP 6 rate. For Swedish kronor, 1.75 per cent is added. Of these surcharges, 0.25 per cent is charged to meet SEK's operating costs. According to a government decree, lending rates in low interest rate currencies may not contain any subsidy element.

Under the M system, lending rates are not subject to the Arrangement or the Understanding. They are based on SEK's cost of funds plus a margin covering operating costs and profit.

In both systems, a commitment fee of 0.5 per cent per annum is charged.

3.3   Interest Subsidies

N/A.

3.4   Other Credit Operations

Financing under the M–system forms the major part of SEK's lending operations at present. They are based on prevailing market rates of interest. Under this system SEK can also offer short term credit.

4.   AID FINANCE PROGRAMMES

4.1   Associated Financing (Mixed Credits)

In order to provide for more flexibility in financial terms, Sweden has introduced a complementary facility that allows it to extend — and report — mixed credits as two separate transactions: an ODA grant and an export credit. During an initial trial period, only a limited number of creditworthy least developed countries are eligible under this new facility (see 3.1). Appraisal criteria and procedures are the same as for concessional credits.

4.2   Integrated Credits

4.2.1   *Funds available*

In 1984, a modified system of "concessional credits" was established to subsidize funds borrowed on international capital markets with grants from the aid budget if they finance projects in developing countries that are of high developmental priority. BITS (see 1.3) administers the scheme and appraises projects to be financed by using an elaborate list of criteria. SEK, acting on behalf of BITS, is the agency responsible for the execution of the financial transactions (borrowing and lending through commercial banks) under the scheme. The amount required for interest subsidy over the life of each loan is transferred from the aid budget to interest bearing accounts opened for each borrower in the National Debt Office. The availability of an export credit guarantee is mandatory.

4.2.2   *Eligibility*

When interest falls due, an amount equivalent to the subsidy is paid to SEK out of the respective borrower's account. The interest subsidy is reported to DAC as an ODA grant. Under the Arrangement, the credits are reported with its concessionality as a single entity, but a cross-reference is made to the DAC report.

Concessional credits are not used for matching. Eligible recipients are creditworthy low income (including LLDCs) and lower middle-income countries (according to World Bank classification). The credits are tied to procurement in Sweden, except for small amounts covering local costs and third country procurement. Concessional credits are only extended to finance contracts awarded under competitive bidding.

4.2.3   *Resulting terms and interest rates*

These are in accordance with Arrangement and DAC guidelines.

Chapter 18

SWITZERLAND

1. ORGANISATION AND STRUCTURE

1.1 Insurance and Guarantees

1.1.1 *Representative organisation*

Geschaftsstelle für die Exportrisikogarantie–ERG
(Office for the Export Risk Guarantee)
Kirchenweg 4
8032 Zurich

Telephone: (41 1) 384 47 77
Telex: 816 519 VSMCH
Telefax: (41 1) 384 48 48

1.1.1.1 *Function*

The Swiss export risk guarantee scheme is ruled by the Federal Law of 26th September 1958 and ordinance of 15th January 1969, as amended.

The aim of the scheme is to create and safeguard employment opportunities and to promote foreign trade. In case of exports to poorer developing countries, the principles of the Swiss development cooperation policy have also to be taken into account.

The office for the Export Risk Guarantee receives and processes applications for guarantee promises and guarantees as well as requests for payment of claims.

1.1.1.2 *Summary of organisation*

See below.

1.1.1.3 *Resources*

ERG is a financially independent body operating on the principle of longer term financial self–sufficiency. The Government may advance the necessary funds to ERG. Such funds bear interest and are repayable.

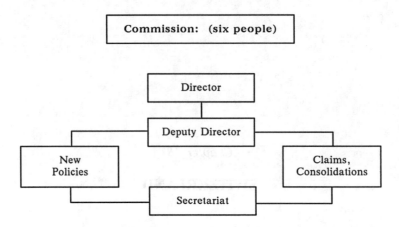

1.1.1.4 *Other organisations involved*

The Board for the Export Risk Guarantee is composed of six members, three each representing the federal administration and economic/industrial associations. The duties of the Board include decisions on requests for guarantee promises and on requests for payment of claims. It proposes to issue guarantees to the Federal Office for Foreign Economic Affairs (for amounts up to 1 million Swiss francs), to the Federal Department of Public Economy (for amounts between one to two million Swiss francs) or to the Federal Department of Public Economy with the concurrence of the Federal Department of Finance (for amounts exceeding one million Swiss francs). Requests of principle or special relevance are to be submitted for decision to the Federal Council (of Ministers).

1.1.1.5 *Relations with the state*

The Government sets the general rules and guidelines for the operation of ERG through the relevant law and ordinance (see 1.1.1.1). In particular, it provides a financial guarantee to the ERG fund (see 1.1.1.3) and lays out the premium structure.

1.1.1.6 *Relations with the private sector*

Swiss and foreign based private insurance companies offer at times export risk guarantee for selected risks and countries. These companies operate on a purely commercial basis.

1.1.1.7. *Additional Structure*

The Investment Risk Guarantee scheme (see 2.3) is available through:

Geschaftsstelle für die Investitionsrisikogarantie IRG
(Office for the Investment Risk Guarantee)
Kirchenweg 4
8032 Zurich

Telephone: (41 1) 384 47 77
Telex: 816 519 VSMCH
Telefax: (41 1) 384 48 48

1.2   Export Finance

Official export credit financing is not available in Switzerland.

1.3   Aid Finance

1.3.1   *Representative organisation*

The Federal Office for External Economic Affairs (OFAEE) of the Federal Department of Public Economy

1.3.1.1   *Function*

OFAEE administers the mixed financing scheme (see 4.1).

2.   INSURANCE AND GUARANTEE PROGRAMMES

2.1   Cover for Exporters

2.1.1   *Policies available*

— Risks covered

The legal framework provides cover for the following risks:
  i) Transfer problems and stand–stills, caused by measures taken by the government of the importing country;
  ii) Commercial risks with regard to public buyers and entities of public utility;
  iii) Commercial risks with regard to public guarantors;
  iv) Political risks, i.e. extraordinary official measures or political events abroad which make it impossible for the private importer to fulfil his contractual obligations;
  v) Risks before delivery, i.e. impossibility to perform due to a subsequent deterioration of the risks mentioned under *i)* to *iv)*.

— Amounts covered

The guarantee is limited by law to 95 per cent of the delivery value plus credit interest. The average guarantee amounted to 78.3 per cent in 1988.

Local cost not exceeding the cash payment may be included in the insurance cover.

— Type of contracts

Only single transaction contracts are available.

2.1.2   *Eligibility*

Criteria for accepting cover

Matters such as the percentage of guarantee coverage, terms of payment, guarantees etc. are examined by the Board of the Export Risk Guarantee according to its country and project risk evaluation. The prevailing rules of the Arrangement are applied where relevant.

Nationality requirement

Applying companies must be domiciled in Switzerland and entered into the register of commerce, but third country suppliers are generally accepted up to 50 per cent of the contract value at the standard premium. Higher third country supplies may be accepted against payment of an additional premium.

2.1.3   *Cost of cover*

Example of premium:

Percentage of cover %	6 months %	two years %	five years %
70	1.32	1.68	2.39
80	0.88	1.12	1.59
95	0.22	0.28	0.40

In the case of public buyer, add 25 per cent for public buyer's commercial risk. Supplements of up to 100 per cent to the above premia may be levied in each case:

— When the commitment with respect to one country represents a large proportion of the overall commitment;
— When the securities and guarantees fall short of the levels generally required;
— Where indicative ceilings for projects in selected countries have been exceeded;
— When there are special delivery risks.

Discounts of up to 75 per cent may be granted where risk assessment permits and where market conditions so require.

Rates of cover exceeding the standard cover (i.e. 50 per cent to 95 per cent) fixed individually for each country on a risk assessment basis may be purchased for an increase in the premium. Standard cover for short term guarantees (up to 12 months) may differ from those for medium and longer term guarantees.

2.2   **Guarantees for Banks**

Cover is available to banks only for buyer credits and only if the bank confirms that all risks which are not covered by ERG are borne by the bank (and not by the exporter).

2.3   Other Insurance Programmes

Protection against losses through dispossession of direct investments in developing countries is available under the Investment Risk Guarantee Scheme which is governed by a separate and special legal framework.

3.   EXPORT FINANCE PROGRAMMES

N/A.

4.   AID PROGRAMMES

4.1   Associated Financing

4.1.1   *Funds available*

Since 1976, a mixed financing scheme provides concessional funds from a special programme to certain developing countries for Swiss capital goods and services required for the implementation of priority development projects. Mixed financing is composed of two components: one financed by the Swiss Government (grant), the other by a consortium of six private banks (commercial loan). Two separate agreements are signed for each mixed financing transaction. The execution of the two agreements is interlinked, as each supply is financed *pari passu* by the two components according to a ratio agreed upon with the beneficiary government. The grants are reported as ODA. The OFAEE administers and co-operates closely with the Export Risk Guarantee and with the consortium of banks providing the commercial credits involved.

4.1.2   *Eligibility*

Mixed financing is tied to procurement in Switzerland, but subcontracting with foreign enterprises is allowed up to an amount of 50 per cent (prior to 1989: 30 per cent) of each credit. Local costs can also be financed up to a maximum of 15 per cent, but the amounts used for this purpose will be deducted from the maximum available for third country procurement. Swiss suppliers of goods and services financed are chosen by the recipient, but their prices have to be competitive internationally.

ERG cover is mandatory for the commercial part of such mixed financing transactions.

A mixed financing transaction can be used in support of Swiss suppliers ("matching") under the following conditions:

— The borrowing country must be eligible for Swiss mixed financing (least developed countries and countries with per capita income of more than US$1 600 are not eligible);

— International competitive bidding must have been organised in which the terms and conditions of financing are to be considered, or in which a competing bid is offering concessional financing;

— The price offered by the Swiss supplier must be the lowest evaluated bid on a cash basis;
— The project must be development oriented and declared by the government of the borrowing country as priority investment (to be ascertained by project appraisal).

4.1.3   *Resulting terms and interest rates*

These are in accordance with Arrangement and DAC guidelines.

Chapter 19

AUSTRALIA

1. ORGANISATION AND STRUCTURE

1.1 Insurance and Guarantees

1.1.1 *Representative Organisation*

Australian Trade Commission
trading as
Export Finance and Insurance Corporation
(AUSTRADE–EFIC)
P.O. Box R65
Royal Exchange
NSW 2000

Telephone: (61 2) 561 01 11
Telex: EFIC AA121224
Telefax: (61 2) 251 38 51

1.1.1.1 *Function*

In 1974, an Act of Parliament set up the Export Finance and Insurance Corporation (EFIC), which succeeded the Export Payments Insurance Corporation (established in 1956 as an independent statutory authority). On 6th January 1986, EFIC became part of the Australian Trade Commission (Austrade), which was established under the Australian Trade Commission Act 1985, as a self supporting statutory authority. This Act provides that EFIC will continue to trade under the name "Export Finance and Insurance Corporation". AUSTRADE–EFIC operates along commercial lines, and the Australian government backs AUSTRADE–EFIC's commitments. In addition to AUSTRADE–EFIC's specialised range of insurance and guarantee facilities against the risks of non–payment, AUSTRADE–EFIC provides overseas investment insurance and export credit financing (see part 3).

1.1.1.2   *Summary of organisation*

Executive

Managing Director, AUSTRADE
Deputy Managing Director, AUSTRADE
General Manager, F.I.P. Group, AUSTRADE

Insurance Division

Divisional Manager
Manager (Underwriting)
Director (Overseas Investment)
Credit Manager
Underwriter (Short Term)
Claims Manager

Group Development and Services Division

Divisional Manager
Chief Economist and Statistician
Manager, Information Services
Manager, Services
Marketing Manager
Manager, Business Development
General Counsel

Finance Division

Divisional Manager
Manager, Lending Operations
Manager, Funding Operations
Senior Funding Analyst
Senior Dealer
Manager, Loans Administration

1.1.1.3   *Resources*

The Australian Trade Commission Act provided for the establishment of an AUSTRADE–EFIC Fund.   The AUSTRADE–EFIC Fund includes, inter alia, AUSTRADE–EFIC's capital prior to joining Austrade, which was made up of appropriations by the government from consolidated revenue.   Interest on this sum, which will continue to be payable yearly, is reviewed periodically, and the rate is determined by the Minister for Finance.   The AUSTRADE–EFIC Fund also includes the bulk of the Corporation's underwriting reserve prior to becoming part of Austrade.   In accordance with Austrade's charter, the AUSTRADE–EFIC Fund will be maintained at a level sufficient to meet AUSTRADE–EFIC's likely liabilities.

The Corporation is required to pursue a policy aimed at securing sufficient revenue to meet all expenditure properly chargeable to revenue (including administration costs).   The Commission's underwriting ceilings (maximum contigent liabilities) for business written on its commercial account are fixed by regulation. The ceilings are currently A$3 000 million for credit insurance, indemnities and guarantees and A$750 million for overseas investment insurance. For loans made by the Commission (direct lending), the current ceiling is A$1 900 million. AUSTRADE–EFIC sources its loan funds on both the domestic and international capital markets.

1.1.1.4   Other Organisations Involved

The Australian Trade Commission Board consists of a Chairman, a Deputy Chairman, up to eight members from Australian commercial interests. The Board is appointed by the Minister for Industry, Technology and Commerce. It is required under the Act to keep the Minister informed of decisions of the Board with respect to matters of policy. The Minister may give directions to the Board.

1.1.1.5   Relations with the state

The Australian Trade Commission Act is administered by the Minister for Industry, Technology and Commerce; his approval is required for the policies of the Commission prior to their adoption by the Board. AUSTRADE is required to make periodical business and financial reports to the Ministers. The government backs AUSTRADE–EFIC commitments.

If the Board considers an application for cover inappropriate on commercial grounds as it would impose upon the Commission a liability that it is not authorised to undertake, or would not undertake in the ordinary course of business on its own account, it may refer it to the Minister for consideration as a "national interest" proposition. In such cases, the Minister for Industry, Technology and Commerce may authorise the Commission to provide cover on behalf of the government with all risks being to the government's account. The Corporation may, at its discretion, participate in "national interest" transactions. Premiums relating to "national interest" business are paid to the government after deduction of operating costs.

1.1.1.6   Relations with the private sector

There are private organisations offering export credit insurance but on a selective and limited basis. Private banks also provide discounting without recourse and confirmation of letters of credit.

1.2   Export Finance

1.2.1   Representative organisation

AUSTRADE–EFIC (see 1.1).

1.3   Aid Finance

1.3.1   Representative organisation

Australian International Development Assistance Bureau (AIDAB)

2.   INSURANCE AND GUARANTEE PROGRAMMES

2.1   **Cover for Exporters**

Insurance is normally provided from the date of contract or of shipment on a comprehensive basis. Where comprehensive cover is not appropriate, specific policies are available. Comprehensive insurance is mostly applied to repetitive business where the terms of credit do not exceed one hundred and eighty days; whereas specific policies are mostly issued for capital goods or services sold on longer supplier credit terms.

Normal credit terms insured or guaranteed are as follows:

Maximum post–shipment credit lengths:

— raw materials and consumer goods — six months (or terms which are normal for the particular trade);

— capital goods and services — up to five years, but extendable, within the context of international understandings;

— major capital goods and projects over five years.

In principle *minimum direct payments from the buyer* of 15 per cent (medium to long term transactions).

Repayments are usually by equal semi–annual instalments with no grace period.

2.1.1   *Policies available*

— Comprehensive Shipments and Comprehensive Contracts Policies

Appropriate for exports of raw materials, primary products, consumer goods and light manufactures on credit terms of up to one hundred and eighty days. Cover commences either from date of shipment or date of contract. Contract cover is appropriate for goods vulnerable to loss if the contract is frustrated prior to shipment. (Percentage of loss payable on commercial risks: 90 per cent; percentage of loss payable on political risks: 100 per cent.)

— Specific Shipment and Specific Contract Policies

Available for large individual contracts of sale usually involving exports of capital or semi capital goods sold on credit terms up to ten years. The contract policy also provides protection during the manufacturing period. (Percentage of loss payable on commercial risks: 90 per cent; percentage of loss payable on political risks: 100 per cent.)

— Extended Terms Policy

A comprehensive type policy designed to cover recurring business transacted on credit terms exceeding six months. (Percentage of loss payable on commercial risks: 90 per cent; percentage of loss payable on political risks: 100 per cent.)

— Services Policy

Appropriate for a wide range of professional or technical services performed for overseas principals. Payments under royalty agreements or patent fees can also be covered. (Percentage of loss payable on commercial risks: 90 per cent; percentage of loss payable on political risks: 100 per cent.)

— External Trade Cover

Covers external trade (merchanting) transactions under which goods of foreign origin are shipped directly from the country of origin to the overseas buyer. Only available if the goods concerned are not competitive with Australian made goods. This facility is available to any exporter that qualifies for a Comprehensive Policy. (Percentage of loss payable on commercial risks: 90 per cent; percentage of loss payable on political risks: 100 per cent.)

— Leasing Policy

Protects lessors of Australian equipment against the failure or inability of overseas lessees to pay amouts due under the leasing or hiring contract. (Percentage of loss payable on commercial risks: 90 per cent; percentage of loss payable on political risks: 100 per cent.)

— Construction Works Policy

Covers non payment of sums due from overseas "employers" for the supply of materials and the performance of services under construction works contracts. (Percentage of loss payable on commercial risks: 90 per cent; percentage of loss payable on political risks: 100 per cent.)

— Agreements to Guarantee

Appropriate for bulk purchase of consumer goods, especially primary products. Involves a commitment to an overseas agency, up to an agreed monetary limit, to insure contracts placed with Australian exporters and to give a supporting guarantee to the Australian bank financing those exports.

— Irrevocable Letter of Credit Cover

Provides cover to exporters for unconfirmed letters of credit. (Percentage of loss payable on commercial risks: 90 per cent; percentage of loss payable on political risks: 100 per cent.)

— Overseas Stocks Cover

Facilitates the holding of stocks overseas for ready sale by indemnifying the exporter if losses arise due to confiscation of the stocks, a ban being imposed on the re–export or destruction of or damage to the goods by war etc. (Percentage of loss payable on political risks: 100 per cent.)

— Processing Stocks Cover

Appropriate for Australian commodities being processed in another country. Cover similar to that applicable to overseas stocks. (Percentage of loss payable on political risks: 100 per cent.)

2.1.2   *Eligibility*

Products and services covered are required to have a majority Australian content, with the exception of goods covered under the external trade endorsement (see 2.1.1).

Under comprehensive cover, exporters have discretionary freedom to a predetermined ceiling provided that they have had satisfactory business experience with the buyer or they have obtained favourable credit reports. For business in excess of this ceiling and/or for terms which are not normal for the business and for specific policies, AUSTRADE–EFIC carries out its own check of the buyer and the country and occasionally may require additional security in the form of a local bank or government guarantee.

If AUSTRADE–EFIC is unwilling or not authorisied to provide cover, the Minister may authorise a policy on the government's account under AUSTRADE–EFIC's "national interest" provisions.

Local costs may be covered or financed, provided the minimum Australian content conditions are satisfied, and the amount of local costs supported on credit terms does not exceed the down payments to be received for the goods and services exported by the completion of the exporter's contractual obligations. Support is not granted for credits or credit guarantees for local costs in developed countries. Neither is it granted for local costs carrying maturity terms more favourable than those supported for the export of goods and services to which local costs are related.

2.1.3   *Cost of cover*

Premiums are payable throughout the life of the policy, and are based on several factors including the credit rating of the buyer and/or country, the type of policy, the goods and payment terms covered. An additional charge is made for unconditional bank guarantees (see 2.2.1).

2.2   **Guarantees for Banks**

In most cases, and especially for medium and long term credit, an AUSTRADE–EFIC payments insurance policy is required by financing institutions as collateral for finance. Exporters, with the agreement of AUSTRADE–EFIC, may assign the proceeds of policies to financial institutions. AUSTRADE–EFIC's unconditional guarantees, which may be issued only in conjunction with a payments insurance policy, in effect guarantees to lenders that portion of the financing not covered by the payments insurance policy. In return the guaranteed institution does not have any recourse on the exporter, but AUSTRADE–EFIC retains recourse on the exporter for any loss not covered by the payments insurance policy.

For supplier credit, AUSTRADE–EFIC may issue to financial institutions making funds available to exporters up to 100 per cent unconditional payment guarantees for political and commercial risks in conjunction with post shipment payments insurance policies. Unconditional guarantees are also provided to cover monies advanced for the production of certain goods.

AUSTRADE–EFIC may unconditionally guarantee, on a buyer credit basis, the repayment of loans made by financial institutions to buyers of capital goods and associated services on credit terms normally exceeding two years. AUSTRADE–EFIC can guarantee Australian or overseas lending institutions which provide foreign currency loans in support of Australian exports of capital goods and related services.

2.2.1   *Policies available*

— Unconditional Guarantees to Banks and Other Financial Institutions

Facilitate the financing of export transactions covered under AUSTRADE–EFIC Specific Shipment or Specific Contract policies. The guarantees to financial institutions can be up to 100 per cent and secure both pre–shipment and post–shipment financing.

— Confirmer/Financier Policy

Covers export business transacted by confirmers/financiers provided that they pay the Australian supplier without recourse. (Percentage of loss payable on commercial and political risks: 90 per cent.)

— Confirming Bank Policy

Provides cover for banks which add their confirmation to letters of credit. (Percentage of loss payable on commercial and political risks: 90 per cent.)

— Buyer Credit Guarantees

Unconditional guarantees are given to Australian lending institutions that finance overseas buyers' purchases of Australian capital goods and associated services.

Buyer credit guarantees are normally available for exports of capital goods and associated services with a minimum loan value in the region of A\$200 000 upwards when credit terms are in excess of two years. This facility may be adapted to embrace a number of individual orders of lower value under a line of credit arrangement.

2.2.2   *Eligibility*

See 2.1.2 and 2.2.

2.2.3   *Cost of cover*

See 2.1.3.

2.3   **Other Insurance Programmes**

2.3.1   *Foreign exchange risk insurance*

There is no programme for insuring foreign exchange risks per se. Australian exporters have, however, access through banks to domestic forward markets. A measure of protection against exchange rate movements is provided under AUSTRADE–EFIC's Reference Rate of Exchange (RRE) facility. This facility determines the exchange rate to be used in converting an exporter's loss to Australian dollars where the export contract has been written in a foreign currency. It is triggered when the exporter has suffered a cause of loss under his policy.

Under the facility, an exporter's loss is converted to Australian dollars using the relevant exchange rate on the due date of payment under the export contract.

AUSTRADE–EFIC's liability has a ceiling of a maximum of 15 per cent more than it would have paid had the rate of exchange been that applying at the date of commencement of cover.

2.3.2   Bond insurance

Bond indemnity and insurance cover for unfair calling of bonds facilities operates in conjunction with AUSTRADE–EFIC's other facilities; hence the underlying export contract must be related to the export of Australian goods and services and must be acceptable for support under AUSTRADE–EFIC's credit insurance, buyer credit or finance facilities.

For bid or tender bonds, the exporter must undertake to insure under the appropriate facility, any insurable risks if it wins the proposed contract.

2.3.3   Bond indemnity

Indemnities issued to financial institutions that provide bonds or guarantees to overseas parties are for 100 per cent of an agreed portion of the bond value. The issue of the indemnity is conditional upon the exporter entering into a recourse agreement with AUSTRADE–EFIC.

Cost:
— A small charge is payable by the exporter on application. Premium is determined on a case by case basis and is payable by the exporter as a single sum on issue of the indemnity to the bank. There is no minimum eligible contract value but a minimum premium of A$250 applies.

Claims:
— AUSTRADE–EFIC reimburses the bank under the indemnity seven days after a claim has been made by the bank that the bond is called. All payments are made in Australian dollars.

Bonds expressed in a foreign currency are converted at the buying rate of exchange on the date of call on the bank under the bond, with AUSTRADE–EFIC's liability being limited to the maximum liability expressed in the indemnity. (This may include provisions for fluctuation of the rate of exchange of up to 115 per cent of a mutually agreed fixed rate of exchange.)

2.3.4   Insurance cover for unfair calling of bonds or guarantees

AUSTRADE–EFIC can provide this insurance where an exporter has properly performed his contract and the calling occurs by reason of circumstances prevailing outside Australia and beyond its control.
— The cover is for 95 per cent of the value of the bond;
— The premium is determined on a case by case basis but would normally be in the region of 0.5 per cent per annum of the value of the bond.

This insurance cover may be issued in conjunction with an AUSTRADE–EFIC bond indemnity.

2.3.5   Investment insurance

The Overseas Investment Insurance Policy provides insurance of Australian overseas investments against the non–commercial risks of loss caused by expropriation;

damage or destruction of property by a war–like operation; inability to transfer to Australia monies received on, or return from, the investment.

3.   EXPORT FINANCE PROGRAMMES

3.1   Direct Credits

3.1.1   *Types of contract available*

In addition to insurance and guarantee facilities, AUSTRADE–EFIC is empowered, under its Export Finance Facility, to provide loans to overseas buyers of Australian capital goods and services.

AUSTRADE–EFIC is also the agent for the government in "national interest" cases, that is loans that would impose on AUSTRADE–EFIC a liability that it is not authorised to undertake or would not undertake in the ordinary course of business. AUSTRADE–EFIC may, at its discretion, participate in such "national interest" transactions.

To the extent that interest rates covered by the Arrangement are below the level of commercial interest rates, the difference in the commercial cost of funds to AUSTRADE–EFIC and the lower interest rate at which it on–lends these funds to the overseas borrower is subsidised by the Australian government.

3.1.2   *Eligibility*

Loans are usually for up to 85 per cent of the value of the Australian export contract. The terms and conditions under which AUSTRADE–EFIC supports export contracts for capital goods and services with credits and guarantees are governed by the OECD Arrangement.

The facility encompasses small orders ranging from A$50 000. To accommodate the smaller loans, AUSTRADE–EFIC uses financial techniques that enable it to avoid some of the extensive documentation and administrative procedures essential for larger overseas loans. In appropriate circumstances, AUSTRADE–EFIC is also able to provide lines of credit, loans in selected foreign currencies and loan drawings during the production or manufacturing period of capital goods that are to be exported.

3.1.3   *Resulting interest rates*

The interest rate on AUSTRADE–EFIC's Export Finance loans is determined in accordance with the provisions of the OECD Arrangement and the exporter is charged a finance fee, determined case by case which is usually included in the contract price. AUSTRADE–EFIC also charges the borrower a once–only establishment fee of 0.3 per cent on the principal loan value and a commitment fee of 0.25 to 0.5 per cent per annum on the undrawn loan balance.

3.2   Refinancing

N/A.

3.3   Interest Subsidies

N/A.

3.4   Other Credit Operations

Since the removal of exchange control regulations in December 1983, available facilities have mostly been determined by the market. AUSTRADE–EFIC is not authorised to accept insurance in foreign currencies. It may insure and guarantee foreign currency transactions for an agreed Australian dollar equivalent, and claims are paid in Australian dollars. By agreement with the exporter, cover for short term supplier credit transactions in foreign currency can be for 115 per cent of the commencement exchange rate. For medium and long term supplier credit transactions and guarantees, higher cover for exchange rate movements can be agreed. Buyer credit guarantees provide full protection against exchange rate movements. Exporters and banks have ready access to forward currency markets.

4.   AID FINANCE PROGRAMMES

4.1   Associated Financing

4.1.1   *Funds available*

ODA grants for mixed credits are channelled through the Development Import Finance Facility (DIFF), which is operated in accordance with the DAC Guiding Principles. An annual ceiling of A$100 million (in real terms) applies on DIFF funding. Actual funding is determined annually. A limit of 40 per cent of total DIFF funds in each year applies for any single country.

4.1.2   *Eligibility*

DIFF funds are tied to procurement in Australia, but local cost up to 15 per cent of the contract value can be financed. As a rule, AIDAB releases the funds if the Australian exporter has been awarded the contract and if AUSTRADE–EFIC is ready to extend an export credit in parallel with the aid grants for the same project.

Mixed credits are available to all developing countries. There is a regional focus in so far as 90 per cent of available funding is reserved for projects within South Asia, South East Asia, China and the South Pacific.

DIFF grants are normally 35 per cent of the Eligible Contract Value, but may exceed 50 per cent in the case of assistance provided for Least Developed Countries.

There is a general requirement for Australian exporters to demonstrate the existence of aid supported competition, although in certain "spoilt markets" where tenders are not normally accepted without an accompanying offer of soft finance, evidence of competition is not necessary. It is Australia's preference that its exporters tender under international competitive bidding conditions. It is recognised that some recipient governments employ other conditions.

To ensure that the development value of projects is well established, Australian suppliers seeking DIFF support are required to provide information on project feasibility. The developmental soundness of projects is a central condition of DIFF.

4.1.3   *Resulting terms and interest rates*

The terms provided under finance packages are influenced by factors such as the loan value, the type of project and whether it is part of a larger development, the standing of the country, the loan terms commonly offered to the country, the loan currency and any particular requirements of the recipient country and its authorities.

Chapter 20

CANADA

1. ORGANISATION AND STRUCTURE

1.1 **Insurance and Guarantees**

1.1.1 *Representative organisation*

Export Development Corporation
P.O. Box 655
Ottawa, Ontario
Canada K1P 5T9

Telephone: (1 613) 598 2500
Telex: EXCREDCORP OTT 053 4136
Telefax: (1 613) 237 2690 (Xerox 495)

1.1.1.1 *Function*

The Export Development Corporation, a Crown corporation fully owned by the government of Canada, was established by the Export Development Act in 1969 to succeed the twenty five year old Export Credit Insurance Corporation (ECIC). EDC provides insurance and guarantees to exporters and financial institutions and extends direct financing to buyers of Canadian exports.

For financial management, for reporting and for auditing, EDC is governed by the Financial Administration Act, legislation that establishes a basic system of controls over Crown Corporations. EDC's current planning, operating and reporting processes meet the requirements of this statute and those of the Export Development Act.

The fifteen members of the Board of Directors of EDC are appointed by the government. Eleven members are from the business community and four are senior government officials: the President of EDC, the Deputy Minister for International Trade, the Deputy Minister for Finance, and the President of the Canadian International Development Agency.

1.1.1.2 *Summary of organisation*

EDC currently operates with six groups reporting to the President: Export Financing, Export Insurance, Finance and Treasury, Human Resources and Administration, Corporate Secretariat and Legal Services, and Marketing. The first two are the Corporation's operations group responsible for the delivery of EDC's financial services to Canadian exporters.

As at 31st December 1988, the Corporation employed 503 persons.

Initial applications can be made to one of EDC's regional or district offices located in Vancouver, Calgary, Winnipeg, London (Ontario), Toronto, Ottawa, Montreal and Halifax.

CORPORATE MANAGERIAL STRUCTURE

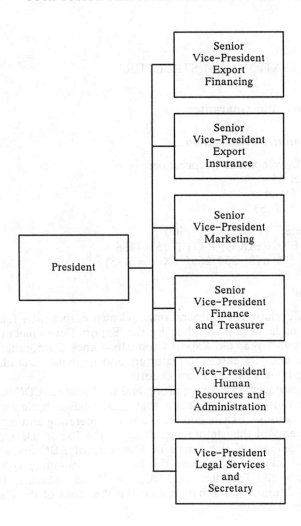

1.1.1.3 *Resources*

EDC's authorised capital stock amounts to C$1.5 billion, of which C$697 million had been subscribed and paid in as at 31st December 1988. There was an insurance reserve of C$44.6 million as at 31st December 1988. The Export Development Act of 1969 establishes financial limits in each area of the Corporation's activity. The limits have been raised twice through amendments to the Act. At present, the limit for EDC's total business is set at C$43 billion. For export credits insurance, the financial ceiling is C$22 billion, of which C$15 billion is for insurance business on EDC's own account (Corporate Account) and C$7 billion for operations specifically authorised by the government (Canada Account).

Under the Export Development Act, EDC may have outstanding loans to foreign borrowers and undisbursed commitments of up to a maximum of C$15 billion. Accounts administered for Canada may have outstanding loans to foreign borrowers and undisbursed commitments of up to a maximum of C$6 billion.

The loans extended on behalf of the government under the Canada Account are written under the same financing principles as loans under the EDC Corporate Account, but are funded through government allocations from the Canadian Government Consolidated Revenue Fund. EDC administers these loans, but the Consolidated Revenue Fund is liable for any losses and receives interest payments after deduction by EDC of associated administrative costs. Certain of these funds may be made available at reduced interest rates, and are used in combination with EDC's own funds to provide a blended interest rate to match, where necessary, financing offered by competitors.

EDC obtains the bulk of the funds required for its lending operations by issuing short and medium term obligations on domestic and international capital markets. It also draws funds from the domestic banking system through lines of credit with private banks. EDC no longer borrows from or rediscounts with the government, but because it is a Crown agency, it can borrow Canadian dollars and other currencies on the international capital markets at virtually the same rates as those at which the government of Canada borrows. EDC does not pay dividends on the capital invested by its shareholder, the government of Canada.

1.1.1.4 *Other organisations involved*

Not applicable.

1.1.1.5 *Relations with the state*

EDC is accountable for its total business activities to the Parliament through the Minister for International Trade. Loans are generally made under the authority of EDC's Board of Directors and at the risk of the Corporation (Corporate Account). In special cases, where EDC's Board of Directors considers the risk or terms associated with the proposed loan to be in excess of that which the Corporation normally would undertake but which the Minister for International Trade considers to be in the national interest, loans may be made under the authority and at the risk of the government (Canada Account).

1.1.1.6   *Relations with the private sector*

When lending for its own account, EDC pursues constructive working relationships with private sector financial intermediaries in order to encourage the maximum availability of a competitive standard of service to exporters.

1.2   **Export Finance**

1.2.1   *Representative Organization*

Export Development Corporation
(See 1.1.1).

1.2.2   *Representative Organization*

Canadian Wheat Board
423 Main Street
Box 816
Winnipeg, Manitoba
R3C 2P5

Telephone: (204) 983–3421
Telex: 0757801
Telefax: (204) 983–3841

1.2.2.1. *Function*

The Canadian government offers a credit programme to countries who are unable to purchase Canadian commodities on a cash basis. The total amount of dollars available to each country is determined by the Department of Finance and other federal departments based on ability to repay the loan.

The Canadian Wheat Board must check with the federal government on a country's line of credit before finalizing a grain deal. The amount of grain that can be bought under credit will vary depending on the price of the grain and other commodities purchased by that country within its line of credit. The federal government guarantees the loans that the Wheat Board takes out to finance its credit sales.

Credit is offered in Canadian or U.S. dollars and is short or medium term at prevailing commercial interest rates. The maximum term offered is three years. Repayment by the customer must be made in the same currency in which the loan is taken.

2.   INSURANCE AND GUARANTEE PROGRAMMES

2.1   **Cover for Exporters**

2.1.1.   *Policies available*

— Risks covered

Cover is normally extended for both commercial and political risks from the date of contract or of shipment. EDC may cover only specified political risks in certain cases. On short term transactions, Canadian exporters may choose to have cover for political risk only.

— Amounts covered

EDC insures exporters on a co–insurance basis, with EDC covering losses for up to 90 per cent of the contract value and the exporter assuming 10 per cent of the risk involved. In cases of contract repudiation or contract termination by the buyer, under Global Comprehensive policies, the exporter must bear the first loss of 15 per cent on the lesser of the gross invoice value or the credit limit for the buyer. The remaining loss is covered up to 90 per cent. Foreign investment insurance covers up to 300 per cent of the initial equity investment and up to 200 per cent for loan investments. EDC will consider coverage of any transaction regardless of the amount.

EDC does not generally extend cover for local cost financing.

— Type of contracts available

Credit Insurance services offered by EDC are as follows:

— The Loan Pre–disbursement Insurance Programme, which is related to EDC financing, provides cover for the production risk from the effective day of financing until disbursement under the financing agreement is made. Foreign investment insurance is also available to protect Canadian companies investing abroad against three broad political risks: inconvertibility or the inability to repatriate earnings or capital, expropriation, war or revolution.

— Global Comprehensive Insurance provides cover to the exporter against both commercial and political risks inherent in export sales made on short–term credit. An exporter is required to insure all export sales unless excluded by EDC.

— Global Political Insurance provides cover to the exporter against specified political risks inherent in export sales made on short term credit. An exporter is required to insure all export sales unless excluded by EDC.

— Selective Political Insurance provides cover to the exporter against specified political risks inherent in export sales made on short–term credit. An exporter may select the countries for which he wants cover but all export sales to buyers in the selected countries must be insured.

— U.S.A. Commercial Risk (Deductible) Insurance provides cover to the exporter against commercial risks inherent in export sales made on short–term credit to the U.S. A choice of deductibles is offered to the exporter and the higher the deductible selected, the lower the premium charged.

— Export Credit Insurance (Small Business) – U.S.A. provides cover to exporters with total sales of $5 million or less against commercial risks of export sales made on short–term credit to the U.S. Features include simplified paperwork, sourcing of credit reports for the exporter by EDC for a small fee, and a free receivables management system operated by EDC's agents to assist with the timely settlement of overdue accounts.

- Export Credit Insurance (Small Business) – Worldwide provides cover to exporters with total sales of $5 million or less against commercial and political risks inherent in export sales made on short–term credits to buyers worldwide. Features include simplified paperwork.
- Documentary Credit Insurance provides cover to Canadian banks against commercial and political risks in respect of documentary credits issued by foreign banks for payment of Canadian export transactions. Banks can select the documentary credits to be insured.
- Bank Export Finance Insurance provides cover for Canadian banks against non–payment of Canadian export receivables discounted or guaranteed by Canadian banks.
- Short–Term Bulk Agriculture Credits Insurance provides cover to the exporter of bulk agricultural products against commercial and political risks inherent in export sales to foreign governments, and in export sales to private buyers under irrevocable letters or credit. Features include competitive premium rates, fast turnaround times, and cover for credit terms of up to 360 days.
- Medium–Term Bulk Agriculture Credit Insurance provides cover to the exporter of bulk agricultural products against political and commercial risks inherent in export sales to foreign governments. Features include competitive premium rates and cover for credit terms of up to three years when warranted by officially supported international competition.
- Specific Transaction Insurance provides cover to the exporter for individual transactions, involving goods and services, either from the effective date of contract or the shipment of goods until payment is received.
- Subsupplier Insurance provides cover to a Canadian firm supplying goods or services to a Canadian exporter selling to a foreign buyer. Provided the export transaction is insured by EDC, the subsupplier can obtain EDC cover against non–payment by the foreign buyer or the exporter as a result of commercial or political risks. Two policies are available: Specific Transaction Subsupplier Insurance (Foreign Risks) and Specific Transaction Subsupplier Insurance (Domestic Risks).

EDC also offers foreign investment insurance to Canadian exporters for new investments that include significant expansion, modernisation or development of an existing enterprise. The investment must be of some economic advantage to Canada and to the host country. In some countries, EDC has entered into a bilateral agreement for investments insured by EDC in that country. The bilateral agreement outlines EDC's rights as recognised and approved by the government of the host country.

2.1.2   Eligibility

Any transactions involving export of goods, services or technology may be insured provided it meets EDC's normal criteria relating to Canadian content, country and buyer risks as well as technical and commercial competence of the exporter. In the case of large projects, EDC may require specific guarantees of governments or other financially creditworthy agencies.

Where a project is not acceptable under normal EDC criteria but is considered by the Minister of International Trade to be in the national interest, the Governor in Council may instruct EDC to underwrite it for the account of the government of Canada.

EDC seeks to optimize the Canadian content in the exports it supports. With this in mind EDC offers advice to exporters on how to meet and exceed Canadian content levels which are determined at the time of the application. Generally, goods and services should have a minimum of 60 % Canadian content.

2.1.3   *Cost of cover*

On short term transactions, EDC's risk grading system takes into consideration commodity classes such as raw materials and luxury manufactured items, as well as terms of payment and country classifications. Pre–shipment factors and underwriting factors based on the exporter's record, the spread of risk and claims are also taken into account.

On medium and long term transactions, EDC considers five country risk categories, the type of buyer (sovereign or commercial) and the exposure term (from first disbursement to last repayment) of the transaction.

2.2   **Guarantees for Banks**

2.2.1   *Policies available*

When deferred payment terms require credit facilities, EDC, in addition to insurance, offers guarantees to banks or other lenders who agree to provide financing.

When one of the above–mentioned insurance services is involved, EDC will agree, if so requested by the exporter, to pay any proceeds payable under an exporter's policy of insurance to a bank or other financial organisation that is financing the export transaction. In addition, when an exporter seeks direct cash flow by discounting an export receivable, EDC's Global Comprehensive Insurance can be assigned directly to any bank that is prepared to discount the receivable from the exporter on a limited recourse basis.

Specific Transaction Guarantees provide a bank with a 100 per cent guarantee against the risks of non–payment under promissory notes that it has purchased from an exporter in connection with an export transaction. The availability of the guarantee to his bank allows an exporter to extend a medium term supplier credit to his foreign buyer and to sell to his bank the resulting promissory notes issued to him by the foreign buyer, thus transforming a sale on deferred credit terms into a cash sale. In addition to the cash proceeds of the transaction becoming immediately available upon the sale of the promissory notes, an attractive feature to the exporter is that neither EDC nor the bank retain recourse to him for payments made under the guarantee. Thus, under the Specific Transaction Guarantee, EDC can provide unconditional cover to banks and other lenders on non–recourse supplier financing. However, the capital goods and services sale must be insured by EDC.

2.2.2   *Eligibility*

See 2.1.2.

2.2.3   *Cost of cover*

See 2.1.3.

2.3   Other Insurance Programmes

2.3.1   *Foreign exchange risk insurance*

There is no official foreign exchange risk insurance programme in operation. Exporters and banks have access to both domestic and international forward markets. Export credits expressed in a foreign currency may be refinanced on the international capital market in the same currency and thus minimise the exchange risk exposure.

2.3.2   *Bond insurance*

In 1978, EDC introduced a programme whereby exporters, financial institutions and surety companies can be covered for risks arising from securities that may be required under the terms of the commercial contract. The programme covers guarantees and bonds for bids, down payments, performance and completion provisions. In the event of a consortium of companies created for the purpose of bidding on international projects, EDC can protect each individual member of the consortium against the risk of a performance instrument being called because of the failure of any one or more of the other consortium members causing a default by the consortium itself under the commercial contract ("cross–consortium insurance"). EDC may also issue a guarantee to a domestic surety company that has issued a surety bond on behalf of the exporter and in favour of a foreign buyer.

The Bid Bond Guarantee gives cover to banks on behalf of exporters provided they have EDC bid bond insurance.

Under the programme, exporters are normally insured up to 90 per cent against unfair calling of a bond. EDC may guarantee the exporter's bank up to 100 per cent against a call of performance security or a bid security.

In the event of a loss and when EDC has issued a guarantee to a bank, EDC does take recourse against the exporter. If the cause of loss is an unjustified call on the bond, EDC's recourse to the exporter is for 10 per cent. However, if the call on the bond is justified, EDC has recourse for 100 per cent.

2.3.3   *Foreign investment insurance*

The Export Development Act gives EDC authority to offer foreign investment insurance on its own account against Canadian investors' political risks of loss of their investments abroad. The programme covers most forms of new foreign investment including investments that are made through a related company based in Canada, the host country or a third country. EDC's foreign investment insurance covers three broad risks: insurrection, revolution or war, expropriation, and inconvertibility. The period of coverage is normally restricted to a maximum of fifteen years, and the investor is required to assume some of the risk of loss.

2.3.4   *Equipment insurance*

Equipment insurance protects exporters against political risks of loss or damage of equipment due to seizures or repatriation restrictions. Canadian exporters can obtain such coverage by an endorsement to the basic insurance policy.

2.3.5   *Performance Security Guarantee*

This is provided to banks only on behalf of exporters who have performance security insurance and credit insurance with EDC.

3.   EXPORT FINANCE PROGRAMMES

3.1   **Direct Credits**

3.1.1   *Types of contract available*

Export financing services are essentially two types: 1. loans made either directly to the buyer or through the purchase of promissory notes issued to the exporter by a foreign buyer, and 2. (according to Canada's interpretation of the term) guarantees of export loans provided by banks or other financial institutions. EDC financing is available for export transactions which would normally warrant medium — or long–term financing support. EDC normally provides funding for up to 85 per cent of the contract value. Funds are disbursed directly to the Canadian exporter on behalf of the foreign buyer, thus creating the equivalent of a cash sale for the exporter.

EDC's financing facilities include loans, lines of credit and note purchases. Specialized financing facilities are also available. Transactions eligible for specialized credit are those for which goods are purchased in Canada by a Canadian buyer that will 1. lease such goods to another person for permanent use outside Canada or 2. will use the goods himself on a permanent basis outside Canada.

EDC strives to be as flexible and responsive as possible to the financing needs of Canadian exporters. The amount and type of financing provided varies with a number of factors including competitive circumstances, the economic life of the goods and services to be exported, project cash flow, the characteristics of the borrower and the nature of the foreign market.

3.1.2   *Eligibility*

EDC's financing services are available to support any person or organization carrying on business in Canada provided EDC is satisfied with the technical and commercial competence of the exporter and the general creditworthiness of the borrower.

Exporters requiring medium and long term export credits submit an application to EDC with sufficient information for an in–depth assessment. In making and guaranteeing loans for the purchase by a foreign buyer of Canadian capital goods and services, EDC assesses the buyer's creditworthiness, the country risk, the Canadian exporter's financial and technical capabilities, and the Canadian material/labour content.

The EDC Board may accept a project for its own account or reject it. In the latter case, the Minister for International Trade may refer the project to the Cabinet for consideration under the Canada Account if it is considered to be in the national interest.

EDC may provide local cost financing on a case by case basis, up to an amount equivalent to the percentage cash payments in accordance with the Arrangement. Financing is only extended when local costs cannot be disassociated from the commercial contract and are thus the exporter's responsibility.

3.1.3   *Resulting interest rates*

Interest rates charged by EDC are set in accordance with minimum rates applicable under the Arrangement and are also guided by EDC's overall earning criteria and by the requirement to match international competition on a case by case basis. Rates vary from transaction to transaction.

EDC charges a commitment fee averaging 0.5 per cent per annum on undisbursed amounts, a management fee that usually ranges between 0.5 per cent and 1.0 per cent flat and legal fees equal to the amount of legal expenses actually incurred together with documentation costs.

In addition, Canadian exporters are required to pay fees to EDC for its financing in order to compensate for the non–payment risks assumed during the disbursement and repayment periods of medium– and long–term export credit financing provided by EDC.

3.2   **Refinancing**

N/A.

3.3   **Interest Subsidies**

N/A.

3.4   **Other Credit Operations**

N/A.

4.   AID FINANCE PROGRAMMES

4.1   **Associated Financing**

Canada has two mechanisms for providing Associated Financing. The first mechanism involves the provision of EDC export financing in parallel with separate aid loans from the Canadian International Development Agency (CIDA), in situations where there are both developmental and commercial interests. The second mechanism involves the use of Canada Account funds at concessional rates in selective cases where it is necessary to match other countries' concessional offers. For this second mechanism, all Canada Account loans are subject to Cabinet approval.

4.2   **Integrated Credits**

N/A.

4.3   **Other Tied or Partially United Aid**

N/A.

Chapter 21

JAPAN

1. ORGANISATION AND STRUCTURE

1.1 Insurance and Guarantees

1.1.1 Representative organisation

Export–Import Insurance Division
Ministry of International Trade and Industry
1–3–1 Kasumigaseki
Chiyoda–ku
Tokyo

Telephone: (81 3) 501–1665
Telex: EIDMITI J 22916
Telefax: (81 3) 508–2624

Export–Import Insurance Division
127 Cheapside
London EC2G 6BP

Telephone: (44 1) 606–2500
Telex: EID LDN 886079
Telefax: (44 1) 600 8107

1.1.1.1 *Function*

The Export–Import Insurance Division (EID) of the Ministry of International Trade and Industry (MITI) began operations in 1930 and now operates under the Export Insurance Law of 1950 (as amended) and the Export Insurance Special Account Law.

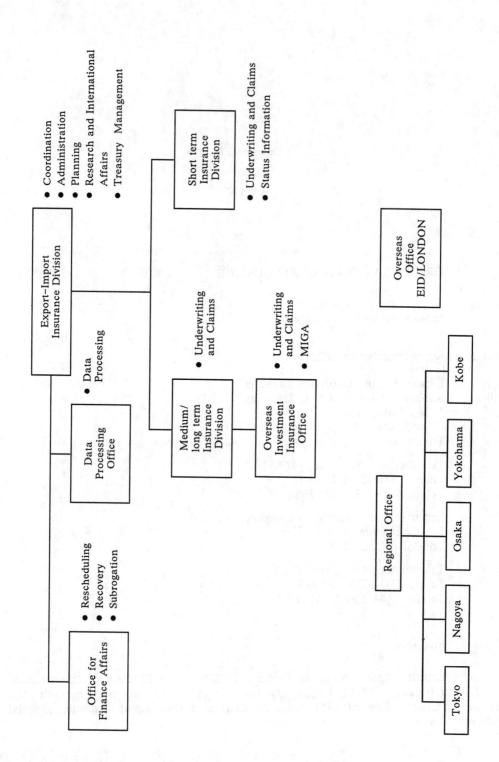

Export–Import Insurance Division
- Coordination
- Administration
- Planning
- Research and International Affairs
- Treasury Management

Office for Finance Affairs
- Rescheduling
- Recovery
- Subrogation

Data Processing Office
- Data Processing

Short term Insurance Division
- Underwriting and Claims
- Status Information

Medium/long term Insurance Division
- Underwriting and Claims

Overseas Investment Insurance Office
- Underwriting and Claims
- MIGA

Overseas Office EID/LONDON

Regional Office
- Tokyo
- Nagoya
- Osaka
- Yokohama
- Kobe

1.1.1.2 *Summary of organisation*

See previous page.

1.1.1.3 *Resources*

EID operates with a capital fund of Yen 17 billion. Annual liability ceilings are fixed by the Diet according to the type of insurance. They were as follows for the fiscal year 1988:

General Export Insurance:	Yen 10 500 billion
Export Proceeds Insurance:	Yen 8 900 billion
Export Bills Insurance:	Yen 1 500 billion
Other:	Yen 1 380 billion
Total:	Yen 22 280 billion

Premiums and losses are credited and debited to the International Trade Insurance Special Account. EID is expected to cover its operating costs, including eventual losses.

1.1.1.4 *Other organisations involved*

The Export–Import Insurance Council advises the Minister of International Trade and Industry on policy questions. The Minister of International Trade and Industry appoints its eleven members chosen from government agencies dealing with foreign trade, finance and insurance.

1.1.1.5 *Relations with the state*

EID/MITI's operations should be self supporting in the long term. The organisation is part of the Ministry of International Trade and Industry.

1.1.1.6 *Relations with the private sector*

The Export–Import Insurance Division (EID) of the Ministry of International Trade and Industry (MITI) insures repayment of export credits. This government–based insurance enables commercial banks, which normally would be unwilling to assume the risk of foreign long term financing, to fund overseas projects. Close co–operation between EXIM, EID, commercial banks and the business community ensures the availability of funds for export financing.

1.1.1.7 *Additional structure*

EID has both specific and comprehensive insurance. In the latter case, the exporter is covered in all export transactions for a fixed time period. EXIM guarantees (see 1.1.2) are available only when EID insurance is not.

1.1.2   The Export–Import Bank of Japan

EXIM (see 1.2 below) runs a programme of guarantees for bank to bank loans and buyer credits that cannot be covered by EID. At the end of fiscal 1987, guarantees were outstanding for Yen 9.3 billion (including guarantees for loans other than export credits given by EXIM).

1.2   **Export Finance**

1.2.1   Representative organisation

The Export–Import Bank of Japan
1–4–1 Ohtemachi
Chiyoda–ku
Tokyo

Telephone: (81 3) 287 1221
Telex: YUGIN J 222 3728
Telefax: (81 3) 287 9539

1.2.1.1   Function

The Export–Import Bank of Japan is a government financial institution. It was established by law in 1950 and began business in 1951.

1.2.1.2   Summary of organisation

See below.

1.2.1.3   Resources

The capital stock of EXIM was yen 967.3 billion as at March 1989. The paid–up capital was wholly subscribed by the government from the Industrial Investment Special Account. After setting aside its reserves (yen 13.3 billion for financial year 1988), EXIM remits its profits to the Treasury.

The total of outstanding credits granted by EXIM may not exceed the sum of its capital and reserves plus its maximum liability limit, which is equivalent to ten times its capital and reserves. The Bank may borrow at a fixed rate (currently 4.85 per cent per annum) at a typical term of ten years from the Trust Fund Bureau, which handles savings received through the government postal savings system. In addition, EXIM has access to foreign currency from the Foreign Exchange Fund. It is also authorised to issue bonds denominated in a foreign currency on the international capital market. EXIM's foreign currency lending is also funded with its yen resources by utilising the forward exchange markets and with its issuing of foreign currency bonds. EXIM cannot borrow from or rediscount with the Bank of Japan.

1.2.1.4   Other organisations involved

N/A.

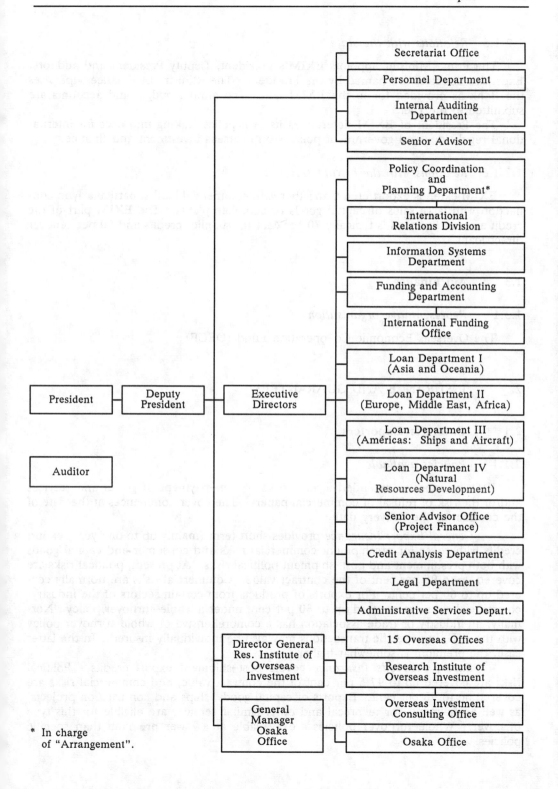

President — Deputy President — Executive Directors

- Secretariat Office
- Personnel Department
- Internal Auditing Department
- Senior Advisor
- Policy Coordination and Planning Department*
- International Relations Division
- Information Systems Department
- Funding and Accounting Department
- International Funding Office
- Loan Department I (Asia and Oceania)
- Loan Department II (Europe, Middle East, Africa)
- Loan Department III (Américas: Ships and Aircraft)
- Loan Department IV (Natural Resources Development)
- Senior Advisor Office (Project Finance)
- Credit Analysis Department
- Legal Department
- Administrative Services Depart.
- 15 Overseas Offices

Director General Res. Institute of Overseas Investment
- Research Institute of Overseas Investment
- Overseas Investment Consulting Office

General Manager Osaka Office
- Osaka Office

Auditor

* In charge of "Arrangement".

1.2.1.5 *Relations with the state*

The Prime Minister appoints EXIM's President, Deputy President and auditors. Executive directors are named by the President. The Ministry of Finance supervises the Bank as provided for in the EXIM law. The annual budget and accounts are submitted to the Diet.

The President of EXIM determines its own policy, taking into account international regulations and government policies on overseas investment and finance.

1.2.1.6 *Relations with the private sector*

EXIM extends export credits together with commercial banks, particularly in connection with large sales of capital goods or complete plants. The EXIM part of the credit amount financed is typically 70 per cent for supplier credits and 60 per cent for direct loans.

1.3 Aid Finance

1.3.1 *Representative organisation*

The Overseas Economic Co–operation Fund (OECF)

2. INSURANCE AND GUARANTEES

2.1 Cover for Exporters

2.1.1 *Policies available*

EID insurance is extended against risks of non–payment of goods and services and/or the risk of refusal of commercial papers. The cover commences at the date of the contract or the delivery date.

— *General Export Insurance* provides short term (mainly up to one year) export credits with cover for preshipment commercial risks and consumer and capital goods with both preshipment and post–shipment political risks. At present, political risks are covered up to 95 per cent of the contract value. Commercial risks are normally covered up to 60 per cent. For exports of products from certain sectors of the industry, commercial risks are covered up to 80 per cent under a whole–turnover policy. Normally, an industry or trade association has a comprehensive or whole–turnover policy with the EID, but specific transactions may also be individually insured. In the latter case, the premium is somewhat higher.

— *Export Proceeds Insurance* covers post–shipment export credits. Political risks are covered up to 97.5 per cent of the contract value, and commercial risks are covered up to 90 per cent. Exports of capital goods, ships and construction projects, as well as payments for technical and other similar services are eligible for this type of cover. Whole–turnover policies are available at a lower premium than specific policies.

2.1.2   *Eligibility*

EID has an established classification for the creditworthiness of different buyer–countries. In principle, no insurance can be issued for a transaction with a "high risk" country or with a country where a default has already occurred. In any event, large projects are submitted to a thorough vetting by EID. Normal credit terms insured are set in line with the OECD Arrangement.

In principle, EID will cover foreign content up to 50 per cent of the contract value, and will extend support to local cost financing in accordance with the provisions on local costs of the Arrangement.

2.1.3   *Cost of cover*

Premia for insurance vary according to the policy scheme to be utilised and the creditworthiness rating of the buyer country. For example, the premium for general export insurance varies from 40 to 60 per cent of the basic insurance premium, depending on the creditworthiness of the buyer country.

2.2   Guarantees for Banks

2.2.1   *Policies available*

— Export Bill Insurance covers banks against default on commercial papers accepted by them on post–delivery export credits. Guarantees for countries with less than a very good credit rating and guarantees for transactions where the insured amount is large relative to the buyer's assets must be referred to MITI for prior confirmation of the amount insured. Cover is up to 82.5 per cent of the paper's face value for political risks, and up to 80 per cent for commercial risks. With respect to these guarantees, additional compensation may be obtained from some local public organisations for losses not covered by EID/MITI.

2.2.2   *Eligibility*

See 2.1.2.

2.2.3   *Cost of cover*

See 2.1.3.

2.3   Other Insurance Programmes

EID/MITI instituted its new international trade insurance programme in October 1987. The programme's aim is to encourage greater capital outflows to foreign countries, especially the developing countries, through overseas investment and assistance to them in earning more foreign exchange by exporting to Japan or third countries. The new programme is comprised of the following types of trade insurance: prepayment import insurance, intermediary trade insurance and enhanced overseas investment insurance.

2.3.1   Prepayment Import Insurance

Prepayment Import Insurance provides an importer with cover in cases of non-refund of prepayments in cases when goods are not delivered despite prepayment being made by an importer prior to shipment. The percentage of indemnity cover is up to 90 per cent of the prepaid amount for political risk, and up to 80 per cent for commercial risk.

2.3.2.   Intermediary Trade Insurance

Intermediary Trade Insurance focuses on the risks of domestic traders engaged in intermediary trade, or those who conclude intermediary trade contracts for the purpose of selling or renting goods manufactured in one foreign country to traders of a third country. This insurance covers risks relating to recovery in such cases as bankruptcies and country restrictions or prohibitions on foreign exchange transactions. Also eligible for this type of insurance cover are domestic financial institutions which lend commodity payment funds to foreign intermediary trade brokers. Cover for political and commercial risks is provided for up to 90 per cent and 80 per cent of the contract value respectively.

2.3.3.   Overseas investment insurance

"General overseas investment insurance" covers political risks for capital invested in overseas subsidiaries or joint ventures or capital goods shipped abroad for the proper execution of a contract. "Mineral resources development–financing insurance" applies to commercial and political risk of long term investments in the development and mining of mineral resources. The applicant must have a long term contract for the import of these resources. If security is demanded by the host country this can be covered by a "suretyship obligation insurance".

Moreover, the Export Insurance Law was amended on March 30, 1987 with a new programme coming into effect on October 1, 1987 under which EID/MITI expanded coverage to include bankruptcy risks incurred from overseas investments other than those related to development of natural resources (loans as well as equity interests). Indemnity coverage percentages are listed below.

	Political risk (%)	Commercial risk (%)
General overseas investment insurance	90	40
Insurance for financing the development of mineral resources	90	80
Suretyship obligation insurance	70	40 (in the case of insurance for financing the development of mineral resources insurance: 60 %)

Cover is normally extended for 5–15 years. A preliminary application for cover must be made before an investment is made. The final application must be submitted at the time funds are committed.

2.3.4.   Foreign exchange risk insurance

Since 1974, EID has operated an exchange risk insurance facility, which covers export contracts denominated in US dollars, pound sterling, French and Swiss francs and German marks. A maximum insurance period of fifteen years can be covered. During the first two years, the insured carries the exchange risk himself but normally covers himself for that time on the forward exchange market. There is a threshold of 3 per cent. Exchange losses that amount to less than the threshold are borne by the insured. However, losses in excess of 3 per cent are indemnified in full up to a ceiling of 20 per cent of the insured amount (maximum liability is thus 17 per cent). Any gain is treated in the same fashion as losses. Hence a part has to be surrendered to the EID. Coverage is limited to some specified goods and services, e.g. plants and plant equipment, ships, aircraft and engineering services.

Premiums charged are 0.4 per cent per half year for comprehensive policies and 0.75 per cent per half year for specific policies.

2.3.5   Bond insurance

Banks and insurance companies are not normally willing to insure exporters' performance or bid bonds against unjustified calling in connection with overseas risk–exposed businesses. In order to cover such risks, EID introduced in 1977 a facility through which performance, bid and refund bonds could be insured. Bonds eligible for cover should be issued by an authorised foreign exchange bank or non–life insurance company, and the creditworthiness of the buyer–country has to be satisfactory. Bond insurance is extended to exports of plants, technical contracts (usually engineering or consulting) and overseas construction projects.

The insurance covers 90 per cent of the bond amount for exporters that have special contracts in which they promise that all of their bonds beyond a certain value in a defined period will be insured. Individual application is also available for exporters who prefer not to file comprehensive contracts. The risk coverage in this case is 70 per cent of the bond amount.

The annual insurance premium for exporters holding a comprehensive policy is 0.1 per cent per annum of the issued amount. For exporters with a specific policy, the annual premium is 0.3 per cent. Bond insurance has mainly been issued in connection with sales to the Middle–East, Asia, etc.

2.3.6.   Technical service supply insurance

This type of cover insures service payments against political and commercial risks. Cover is obtainable for up to 90 per cent for equipment and up to 97.5 per cent for services.

3.   EXPORT FINANCE PROGRAMMES

3.1   Direct Credits

3.1.1.   *Types of contract available*

Buyer credits and bank to bank loans are extended to foreign governments, foreign banks, foreign corporations and international or regional agencies. In the case of buyer credits and bank to bank loans, EXIM carries the risk itself for its portion of the financing. For the bank–financed part, however, an EID insurance is in principle required.

3.1.2.   *Eligibility*

When extending buyer credits or bank to bank loans, EXIM takes account of the requests of borrowers, types of project, etc. on a case by case basis. Terms of financing are determined in the same way as for supplier credits.

3.2   Refinancing

3.2.1.   *Types of contract available*

Export credits with a repayment term not exceeding six months are provided entirely by commercial banks. Most medium and long term supplier credits are refinanced by EXIM at the relative Arrangement rate in combination with commercial bank participation at market rates. All supplier credits are eligible for refinancing provided that the minimum duration exceeds six months and sales of capital goods are involved.

3.2.2.   *Eligibility*

Refinancing is not automatic. Each transaction is separately screened by EXIM, which makes the decision to refinance on a case–by–case basis.

3.3   Interest Subsidies

No official interest rate subsidy scheme is operated.

3.4   Other Credit Operations

About one fifth of medium or long term export contracts are denominated in a foreign currency. These contracts are almost entirely expressed in US dollars. EID is authorised to insure credits in a foreign currency. Banks and exporters have access both to domestic and international forward exchange markets. For periods exceeding two years, the exchange risk may be covered by the exchange risk insurance scheme operated by EID.

4.   AID FINANCE PROGRAMMES

4.1   **Associated Financing** (Mixed credits)

4.1.1.   *Funds available*

OECF cooperates with commercial banks to extend concessional aid credits to developing countries. The terms are in accord with Arrangement guidelines.

In addition, aid funds can occasionally be combined with EXIM export credits to provide concessional facilities to support Japanese exporters in matching situations. Only a limited number of such cases has occurred in the past and decisions are taken on a case–by–case basis. The ODA component of these transactions is extended by the OECF which appraises projects to be financed against developmental criteria. Local costs can be financed to a certain extent.

Chapter 22

NEW ZEALAND

1. ORGANISATION AND STRUCTURE

1.1. Insurance and Guarantees

1.1.1 Representative organisation

Export Guarantee Office (EXGO)
P.O. Box 5037
Wellington

Telephone: (64 4) 720 265
Telex: STATINS NZ 31239, For EXGO
Telefax: (64 4) 725 824

1.1.1.1 Function

The Export Guarantee Act of 1964 instituted the Export Guarantee Office (EXGO) as a government agency under the administration of the State Insurance Office, which is responsible for day to day operations.

1.1.1.2 Summary of organisation

[Organisation Chart not available].

1.1.1.3 Resources

EXGO operates under a government guarantee but without capital. Surpluses on its operations, which are to cover expected losses, and administrative expenses are paid into the State Insurance account, and, where possible, investments are made in the name of the Export Guarantee Office.

1.1.1.4 Other organisations involved

The Export Guarantee Advisory Committee, the functions of which were to advise the Minister of Overseas Trade on matters relating to the export trade of New Zealand insofar as they related to the functions of EXGO, was disestablished in July 1988.

1.1.1.5   *Relations with the state*

Claims that result from the operations of EXGO and for which the funds in the State Insurance account are insufficient are reimbursed from the Consolidated Revenue Account of the New Zealand government. From time to time risks can be covered in the National Interest which impose a direct liability on the Consolidated Revenue Account.

1.1.1.6   *Relations with the private sector*

Private banks can insure export credits under a confirming bank policy where the bank agrees to confirm an irrevocable letter of credit and to pay the exporter without recourse.

1.2   **Export Finance**

No government sponsored export credit facilities are available. Export Finance is processed through normal banking channels.

2.   INSURANCE AND GUARANTEE PROGRAMMES

2.1   **Cover for Exporters**

2.1.1   *Policies available*

Insurance policies on specific transactions are available to cover political risks or commercial and political risks from date of contract or from date of shipment and are normally used where the period of credit exceeds six months. Comprehensive policies are also available where credit does not exceed one hundred and eighty days and on a whole turnover basis. Both supplier and buyer credits may be covered.

Local cost financing may be covered within the limits of the Arrangement. Credit terms may be more favourable than those normally supported in cases of matching officially supported or other competition.

The usual maximum credit lengths are as follows, within the limits of the Arrangement:

— Raw materials, semi–manufactures and consumer goods: up to six months;
— Consumer durables: up to three years;
— Quasi–capital goods: up to five years;
— Capital goods: up to eight years depending upon value.

Repayment is normally in equal semi–annual instalments with no grace period.

2.1.2   *Eligibility*

The main criteria are satisfactory creditworthiness of the buyer and the country of destination. These are determined by EXGO.

Cover is given on contracts for the sale of goods and services, or a combination of both, wholly or partly produced or manufactured in New Zealand provided that the terms of payment are consistent with those for the product in international trade.

2.1.3 *Cost of cover*

Premium and guarantee fees depend upon the categories of risks covered, the period of credit and the creditworthiness of both the buyer and the country of destination.

Open Declaration Policies attract an average rate of 0.42 per cent. A fee towards the cost of administration and obtaining credit reports is also levied. Specific policies covering export of capital goods and services are typically considered on a case by case basis, and charges vary according to term of contract and other underwriting factors.

2.2 **Guarantees for Banks**

2.2.1 *Policies available*

There are three ways in which EXGO policies and guarantees can affect the mobilisation of financing for exports:

— The exporter may assign the proceeds of his policy to any financier providing financing. This applies especially to short term credits;

— Comprehensive guarantees to financial institutions who will discount bills in respect of short term export contracts without recourse to the exporter. This mechanism effectively gives the exporter additional working capital up to the amount of the guaranteed facility;

— Specific guarantees to financial institutions under which they discount bills in respect of a specific contract without recourse to the exporter. These guarantees are usually in respect of contracts where the period of credit exceeds twelve months.

2.2.2 *Eligibility*

See 2.1.2 and 2.2.1.

2.2.3 *Cost of cover*

Competence Guarantees	0.15 per cent
Specific Guarantees	0.50 per cent

2.3 **Other Insurance Programmes**

2.3.1 *Bond insurance*

EXGO offers 100 per cent cover on losses arising from unfair calling (political risks) of a bond for tender, advance payment performance, progress payment and maintenance bonds. A charge of one half of one per cent of the face value of the bond is made.

3. EXPORT FINANCE PROGRAMMES

N/A.

4. AID FINANCING PROGRAMMES

New Zealand has no aid–related transactions combining aid and other funds.

Chapter 23

UNITED STATES

1.   ORGANISATION AND STRUCTURE

1.1   Insurance and Guarantees

1.1.1   *Representative organisation*

The Export–Import Bank of the United States (Eximbank)
811 Vermont Avenue, N.W.
Washington, D.C. 20571

Telephone: (202) 566–8990 Public Affairs Office
Telex: EXIMBANK 89 461
Telefax: (202) 566–7524

1.1.1.1 *Function*

The Export–Import Bank of the United States, chartered in 1934 as an independent government agency, facilitates U.S. exports by providing gurantee and insurance financing support in coordination with the Foreign Credit Insurance Association (FCIA) (see 1.1.2 below), and providing some direct credits. The guarantee and insurance coverage offered by Eximbank and FCIA on both short and medium term transactions is designed to protect the exporter against political and commercial risks.

Through its programmes Eximbank fills gaps left by private sector export credit financing sources. For example, Eximbank provides longer maturities in the face of commercial bank preference for short terms, assumes foreign credit risks that the private sector finds unacceptable within the limits of its information on creditworthiness grounds, and neutralises the export credit subsidies of foreign governments.

1.1.1.2 *Summary of organisation*

See below.

1.1.1.3 *Resources*

With the exception of the tied aid credit War Chest (see section 4.1.1), Eximbank does not receive any appropriated funds and has no access to any other "special" fund. Eximbank funds its operations by constantly rolling over its capital and reserves,

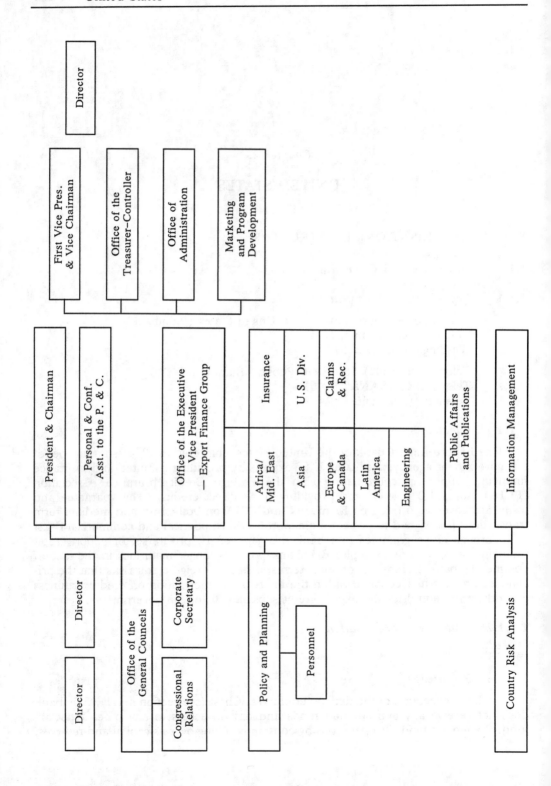

quarterly borrowing of long term debt at market rates from the Federal Financing Bank of the U.S. Treasury, and from revenues earned through payment of interest, fees and principal on its insurance, guarantees and direct loans. At the end of fiscal 1988 an amount of $11.0 billion was owed to the FFB. Eximbank also has authority under its Act to borrow directly from the U.S. Treasury and to have outstanding up to $6 billion of such borrowings. This authority is used for short term borrowing.

In fiscal year 1988 (which ended 30th September 1988) Eximbank reported a net loss of $428.2 million. Losses in the previous seven fiscal years reduced the total of capital and accumulated reserves of profitable years to $968.7 million.

Eximbank operates under both overall and annual budget ceilings. Overall limits on the amounts of loans, guarantees, and insurance are established in the Export–Import Bank Act. The Bank can have committed loans, guarantees, and insurance in the aggregate not exceeding $40 billion. For purposes of this limitation, the first $25 billion of guarantees and insurance commitments are only counted at 25 per cent of Eximbank's liability for principal. At the end of September 1988, the total committed authority was $27.9 billion so that $12.1 billion remained available.

The annual ceiling of new commitments has a crucial impact on the Bank's activities. Ceilings on Eximbank's guarantees are also determined as part of the institution's overall maximum liabilities. The ceiling for the fiscal year 1988 was $15.3 billion including $14.6 billion for all types of guarantees and insurance. For fiscal year 1989, the ceiling for guarantees was $17.9 billion.

1.1.1.4 *Other organisations involved*

The Bank's Board of Directors consists of seven members, a chairman, a vice–chairman and three directors appointed by the President from the private sector, the Secretary of Commerce (*ex officio*) and the United States Trade Representative (*ex officio*).

The National Advisory Council on International Monetary and Financial Policies (NAC) reviews all loans and guarantees involving over $30 million and insurance cases involving more than $50 million. Congressional review is also required on all transactions involving $100 million or more. The NAC also advises on Eximbank policy in general. The NAC includes representatives from the Departments of the Treasury, State and Commerce as well as the Export–Import Bank, the Office of the U.S. Trade Representative, the Federal Reserve Board and the umbrella agency which includes the Agency for International Development (AID). On questions pertaining to tied aid credits, the NAC also includes the Trade and Development Program (TDP). Eximbank also receives recommendations from an Advisory Committee that meets four times per year and contains twelve members representing private industry, agriculture, labour, education and state government, including three members from small businesses.

1.1.1.5 *Relations with the state*

Although Eximbank is an independent government agency, the United States Congress and several government agencies do play a significant role in policy related issues. Eximbank's annual budgetary limits for all of the Bank's major programmes are established through the federal budget process by the Office of Management and Budget and are authorised by the U.S. Congress.

1.1.1.6 *Relations with the private sector*

Commercial and political risk cover is available in certain markets from a small number of private insurance companies.

If commercial banks wish to participate in part of the risk, Eximbank may reduce its portion of cover to accommodate the bank participants.

1.1.2   FCIA

Foreign Credit Insurance Association (FCIA)
40 Rector Street, 11th Floor
New York, N.Y. 10006

Telephone: (212) 306-5000
Telex: 428 807 and 428 818 FCIA NYK
Telefax: (212) 513-4704

1.1.2.1 *Function*

The FCIA is an association of leading private insurance companies, operating in co-operation with and as an agent of Eximbank. Through FCIA, Eximbank insures exporters against political risk and either insures or reinsures exporters against all commercial risks. FCIA, as Eximbank's agent, is responsible for marketing, servicing, and administering a variety of insurance policies, and for processing most buyer credit requests and claim filings.

1.1.2.2 *Summary of organisation*

FCIA's main operating division, Corporate Underwriting, is divided into the following three sections: Exporter Underwriting, Buyer Underwriting and Supplier Support. Further information on programmes can be obtained from FCIA's New York headquarters or any of its five regional offices (Chicago, Houston, Los Angeles, Miami and New York).

1.1.2.3 *Resources*

The ceilings on FCIA operations are a function of statutory Eximbank liability ceilings. Eximbank acts as a total reinsurer on all risks assumed by FCIA acting in its capacity as agent. The ceiling for Eximbank/FCIA insurance operations for fiscal year 1988 was $6.5 billion. Approximately 77 per cent of available insurance authority was utilised in FY 1988.

1.1.2.4 *Other organisations involved*

FCIA is an agent of Eximbank (see sections 1.1.2.1 and 1.1.2.5).

1.1.2.5 *Relations with the state*

FCIA operates as the sole agent of Eximbank, which assumes all commercial and political risks. FCIA has been delegated a high degree of independence, but Eximbank restricts its authority in certain areas (markets, types of buyers, types of products, etc.).

1.1.2.6 *Relations with the private sector*

Eximbank underwrites *all* risk assumed by FCIA. Private sector insurance agents do not participate in underwriting FCIA activity.

1.1.3 *Commodity Credit Corporation (CCC)*

CCC Operations Division
Room 4503–S, Foreign Agricultural Service
Department of Agriculture
Washington, D.C. 20250

Telephone: (202) 447–3224
Telefax: (202) 382–8238 and (202) 382–0441

1.1.3.1 *Function*

The Commodity Credit Corporation (CCC) was established "for the purpose of stabilising, supporting, and protecting (U.S.) farm income and prices, of assisting in the maintenance of balanced and adequate supplies of agricultural commodities, products thereof, foods, feeds, and fibres..., and of facilitating the orderly distribution of agricultural commodities..." (Commodity Credit Corporation Charter Act). The CCC operates two commercial guarantee programmes to assist U.S. exporters of agricultural commodities (see 2.3.4), under which it guarantees U.S. exporters of their assignees against risk of non–payment on U.S. dollar–denominated irrevocable letters of credit opened in payment for exports of U.S. agricultural commodities by approved banks in importing countries. The purpose of these credit guarantee programmes is to expand or maintain foreign markets for U.S. agricultural commodities.

1.1.3.2 *Summary of organisation*

The CCC is a U.S. government corporation staffed and operated by the U.S. Department of Agriculture. The export credit guarantee programmes are operated by USDA offices reporting to the Under Secretary for International Affairs and Commodity Programs, specifically the Foreign Agriculture Service (FAS) and the Agricultural Stabilization and Conservation Service (ASCS).

1.1.3.3 *Resources*

For export credit guarantee programmes, the annual guarantee exposure ceiling (in U.S. fiscal year 1989) was $5.0 billion for the GSM–102 Export Credit Guarantee Program and $500 million for the GSM–103 Intermediate Export Credit Guarantee Program. Ceiling levels are determined annually by the executive branch of the U.S. government, and incorporated in budget proposals submitted to the Congress of the United States. Payment guarantees are extended under regulations published at 7 CFR (U.S. Code of Federal Regulations) 1493.1 – 1493.17.

1.1.3.4. *Other organisations involved*

International credit operations of the Corporation are subject to advisory review by the National Advisory Council on International Monetary and Financial Policies (NAC).

1.1.3.5 *Relations with the state*

See section 1.1.3.2 above.

1.1.3.6 *Relations with the private sector*

CCC's export credit guarantee programmes support commercial financing of U.S. agricultural exports by taking on most of the risk of registered sales. (See section 2.3.4 for details on the coverage provided.)

1.2   Export Finance

1.2.1 *Representative organisation*

The Export–Import Bank of the United States (see 1.1.1 above).

1.2.1.1 *Function*

Eximbank administers the official export credit programmes of the United States. Eximbank also frequently co–operates with private commercial banks in financing export transactions. (See also section 1.1.1.1.)

1.2.1.2 *Summary of organisation*

See section 1.1.1.2.

1.2.1.3 *Resources*

See section 1.1.1.3. For FY 1989, the budget ceiling for direct credits was $695 million.

1.2.1.4 *Other organisations involved*

See section 1.1.1.4.

1.2.1.5 *Relations with the state*

See section 1.1.1.5.

1.2.1.6 *Relations with the private sector*

Eximbank encourages participation by the private sector (e.g. commercial banks, PEFCO) in export loans.

1.2.2   *Private Export Funding Corporation (PEFCO)*

280 Park Avenue
New York, N.Y. 10017

Telephone: (212) 557–3100
Telex: 1–2250
Telefax: (212) 687–9351

1.2.2.1 *Function*

PEFCO is a major source of capital for medium and long term fixed rate financing for U.S. exports. PEFCO serves as a supplemental source of such financing for foreign buyers of U.S. goods and services. The high cost and long economic lives of some exports — aircraft, industrial plants, and conventional or nuclear power plants, for example — require large amounts of money for extended terms.

1.2.2.2 *Summary of organisation*

PEFCO is a private corporation owned by forty–six commercial banks, six industrial firms and one investment banking firm.

1.2.2.3 *Resources*

PEFCO raises funds through the public sale of its debt obligations which are secured through pledges of its Eximbank guaranteed loans. Interest on the PEFCO obligations is guaranteed directly by Eximbank. Since its inception in 1970, PEFCO has supported transactions in excess of $5 billion.

1.2.2.4 *Other organisations involved*

PEFCO works in conjunction with its Board of Directors, Advisory Board and Exporters' Council. (See section 1.2.2.5 for PEFCO's relationship with Eximbank).

1.2.2.5 *Relations with the state*

Eximbank coordinates its various programmes with the Private Export Funding Corporation. Eximbank unconditionally guarantees PEFCO loans and therefore maintains a measure of control over PEFCO's loan commitments as well as borrowings. PEFCO is, however, a private corporation and its management is responsible to its Board of Directors and to its stockholders.

1.2.2.6 *Relations with the private sector*

Eximbank encourages PEFCO to participate with commercial banks in export loans. PEFCO traditionally lends in conjunction with one or more commercial banks and will cover up to 85 per cent of export value.

1.2.3 *Overseas Private Investment Corporation*

Overseas Private Investment Corporation (OPIC)
1615 M Street, N.W.
Washington, D.C. 20527

Telephone: (202) 457–7200
Telex: OPIC UI 440 227

1.2.3.1 *Function*

The Overseas Private Investment Corporation is a U.S. government agency organised in corporate form. Its function is to encourage the investment of U.S. private long term capital and technology in developing countries and areas, as a complement to other types of official aid programmes (see section 4).

The Foreign Assistance Act of 1969 authorised creation of OPIC to conduct insurance and finance programmes, including direct lending, in order to encourage U.S. private investment in the "economic and social development of less developed friendly countries and areas".

OPIC's legislative authorisation requires OPIC, in determining whether to provide insurance, financing, or reinsurance to a project, to be "guided by the economic and social development impact and benefits of such a project and the ways in which such a project complements, or is compatible with, other development assistance programmes or projects of the United States or other donors," and to concentrate its efforts in the least developed countries.

OPIC's incentive tools include pre–investment services, investment insurance against political risks, direct loans from its own capital, and guarantees of repayment of loans contracted from private U.S. lenders.

1.2.3.2 *Summary of organisation*

OPIC's major programmes are carried out by its Insurance and Finance Departments. Application should be made to the appropriate office.

1.2.3.3 *Resources*

While OPIC is a self–sustaining USG agency, and does not require appropriation of funds, programme levels for finance activity are established by appropriation acts. For FY 1989, for example, the ceiling on direct loans was established at $23 million and the ceiling on guarantees at $175 million. As has always been the case in recent years, in FY 1989 these ceilings were reached; i.e. programme utilisation was 100 per cent. Programmes are funded with the revenue from OPIC's activity.

Should claims payments on insurance and guarantees exceed OPIC's reserves, OPIC has the authority to borrow up to $100 million from the U.S. Treasury. This authority has never been used, and OPIC currently has reserves of over $1 billion. In addition, OPIC's insurance and guarantee programmes are supported by the full faith and credit of the U.S. government.

1.2.3.4 *Other organisations involved*

OPIC is governed by a fifteen–member Board of Directors. Eight of OPIC's directors are appointed by the President from the private sector, including one experienced in organised labour, one in co–operatives, and two in small business. The chairman is the Administrator of AID, *ex officio*, its vice–chairman is the Deputy U.S. Trade Representative and the State, Treasury, Commerce and Labor Departments are represented at the sub–cabinet level. OPIC's president is also a member of the Board.

OPIC is under the foreign policy guidance of the Secretary of State, and is a member of the International Development Coordination Agency (IDCA), a U.S. umbrella agency.

1.2.3.5 *Relations with the state*

OPIC liabilities are backed by the full faith and credit of the U.S. government.

1.2.3.6 *Relations with the private sector*

One of OPIC's legislative mandates is to encourage development of the private sector political risk insurance industry. For that purpose, OPIC works closely with an advisory group of representatives of the private sector political risk insurance industry to develop co-operative programmes to enhance the ability of the private political risk insurance indstry to meet the political risk insurance needs of U.S. investors.

A majority of members of the Board of Directors are from the private sector and all users of OPIC's programmes are from the private sector.

1.3   **Aid finance**

1.3.1   *Representative organisation*

The U.S. Agency for International Development
2201 C Street, N.W.
Washington, D.C. 20523–0062

Tel.: (general inquiries) (202) 647–1850
Telex: 24 83 79 (by RCA)
Telefax: (202) 647–8518

1.3.1.1 *Function*

The Agency for International Development (AID), established in 1961, has operational responsibility for implementing the U.S. development assistance programme. It is a sub-unit of the International Development Cooperation Agency, the other constituent elements of which are the Overseas Private Investment Corporation and the Trade and Development Program. At present, the only active programme making loans with concessionality levels below 50 per cent is the Private Sector Revolving Fund, administered by the Office of Investment in AID's Bureau for Private Enterprise (see 4.3.1).

1.3.1.2 *Summary of organisation*

Headquarters staff are divided among three regional bureaus (Africa, Asia/Near East, and Latin America/Caribbean) and a number of functional bureaus of which the Bureau for Private Enterprise is one. AID also has representatives in recipient countries overseas.

1.3.1.3 *Resources*

AID prepares a programme budget annually for submission to Congress which authorises and appropriates funds to be used on a fiscal year basis (beginning the 1st of October). The Private Sector Revolving Fund is financed by principal repayments and fee income which are invested in U.S. securities.

1.3.1.4 *Other organisations involved*

AID co-operates closely with the Departments of State and Agriculture on U.S. development assistance programmes. AID also works with the Trade and

Development Program on tied aid credit programming involving ESF grants, and co-operates on an *ad hoc* basis with Eximbank on tied aid credit programming where possible (see section 4.1).

1.3.1.5 *Relations with the state*

The provisions of the Foreign Assistance Act hold AID closely accountable to the Congress for all programmes.

1.3.1.6 *Relations with the private sector*

AID is committed to maximum involvement of the private sector in development assistance activities. However, AID's major programme emphasis is on promoting the role of the indigenous developing country private sector in development.

1.3.2   *The U.S. Trade and Development Program*

Mailing	Courier
SA-16 Room 309	1621 N. Kent Street
Washington, D.C. 20523-1602	Suite 309
Tel: (703) 875-4357	Rosslyn, VA 22209
Telefax: (703) 875-4009	

1.3.2.1 *Function*

The U.S. Trade and Development Program (TDP) was created in 1980, and established as an independent agency by the Omnibus Trade and Competitiveness Act of 1988. TDP has two objectives: (1) to assist in the economic development of friendly developing and middle-income countries and (2) to promote the export of U.S. goods and services to those countries. TDP accomplishes these objectives by providing ODA grants for feasibility studies and planning services for public sector development projects. TDP acts as a catalyst to encourage U.S. private sector involvement in infrastructure development. TDP grants are untied to follow-on procurement.

1.3.2.2 *Summary of organisation*

The Trade and Development Program (TDP) is divided into regional operational areas. Application should be made directly to TDP.

1.3.2.3 *Resources*

TDP's annual budget, appropriated by Congress, was $25 million in both FY 1988 and FY 1989. This funding is used primarily for feasibility studies. In addition, up to $5 million in Economic Support Fund monies is available for TDP's mixed credit programme, with the concurrence of the State Department and AID. With a Presidential waiver, TDP programming of ESF funds can exceed the $5 million cap.

1.3.2.4 *Other organisations involved*

TDP is a sister agency to the Agency for International Development and the Overseas Private Investment Corporation under the umbrella of the International Development Cooperation Agency (IDCA).

TDP is a voting member of the National Advisory Council on International Monetary and Financial Policies (NAC) (see section 1.1.1.4) on matters relating to mixed credits. Mixed credit transactions under the Tied Aid Credit Program (see section 4.1) must receive unanimous consent of the NAC.

1.3.2.5 *Relations with the state*

TDP is an independent U.S. government agency. TDP does coordinate with other agencies on significant policy issues.

1.3.2.6 *Relations with the private sector*

TDP always funds feasibility studies on a stand–alone basis.

2.   INSURANCE AND GUARANTEES

2.1   **Insurance** (see also section 2.3)

2.1.1 *Policies available*

Comprehensive short and medium term cover for commercial and political risks (or the latter separately) is provided by the Foreign Credit Insurance Association (FCIA). FCIA helps U.S. exporters develop and expand their overseas sales by protecting them against loss should a foreign buyer or other foreign debtor default for political or commercial reasons. With an FCIA policy, exporters can also obtain export financing more easily because with prior approval the proceeds of the policy can be assigned to a financial institution as collateral.

To encourage the export of U.S. goods and services, FCIA tailors its policies to the insurance needs of exporters and financial institutions. For example, FCIA policies may apply to shipments to one buyer or to many buyers, insure comprehensive credit risks or only specific political risks, or cover short term as well as medium term sales.

Exim can also issue financial guarantees for large (over $5 million) leasing deals on credit terms over five years. Cover includes commercial and political risks including expropriation and confiscation. Smaller deals and shorter terms can be insured by FCIA. The policy can be used for second hand as well as new equipment as well as for operating leases (where the asset is returned to the lessor and no cash payment is required) and financial leases (where the assets are retained by the lessee and a minimum 15 per cent cash payment is required).

Types of policies: In conjunction with Eximbank, FCIA offers a wide range of policies to accommodate many different export credit insurance needs:

— *Policies for new exporters,* affording enhanced protection for short term sales of U.S. companies with relatively little export credit experience. Applicants must meet export sales volume criteria and must not have held an FCIA insurance policy in the past two years.

— *Multi–buyer policies*, providing FCIA's regular coverage for exporters' short term, medium term, or combined short and medium term sales to many different buyers. Under multi–buyer policies, exporters must in most cases insure all their eligible export credit sales. Sales on confirmed letters of credit or for cash in advance can be excluded. Shipments to subsidiaries and affiliates can only be covered for political risks or can be excluded entirely.

— *Single–buyer policies*, insuring short or medium term sales to one buyer. Also, companies exporting to dealers can use the policy to insure short term inventory financing followed by medium term receivables financing.

— *Financial institution buyer credit policy*, protecting financial institutions against losses on short term direct credit loans or reimbursement loans to foreign entities for the importation of U.S. goods and services.

— *Bank letter of credit policy*, protecting banks against losses on irrevocable letters of credit issued by foreign banks in support of U.S. exports.

— *Leasing policies*, for operating and finance leases, insuring both the stream of lease payments and the fair market value of the leased product.

— *Special coverage policies*, providing political risk insurance only, insurance on exported services, and insurance administered by trade associations.

Special coverages: Special coverages are also available to FCIA policyholders. Certain agricultural commodities may be covered at 98 per cent of the commercial risk and 100 per cent of the political risk (except when the equalized coverage option is selected, then coverage is 98 per cent for both risks). Eligible products include grains, corn, raw sugar, sunflower seeds, rice, tallow, peanuts, cotton, cottonseeds, and the oils or meal derived from such products.

Exporters can also obtain special endorsements to cover sales into or out of consignment, sales made from an overseas warehouse, non–acceptance of shipments, preshipment on a select or whole turnover basis, payments in a foreign currency, sales out of foreign trade fairs, used equipment sales, and dairy/breeding cattle sales.

2.1.2 Eligibility

Nationality requirements — Foreign content

Eximbank will support foreign content as follows:

— Short term: up to 50 per cent may be covered.

— Medium and long term: Eximbank's medium and long term export loans and guarantees may support U.S. export *items* that contain foreign made components subject to the following guidelines:

— U.S. content must be at least 50 per cent of the total contract price of the item;

— Eximbank's loan or guarantee may support up to 100 per cent of the U.S. content of the item, but may not exceed 85 per cent of the total contract price of the item;

— A cash payment of at least 15 per cent of the total contract price of the item is requested;

— All foreign components must be incorporated into the item in the United States; and

— The "total contract price of the item' used for this purpose includes the supply of foreign items that are not deemed components of the U.S. item.

Eximbank could consider reciprocal agreements on co–insurance or re–insurance on a general or case–by–case basis particularly for short and medium term transactions.

Criteria for cover

— FCIA provides insurance for supplier credits of maturities up to five years (longer for certain products, e.g. executive aircraft and locomotives);
— Minimum cash payment requirement for medium term (one hundred and eighty one days to five years) credit for all markets is 15 per cent;
— Regular (equal semi–annual) principal and interest instalments with no extended grace periods for the duration of the credit are required.

Restriction on sales

A policy may not provide insurance for goods or services destined for military use. Neither may a policy insure exports to or for use in a Marxist–Leninist country unless the President of the United States has determined that FCIA–insured sales to that country are in the national interest. Eximbank's charter also places some restrictions on FCIA support of exports to South Africa.

2.1.3   Cost of cover

Exporter retention and deductible: In general, FCIA policies cover 90 to 95 per cent of the commercial risk and 95 to 100 per cent of specified political risks. In addition to retaining a percentage of the risk on each transaction, the exporter also may be required to absorb a first dollar loss, called the deductible, on losses that relate to transactions insured in a given policy. There is no first loss deductible for single–buyer policies.

Premiums: Premiums vary with the credit terms, exporter experience, the quality and number of buyers being insured, and the importing countries. Most policies require a minimum premium to be paid in advance at the beginning of every policy year. Premiums for multi–buyer policies are generally paid monthly in tandem with submission of the report of premiums payable. Premiums for single–buyer policies are paid in advance of shipment.

2.2   Guarantees

2.2.1.   Policies available

Eximbank's guarantees provide repayment protection for private sector loans to creditworthy buyers of U.S. exports. The guarantees cover the repayment risks on the foreign buyer's debt obligations. Eximbank guarantees that, in the event of default, it will repay all of the principal and most of the interest on the loan. Eximbank requires that the foreign buyer make a cash payment to the exporter equal to at least 15 per cent of the U.S. export value.

As described below, Eximbank's comprehensive guarantee covers 100 per cent of the commercial and political risk for principal and eligbile interest. Guarantees covering only political risks are also available and are the only type of guarantee available where there is common ownership between the supplier (or exporter) and the foreign buyer (or guarantor). Eximbank's guarantees commit the full faith and credit of the U.S. Government. Notes guaranteed by Eximbank are freely transferable.

One particular application of Eximbank's guarantees in the guarantee of medium and long term credits made available by the private corporation PEFCO. PEFCO's credits are generally made at fixed rates of interest set by PEFCO on the basis of several factors including the cost of PECFO's funds. During 1988, PEFCO rates ranged from 9.25 per cent to 14 per cent. PEFCO's interest rates are not subject to Arrangement guidelines. Repayment terms are generally five to ten years.

Eximbank also guarantees lease financing.

Comprehensive guarantees: Eximbank's comprehensive guarantee covers all risks of non–payment of principal.

In such cases where the guarantee covers a loan value of $10 million or less with a repayment term of seven years or less, and the obligor or guarantor does not commit the full faith and credit of it government, the exporter (or lender) must give Eximbank a counter–guarantee for 2 per cent of any amounts paid by Eximbank for claims resulting from commercial defaults.

Commercial risk is non–repayment for reasons other than specified political risks. Examples include deterioration of the buyer's market, fluctuations in demand, unanticipated competition, shifts in tariffs, technological change, buyer insolvency, and natural disasters. Losses due to currency devaluation are considered a commercial risk.

Political risk only guarantees: A guarantee covering only political risks of non–payment of principal is available for transactions with private or non–soverign public buyers. It is the only type of guarantee available where there is common ownership between the supplier (or exporter) and the foreign buyer (or guarantor).

Political risks include war risks, cancellation of an existing export or import licence, expropriation, confiscation or intervention in the buyer's business, or transfer risk (failure of the appropriate foreign government authorities to transfer the local deposit into dollars).

Foreign currency guarantees: Comprehensive and political risk only guarantees of non–payment of principal are available for loans denominated in readily convertible foreign currencies acceptable to Eximbank.

Coverage provided under Eximbank guarantees:

— *Principal.* Eximbank will guarantee up to 85 per cent of the U.S. export value.
— *Interest.* Lenders are free to charge a market rate of interest on guaranteed loans. (Intermediary lenders are an exception to the rule.) Eximbank's guarantee is available for fixed– or floating–rate loans. Interest on dollar loans will be guaranteed at the following rates:
  For fixed rate loans: the lesser of the rate on the note minus 50 basis points, or the Treasury rate at the time of loan pricing for a comparable term plus 50 basis points.
  For floating–rate loans: the lesser of the rate on the note minus 50 basis points, or a rate determined on the basis of one of the following options, which the guaranteed lender chooses at the time it enters the transaction:

  • Prime rate less 200 basis points
  • LIBOR less 25 basis points
  • Treasury rate plus 50 basis points

For foreign currency loans: The guarantee covers interest (fixed or floating) at a rate based on comparable government borrowing or other capital market rates depending upon the foreign currency used.

Repayment: Repayment terms on transactions supported by loans guaranteed by Eximbank normally range from one to 10 years, depending on the contract value, the country, the terms offered by officially supported competitors. However, maximum repayment terms are in line with those agreed under the OECD Arrangement. Payments are usually made in semi–annual instalments, on the 15th of the month, beginning six months after final delivery, the mid–point of deliveries or completion of the project, whichever is appropriate.

Special coverages

Bank–to–bank line of credit guarantees: Banks can obtain guarantees to cover revolving lines of credit established with foreign banks. The foreign bank must be in a non–industrialised country. Eximbank does not limit the number of line of credit guarantees available, but it encourages banks to limit their applications to foreign banks that will actively use the programme.

Guarantees on repetitive sales: Some U.S. suppliers repeatedly sell to the same dealer, distributor, or ther foreign buyer. Agricultural and construction equipment are examples of products frequently sold in such a manner. Eximbank will guarantee a revolving line of credit to such repeat buyers. Dealers and distributors may be granted terms of up to five years, although individual sales of equipment may be reapid on shorter terms.

Lines of credit are established on the basis of their customers' estimated sales to the non–industrialised country over the coming 12–month period.

Eximbank's standard conditions for guarantees apply to this special coverage, except:

— The bank must act as the exporter of record and must assume the counter–guarantee for 2 per cent of the amounts paid out under a commercial default. When a bank acts as the exporter of record, the transaction is altered, and the bank assumes additional responsibilities, including signing the supplier's Certificate. Lenders should note that they assume additional liability under the Supplier's Certificate.

— The foreign bank, not the buyer, is the obligor in the transaction.

— Once the line is established, individual transactions can move ahead without prior Eximbank approval.

2.2.2   Eligibility

Any U.S. or foreign bank, other financing institution, or other responsible party, including the exporter, can be a lender under the guarantee programme. Lenders may be located in the United States or overseas. The borrower must be a creditworthy entity in a country eligible for Eximbank assistance.

Lenders may receive Eximbank guarantees on 1) loans extended directly to foreign buyers or 2) foreign buyers' debt obligations (in the form of a promissory note) purchased from the exporter and without recourse to the exporter. Eximbank guarantees financing for U.S. capital equipment, projects, and services.

Eximbank Exposures Fees
($ Fee per $100 of Eximbank Loan or Guarantee Principal)

Repayment Term (Yrs)	Country – Category														
	A			B			C Borrower Guarantor			D			E		
	I	II	III	I	II	III	I	II	III	I	II	III	I	II	III
1	0.50	0.60	1.00	0.75	0.90	1.50	1.13	1.35	2.25	1.69	2.03	3.38	2.53	3.04	5.06
2	0.63	0.75	1.25	0.94	1.13	1.88	1.41	1.69	2.81	2.11	2.53	4.22	3.16	3.80	6.33
3	0.75	0.90	1.50	1.13	1.35	2.25	1.69	2.03	3.38	2.53	3.04	5.06	3.80	4.56	7.59
4	0.88	1.05	1.75	1.31	1.58	2.63	1.97	2.36	3.94	2.95	3.54	5.91	4.43	5.32	8.86
5	1.00	1.20	2.00	1.50	1.80	3.00	2.25	2.70	4.50	3.38	4.05	6.75	5.06	6.08	10.13
6	1.13	1.35	2.25	1.69	2.03	3.38	2.53	3.04	5.06	3.80	4.56	7.59	5.70	6.83	*
7	1.25	1.50	2.50	1.88	2.25	3.75	2.81	3.38	5.63	4.22	5.06	8.44	6.33	7.59	*
8	1.38	1.65	2.75	2.06	2.48	4.13	3.09	3.71	6.19	4.64	5.57	9.28	6.96	8.35	*
9	1.50	1.80	3.00	2.25	2.70	4.50	3.38	4.05	6.75	5.06	6.08	10.13	7.59	9.11	*
10	1.63	1.95	3.25	2.44	2.93	4.88	3.66	4.39	7.31	5.48	6.58	10.97	8.00	9.60	*

* Because of the level of risk, fees for this category may change. Therefore, applicants are requested to contact Eximbank on a case-by-case basis.

2.2.3   *Cost of cover*

Fees

Eximbank charges the following fees in connection with a guarantee:

— *Processing fee.* A $100 processing fee must accompany each Preliminary Commitment application and each application for a Final Commitment that is not a conversion of a Preliminary Commitment.

The fees described below are not incurred until Eximbank authorises a Final Commitment.

— *Commitment fee*: Eximbank charges the lender a commitment fee of one–eighth of one per cent per annum on the undisbursed balance of a guaranteed loan. If an intermediary loan of $10 million or less and a repayment term of seven years or less is combined with a guarantee covering the intermediary's loan to the foreign borrower, a one–half per cent per annum commitment fee is charged on the undisbursed balance of the guaranteed loan. Commitment fees begin to accrue 60 days after Eximbank's Final Commitment for the guarantee.

— *Exposure fee.* Eximbank charges a front–end exposure fee, calculated and payable as the guaranteed loan is disbursed. The exposure fee is the responsibility of the exporter and is paid through the guaranteed lender. The fee may be included in the contract price.

For exposure fees purposes, Eximbank classifies countries in five country categories. The countries within each category are not published. Under each country category, there are three borrower/guarantor classifications:

Class I   : Sovereign borrowers of guarantors.
Class II   : Creditworthy non–sovereign public institutions or banks, or highly creditworthy private buyers.
Class III : Other creditworthy private buyers.

(See previous page.)

Country categories and exposure fees are reviewed and adjusted periodically. Fee information for individual transactions should always be obtained by contacting an Eximbank loan officer at an early stage.

2.3   Other Insurance Programmes

2.3.1   *Investment and bond insurance*

Eximbank does not provide any type of bond insurance. Exporters are referred to private companies extending bond insurance or to the Overseas Private Investment Corporation for investment insurance (see section 1.2.2).

OPIC provides political risk insurance to eligible U.S. businesses investing in projects located in a developing country in which OPIC operates. The projects must be developmentally beneficial to the host country, consistent with the economic interests of the United States, and not have significant adverse effect on the U.S. economy or levels of employment in the United States. The project should also be privately controlled and managed, but minority foreign government participation will not render the project ineligible. In addition to these criteria, OPIC does not insure loans of less than three year's average maturity.

Within these constraints, OPIC insurance is available to investors in almost all types of projects, one major exception being projects which produce armaments. Special OPIC insurance coverages are available to protect U.S. exporters, lessors and construction contractors. OPIC insurance is available only for new investment in new or expansion projects. To be eligible, the investor must be a U.S. citizen; a business organised in the U.S. and more than 50 per cent beneficially owned by U.S. citizens; or a foreign corporation, partnership or association wholly owned by one or more U.S. citizens, corporations, partnerships or other associations.

OPIC insurance is offered against three types of political risk: inability to convert local currency earnings or returns of capital into U.S. dollars; expropriation or confiscation of the investment; and damage due to war, revolution, or insurrection. OPIC political risk insurance does not offer any protection against commercial risks or devaluations of local currencies.

Additionally, before OPIC will insure or guarantee any investment, the host government must give its specific approval for OPIC to do so. This is one of the features of the bilateral agreements under which OPIC programmes are instituted. Among other things, these agreements, which have been negotiated with over 100 developing countries, provide for subrogation of OPIC to the interests or claims of the OPIC-insured or guaranteed U.S. investor, with provision for international arbitration of certain types of disputes between OPIC as subrogee/successor and the host government.

2.3.2   Working Capital Guarantee Programme

The Working Capital Guarantee Programme was established 1st October 1982, as a result of Eximbank's mandate to assist small to medium sized exporters. Eximbank issues guarantees to U.S. commercial banks or providers of private credit to cover the repayment of short term secured loans extended to U.S. companies. The loan funds must be used for export-related activities such as purchasing inventory for export or foreign business development but may not be used to pay existing debts. Eximbank covers up to 90 per cent of the principal amount as well as interest.

Interest covered is, up to the date of the claim payment, at the stated rate on the loan or one per cent over the Treasury borrowing rate for comparable maturities, whichever is lower. Eximbank requires that the loan balance not exceed 90 per cent of the collateral value. Eximbank does not impose any interest rate ceilings or limits of fees the lender may charge.

Fees

Eximbank charges the following fees in connection with a working capital guarantee:
- *Processing fee.* A non-refundable processing fee of $100 is payable with the submission of each application.
- *Facility fee.* The lender must pay one-half of one per cent of the loan amount within 90 days of Eximbank's authorisation of the Final Commitment or prior to the first disbursement, whichever is earlier.

— *Usage fee*. The lender pays one–quarter of one per cent of the average ous-
tanding balance for each calendar quarter within 15 days following the end of
each quarter. For guarantee periods beginning or ending mid–quarter, usage
fees must be pro–rated accordingly. If there are balances outstanding under
the guaranteed loan subsequent to the "expiration date", usage fees on the
outstanding balance must continue to be submitted until said balances are
reduced to zero.

During fiscal year 1988, Eximbank authorised $76.0 million in guarantees under
this programme.

2.3.3   *Guarantee for Foreign Currency Swap Transactions*

If either party to a swap defaults, the intermediary incurs the cost associated with
replacing the defaulting party if market exchange rates and/or interest rates have
moved against the intermediary. Exim's foreign exchange default guarantee will cover
most of the present value of the costs incurred by the intermediary in replacing the
foreign buyer if this party defaults under a currency swap. Eximbank expects the
recipient of its guarantee to assume some risk sharing throughout the life of the swap.

Because the maximum loss under a swap guarantee is likely to be only a portion of
the underlying loan's principal value, Eximbank's charge for a foreign exchange default guarantee will vary from case to case, averaging approximately 40 per cent of the
comparable Eximbank loan guarantee fee.

In most standard export credit transactions, the foreign exchange default guarantee would *not* be offered in combination with either an Eximbank credit or a financial
guarantee. In this way, Eximbank avoids supporting *both* the dollar funding cost and
all swap risks in an individual transaction. This is to ensure that Eximbank is not
normally associated as both lender or guarantor of the original dollar transaction and
as facilitator of the swap in any financing which yields an interest rate below Arrangement minimum interest rates. However, there may be some cases in which both lending risk and swap risk support is required. The Board will consider these on a case by
case basis.

2.3.4   *Guarantee programmes for agricultural exports*

The programmes administered by CCC (see section 1.1.3) are as follows:

— The GSM–102 programme (which became operational in 1981) provides
credit guarantees on credit terms of up to three years. Under this programme,
CCC will cover 98 per cent of the port value (principal) and, since November 1986, up to 4.5 percentage points of interest on the guaranteed value.
Interest rate coverage may be adjusted as U.S. capital market conditions
change. The annual GSM–102 guarantee ceiling for U.S. fiscal year 1989
was $5 billion.

— The Intermediate Export Credit Guarantee Programme (GSM–103), which
became operational ·in 1986, offers credit guarantees on commercial credit
with terms longer than three, but not longer than ten years. Under the
GSM–103 programme, CCC agrees to cover 98 per cent of principal and interest up to 80 per cent of the average rate of the most recent 52–week Treasury bill. The annual GSM–103 guarantee ceiling for U.S. fiscal year 1989
was $500 million.

Interest rates charged on a CCC–guaranteed loan are commercial rates set by the financing institution and are usually based on LIBOR plus a premium. CCC's official guarantees cover both commercial and non–commercial risks. Maritime freight and other charges arising after export are generally not covered by CCC, but freight costs for breeding animals usually are covered. CCC considers requests for guarantee programmes and issues a press release when coverage is to be made available. Upon issue of such a release, CCC is prepared to receive U.S. exporters' applications for cover on their qualifying export credit transactions.

Cover is provided only on exports of U.S. agricultural commodities. CCC operations are not subject to Arrangement guidelines because the Arrangement does not cover export credits for agricultural products.

3.   EXPORT FINANCE PROGRAMMES

3.1   *Direct Credits*

3.1.1   *Types of contract available*

Eximbank offers fixed rate loans directly to foreign buyers of U.S. goods and services to help U.S. exporters compete against foreign suppliers offering officially supported subsidised financing.

Cash payment: Eximbank requires that the buyer make a cash payment to the U.S. exporter equal to at least 15 per cent of the U.S. export value. The cash payment may be paid in a lump sum prior to disbursement of the financing, or it may be paid in instalments equal to at least 15 per cent of the value of each completed shipment and related disbursement under the contract. The alternative selected is negotiated between the buyer and the seller.

Cover: Eximbank will consider extending a loan to the foreign buyer covering up to 85 per cent of the U.S. export value.

Participating lenders: Eximbank's direct loans may in some cases be issued in participation with private sector lenders. (Eximbank's Guarantee Program is also available to participating lenders.) Generally, the participating lender is a domestic or foreign commercial bank or the Private Export Funding Corporation (PEFCO). The U.S. supplier or an affiliated company may also in some instances extend credit to the buyer as part of the financing package supported by Eximbank.

Repayment: Repayment terms on transactions supported by direct loans normally range from 5 to 10 years, depending on the export value, the product or project being financed, the importing country, and the terms offered by officially supported competitors. However, maximum repayment terms are in line with those agreed under the OECD Arrangement.

Payments are usually made in semi–annual instalments, on the 15th of the month, beginning six months after final delivery, the mid–point of deliveries, or completion of the project, whichever is appropriate.

PEFCO: PEFCO provides substantial volumes of medium and long term direct credit financing to U.S. exporters. It is not, however, a U.S. government agency. Eximbank guarantees PEFCO financing (see section 2.2.1).

3.1.2   Eligibility

Capital equipment, large–scale projects, and related services are eligible for direct loan financing.

Eximbank direct loans generally involve loan amounts over $10 million or a repayment term of more than seven years. Transactions involving loan amounts of $10 million or less and financed on terms of seven years or less are ordinarily financed by a private or third party, and Eximbank support usually takes the form of an intermediary loan or a guarantee, or both.

Eximbank must examine the competition the U.S. exporter faces on the transaction. The only exception is for small business exports.

The buyer must be a creditworthy entity in a country eligible for Eximbank assistance.

3.1.3   Resulting interest rates

Interest rates on direct loans are fixed for the life of the loan at the time of Eximbank's finance commitment. Interest is payable on the instalment dates on outstanding balances.

Eximbank charges the minimum OECD rate applicable to the category of the importing country and the repayment period.

Fees

Eximbank charges the following fees in connection with a direct loan:

— *Processing fee:* A $100 processing fee must accompany each Preliminary Commitment application and each application for a Final Commitment that is not a conversion of a Preliminary Commitment.

The fees described below are not incurred until Eximbank authorizes a final Commitment.

— *Commitment fee.* Eximbank charges the borrower a commitment fee of one–half of one per cent per annum on the undisbursed balance of a direct loan. This fee begins to accrue 60 days after Eximbank's Final Commitment for the loan.

— *Exposure fee.* Eximbank charges a front–end exposure fee assessed on each disbursement of a direct loan. The exposure fee is the responsibility of the exporter, and may be included in the contract price. For additional information on exposure fees, and for the exposure fee table, see section 2.2.3.

Eximbank does not normally charge for legal services in the preparation of loan documents; however, the cost of printing loan documents is the borrower's responsibility and will be billed directly by the printing firm.

3.2   Refinancing

3.2.1   Types of contract available

The Intermediary Credit Programme provides fixed interest rate support for those medium term export sales facing subsidised officially supported export credit competition from abroad.

The Small Business Credit Programme was established 1st October 1982, as a result of Eximbank's mandate to assist small business. Eximbank will make a fixed interest loan commitment to a U.S. bank in support of exports of a U.S. manufacturer qualifying as a small business (as determined by the Small Business Administration's guidelines). The manufacturer need not show evidence of officially supported foreign competition.

3.2.2   Eligibility

Under the Intermediary Credit Programme, each medium term transaction is limited to a maximum Eximbank liability value of $10 million. Each small business credit transaction is limited to a contract value of $2.5 million and there is a $10 million maximum limit on availability to each manufacturer per year.

3.2.3   Resulting interest rates

Under the Intermediary Credit Programme, once evidence of competition is established, Eximbank will make a fixed interest rate loan commitment at below the current Arrangement minimum rate to a U.S. bank that is financing the export sale. The commercial bank is required to charge the Arrangement rate to the borrower. The commitment fee is an up–front fee based on the loan amount (85 per cent of contract price) and the total term of the commitment, which is the period from Eximbank authorisation through final payout. Eximbank authorisations under this programme for fiscal year 1988 were $220 million.

Fees

Eximbank charges the following fees in connection with an intermediary loan:
- *Processing fee*. A $100 processing fee must accompany each Preliminary Commitment application and each application for a Final Commitment that is not a conversion of a Preliminary Commitment.
  The fees described below are not incurred until Eximbank authorises a Final Commitment.
- *Commitment fee*. No commitment fee is charged on Eximbank intermediary loans of up to $10 million and repayment terms of seven years or less that are not combined with a guarantee. However, if such a loan is combined with an Eximbank guarantee, a one–half of one per cent per annum commitment fee is charged on the undisbursed balance of the guaranteed loan.
  A commitment fee of one–half of one per cent is charged on all intermediary loans over $10 million or with a repayment term of over seven years, whether or not they are combined with an Eximbank guarantee. Thus, such a loan, if combined with a guarantee, would have both a one–half of one per cent commitment fee on the Eximbank intermediary loan and a one–eighth of one per cent commitment fee on the guaranteed loan.
  Commitment fees begin to accrue 60 days after Eximbank's Final Commitment for the loan.
- *Exposure fee*. Eximbank charges a front–end exposure fee to compensate for the risk it is taking. The fee is assessed on the amount of each disbursement of the underlying export loan, payable on the date on each such disbursement. For an Eximbank intermediary loan not combined with a guarantee, the

exposure fee is a function of the country and classification of the intermediary lender and the repayment term of the loan. When an intermediary loan is combined with an Eximbank guarantee, the exposure fee is based on the country and classification of the foreign obligor (or guarantor) and the repayment term.

The exposure fee is the responsibility of the exporter and is paid to Eximbank through the intermediary. The fee may be included in the contract price. For additional information on exposure fees, and for the exposure fee table, see section 2.2.3.

Eximbank does not normally charge for legal services in the preparation of loan documents; however, the cost of printing loan documents is the intermediary borrower's responsibility and will be billed directly by the printing firm.

4.   AID FINANCE PROGRAMMES

4.1   Associated Financing

4.1.1   Funds available

Eximbank/War Chest

In October 1986, Congress authorised a two-year, $300 million War Chest to be used in support of the U.S. government's negotiating efforts on the tied aid credit issue. Subsequently, Congress appropriated $100 million for FY 1987 and $110 million for FY 1988 for the War Chest. The Omnibus Trade Act of 1988 extended the War Chest for another year, and Congress provided War Chest funding of $110 million for FY 1989.

The War Chest provides grant resources which may be combined with direct loans and/or guarantees to generate a tied aid credit. Since the March 1987 tied aid credit agreement, Eximbank has used the War Chest on a selective basis, generally in response to a competitor country tied aid credit offer that breaches either the spirit or the letter of that agreement.

Eximbank can also combine resources with TDP and AID to offer a tied aid credit.

Trade Financing Facility

The Trade Financing Facility, established in 1981, provides associated financing for Egypt only. Funding for the TFF comes from Economic Support Fund/Commodity Import Program (ESF/CIP) funds available through AID to Egypt. A portion of Egypt's ESF/CIP funds — usually $20–30 million — is set aside each year to fund the grant portion of TFF transactions. These funds are combined with Eximbank and/or commercial bank credits; unused amounts revert to ordinary ESF/CIP uses.

TFF is used to match tied aid offers to the Government of Egypt which are encountered by U.S. exporters in international trade competition. There have been no transactions under this facility since 1982.

Tied Aid Credit Program

The Trade and Development Enhancement Act of 1983, in sections 644 and 645, authorised Eximbank and AID jointly to provide tied aid credits. These sections were amended by the Omnibus Trade and Competitiveness Act of 1988 which transferred AID's tied aid credit authority under these provisions to TDP.

To date, the Economic Support Fund has been the only source for grant funding under the Tied Aid Credit Program. These funds are combined with credits from Eximbank and/or private sources. In general, funds are available in any given fiscal year only for those developing countries with active ESF/CIP programmes. Appropriation legislation in U.S. fiscal years 1988 and 1989 limited total funding of the Tied Aid Credit Program to $5 million per year — unless the President determined that it was in the national interest to provide more. In neither year, however, were funds actually appropriated for the tied aid credit programme.

AID, under its general authorities, is able to offer the grant portion of a mixed credit. TDP, in addition to its authority under the tied aid credit programme, can also offer the grant portion of a mixed credit under its general authorities.

4.1.2   Eligibility

Eximbank/War Chest

An interested exporter should bring to Eximbank's attention a possible export sale for War Chest financing. Eximbank considers such applications on a case–by–case basis in relation to the U.S. government's negotiations and agreements in the OECD on the tied aid credit issue. Eximbank makes its decisions in accordance with the advice of the Secretary of the Treasury and in consultation ith the NAC.

Trade financing facility

This facility is for projects only in Egypt. An interested exporter should contact the Assistant Administrator of AID's Asia/Near East Bureau, or an AID representative in Egypt. Transactions under the Trade Financing Facility must be approved by both the U.S. Government and the Government of Egypt.

Tied aid credit programme

Guidelines on AID's use of this programme stipulated that funding could be used defensively (e.g. by matching) where it would contribute to the development objectives of the importing country and where it would be consistent with country criteria for utilisation of the Economic Support Fund. Under TDP, there are no a priori requirements or limitations.

An interested exporter should approach TDP directly. Tied aid credit programme transactions are subject to review by an inter–agency body, the National Advisory Council on International Monetary and Financial Policies, which must give unanimous approval before an offer is made.

4.1.3   Resulting terms and interest rates

Eximbank/War Chest

A variety of packages have resulted from use of the War Chest, including both credit lines and individual concessional packages. A resulting package must conform with the March 1987 Tied Aid Credit Agreement negotiated by Participants in the OECD Arrangement on Export Credits.

Trade Financing Facility

The Trade Financing Facility has been used only twice, both in 1982. In each of these two instances, a grant of under $4 million was combined with Export–Import Bank export credits and private bank loans. The resulting packages had grant elements of less than 20 per cent.

Tied aid credit programme

AID grants under the tied aid credit programme were used to offer financing in support of the sale of U.S. exports substantially as concessional as the financing available from foreign competitors.

Although several offers have been made under the tied aid credit programme, there have been no commitments to date.

Mixed credits in which TDP participates typically are to support training and include a TDP grant portion that meets the *de minimus* requirements of the OECD Arrangement on Export Credits (i.e., it is not greater than 3 per cent of the total transaction or greater than $1 million).

4.2   Integrated Credits

N/A.

4.3.   Other Tied and Partially Untied Aid

4.3.1.   Funds available

AID's Private Sector Revolving Fund

The Private Sector Revolving Fund of AID's Bureau for Private Enterprise provides non–concessional loans to intermediate credit institutions (and, in some cases directly to small businesses) in developing countries. The goal of these transactions is the increased availability of market rate credit to developing country entrepreneurs.

OPIC

OPIC's finance programme provides medium to long term financing to overseas ventures with U.S. participation (generally U.S. equity) through its direct loan and investment guarantee programme. (See section 1.2.3.3 for dollar ceilings for these programmes.) Under the latter programme, OPIC furnishes an "all risk" guarantee of the repayment of debt from U.S. banks and other financial institutions, and thus includes protection against both commercial and political risk. In either case, however, OPIC's financing commitment to a new venture may extend to, but not exceed, 50 per cent of the total cost. A larger participation (up to 75 per cent) may be considered for an expansion of a successful existing enterprise. Investors must be willing to establish a sound debt/equity relationship, typically in a ratio of 60 per cent debt to 40 per cent equity.

Under OPIC's new pilot equity programme, the Corporation can also invest in common or preferred stock of projects in two geographic regions: sub–Saharan Africa and Central America and the Caribbean.

4.3.2   Eligibility

AID's Private Sector Revolving Fund

Interested credit institutions and small businesses should contact AID's in–country representatives.

OPIC

An interested organisation should apply directly to OPIC, which considers applications on a case–by–case basis.

4.3.3   Resulting terms and interest rates

AID's Private Sector Revolving Fund

Support for any individual project is limited to $3 million, and no more than 20 per cent (or about $14 million) of the revolving fund's total assets may be invested in any one country.

A typical loan package would be untied and would be made at market interest rates with a life of five years including a grace period of two years.

OPIC

Interest rates on OPIC direct loans vary according to a project's financial and political risk, but generally parallel commercial rates. Interest rates on guaranteed loans are comparable to those of other U.S. government–guaranteed issues, and OPIC charges the borrower a guarantee fee as well as facility and commitment fees.

Chapter 24

TURKEY

1. ORGANISATION AND STRUCTURE

1.1 Insurance and Guarantees

1.1.1 *Representative organisation*

Turk Eximbank
Export Credit Bank of Turkey
Müdafaa Cad. 20
Bakanliklar
06100 ANKARA, Turkey

Telephone: (4) 117 13 00
Telex: 42 606 DYB TR
46 751 EXMB TR
Telefax: (4) 125 78 96
Teletex: 44 803 EXIMBA–TR

1.1.1.1 *Function*

Turk Eximbank's main objective is to promote Turkey's exports through the diversification of exported goods and services by increasing the share of Turkish exporters in international trade, finding new markets for traditional and non–traditional export goods and providing exporters and overseas contractors with support thereby increasing the competitiveness and security in international markets. As a means of aiding export development, Turk Eximbank offers credit, insurance and bank guarantee financing. Through finance programmes, credit support is extended to exporters at such costs as will enable them to be competitive on the international market. Guarantee programmes provide guarantees so that exporters can obtain credit from local and foreign banks as well as financial institutions in order to finance exports.

Through insurance programmes, Turk Eximbank provides export credit insurance by securing exports against losses that may arise out of commercial and political risks.

1.1.1.2 *Summary of organisation*

Turk Eximbank's executive and supervisory organs are: the General Assembly, the Board of Directors, the General Directorate, the Credits Committee and the Board of Auditors. The Bank is managed by the Board of Directors, comprising seven members and including the General Director.

The General Directorate manages the Bank according to principles agreed by the Board of Directors. The General Directorate comprises the General Director and the Deputy General Directors, who are responsible respectively for credits, insurance, finance, state economic enterprises, systems and coordination.

Initial enquiries should be made directly to the Head Office of the Bank, which is located in Ankara.

1.1.1.3 *Resources*

The Bank has a share capital of Turkish Lira 500 billion. External resources are credits and advances made available by the Central Bank and the Council of Ministers and funds raised by borrowing in the domestic and international money and capital markets or borrowed from international financial institutions such as the Islamic Development Bank, the World Bank and the I.M.F.

In 1988, the Bank participated in four successful bond issues in the Tokyo and Frankfurt capital markets, raising a total of DM 200M and yen 28.5 billion. Additionally, the amounts raised through credit lines with various Japanese and European banks are yen 3 billion, £ 5M and DM 100M.

1.1.1.4 *Other organisations involved*

Four members of the Board are from the Prime Minister's Undersecretariat of Treasury and Foreign Trade which holds not less than 51 per cent of the capital.

1.1.1.5 *Relations with the State*

The State Investment Bank was reorganised as the Export Credit Bank of Turkey, Turk Eximbank, as from 21st August 1987. The Eximbank operates within the principles set forth in a Council of Ministers Decree dated 17th June 1987 and under the Turkish Commercial Code and the Banking Act as a joint stock company.

1.1.1.6 *Relations with the private sector*

1.2   Export finance

See section 1.1 above.

2.   INSURANCE AND GUARANTEE PROGRAMMES

2.1   Cover for Exporters

2.1.1   *Policies available*

To increase the competitiveness and security of Turkish exporters, contractors and investors in international markets, Turk Eximbank plans to offer two types of export insurance programmes for exporters, namely:
— A short–term wholeturnover insurance programme;
— A specific shipment insurance programme.

The short–term wholeturnover insurance programme and the specific shipment insurance programme are designed to meet some of the most urgent needs of the exporters.

2.1.1.1   *Short–term wholeturnover insurance programme*

The short–term wholeturnover policy is a continuous insurance programme subject to a simple annual renewal procedure.   Through the wholeturnover insurance programme, Turk Eximbank aims to provide insurance on a continuous basis for sales made on credit terms of up to 6 months.

Under the terms of this policy, the exporter is obliged to insure all the shipments made during the 12 months after its commencement.   The wholeturnover policy is a "post–shipment" policy, i.e. the liability of Turk Eximbank will arise only if the loss occurs on or after the date of shipment.   The goods covered under this programme are durable and non–durable consumer goods, raw materials, agricultural products and other goods exported on a short–term basis.

The short–term wholeturnover insurance programme provides cover for non–payment of the goods dispatched overseas under a contract of sale made with a buyer outside Turkey due to certain commercial and political events.

The commercial occurences specified as commercial risks in the policy are: non–payment due to the insolvency of the buyer, the buyer's failure to pay for the goods that he has accepted, and refusal or the failure of the buyer to take delivery of the goods that have been dispatched to him.

The political occurences specified as political risks in the policy are those that may occur outside the control of the exporter and the buyer.   These are mainly: cancellation of import permits and licences, losses that may arise as a result of war, revolution and civil war, and transfer difficulties.

Risks which can be covered under marine insurance: failure of the exporter to fulfil the terms of the export contract or any negligence on his part, default or insolvency of any agent of the exporter or of the collecting bank, deterioration in the quality of the goods and fluctuations in the exchange rate of the currency of the invoice are some of the risks which are not covered under this insurance programme.

During the policy period, the exporter is obliged to prepare a monthly declaration of shipments for each calendar month and send it to Turk Eximbank before the 10th of the following month.   The exporter should also by the 10th of each month send Turk Eximbank a declaration of all payments not received within 30 days of the payment date.

The short–term wholeturnover insurance programme gives cover against commercial and political risks of 80 per cent and 90 per cent respectively.

2.1.1.2   *Specific shipment insurance programme*

The specific shipment insurance programme is a post–shipment facility protecting exporters from losses that may arise as a result of commercial and political risks. It is designed to provide insurance coverage for shipments of capital goods and semi–capital goods, including construction machines, transportation vehicles, mining and agricultural equipment and motor vehicles to a single buyer with a credit period of up to 5 years.

This programme embodies most of the elements and conditions of the short–term wholeturnover policy. The main differences may be stated as follows:

— The specific policy applies to individual contracts carried out with a single buyer, whereas the wholeturnover policy provides cover for goods exported on a repetitive basis to a number of buyers in different countries;
— The specific policy covers the export of goods sold on credit terms up to 5 years, whereas under the wholeturnover policy, goods exported on terms of up to 180 days are covered;
— Under the specific policy, the premium is paid in advance whereas under the wholeturnover policy premiums are paid after the shipments have been made.

2.1.2   *Eligibility*

Both for the short–term wholeturnover insurance programme and the specific shipment insurance programme, Turk Eximbank sets a maximum liability, which is the limit up to which Turk Eximbank will meet claims. The maximum limit is a rather hypothetical and flexible concept, being an estimate of likely total outstanding covered by Eximbank, rather than an accurate figure. Depending on the operation of the policy, the maximum liability can be amended. Apart from this, under the short–term wholeturnover policy, the exporter must obtain from Turk Eximbank a credit limit on each one of his buyers to whom he makes shipments. The credit limit is the limit for which Turk Eximbank accepts liability for losses arising from commercial risks.

2.1.3   *Cost of cover*

Under the short–term wholeturnover policy, premiums for shipments covered become payable at the date the shipment is made. On the other hand, under the specific shipment insurance policy, the premium is paid in advance.

The amount of the premium to be paid is calculated in accordance with premium rates set by Turk Eximbank. In the determination of premium rates, the risk classification of the buyer's country, the terms and conditions of payment and the type of buyer (public or private) are the three main factors that are taken into account.

2.2   Guarantees for banks

2.2.1   *Policies available*

Apart from the above insurance programmes, a bank guarantee programme is designed to encourage commercial banks to finance exporters by purchasing export receivables.

This programme covers the foreign buyer's debt obligations that a bank purchases without recourse from the exporter.

Like the specific shipment insurance programme, the bank guarantee programme is designed on a single buyer and a specific contract basis.

Both political and commercial risks are covered under the bank guarantee programme.

Political risks include war, cancellation of an existing export or import licence and transfer risks. Commercial risks covered under this programme are those which are not specified as political. However, losses due to currency devaluations are not covered.

For public buyers, Turk Eximbank's guarantee covers 100 per cent of the commercial and political risk. For private buyers, Turk Eximbank provides cover for 100 per cent of the political risks and 85 per cent of the commercial risks.

2.2.2   *Eligibility*

See section 2.1.2 above.

2.2.3   *Cost of cover*

The guarantee fee is determined according to the type of buyer, the terms of credit and risk classification of the buyer's country and is paid in advance.

2.3   Other insurance programmes

2.3.1   The *overseas construction works insurance policy* covers civil construction jobs as well as turn–key projects involving supplies and services. It provides cover against non–payment for both the supplies and services elements of constructional works contracts.

Turkish construction companies selected as a result of a tender opened by an overseas employer to undertake turn–key projects or construction, extension, erection and repair and maintenance of schools, residential construction and infrastructural investments such as roads, bridges, dams, waterways, channels and all kinds of industrial establishments such as factories, power plants, refineries and the like, may utilise this programme.

As with other insurance programmes, the risks covered under this programme are both political and commercial.

The overseas construction works insurance programme gives cover against 80 per cent and 90 per cent of losses incurred as a result of commercial and political risks, respectively.

Policies issued within this programme are based upon the estimated contract and interest rates, as well as upon other payments due. Premiums are payable at the commencement of the contract. Turk Eximbank shall either refund or request an additional premium in accordance with whether the actual contract price is above or below the estimate.

2.3.1.2   The *overseas investment insurance programme* covers overseas investments to be made by Turkish investors against losses that may arise from political risks.

Eligible investment includes the allocation against a share of capital in cash or kind to a new investment overseas. As the aim of an insurance programme relating to overseas investments is to encourage long term and permanent investments, the term of investment should be at least three years.

The investor is required to elect annually a current insured amount, which states a ceiling on Turk Eximbank's liability for the following twelve months. This amount should be sufficient to cover the initial contribution plus earnings already retained in the business together with expected earnings during the insurance year.

Risks covered under this policy are expropriation, war damage and restrictions on remittances.

Turk Eximbank will indemnify up to 90 per cent of the losses that the investor may incur because of the above–mentioned political risks.

Premiums are determined on the basis of the risk rating of the country where the investment is to be made, the field of investment and the period of the policy.

2.3.3   Preshipment credit guarantee

Aim: to facilitate extension of credits by commercial banks for the production and preparation of the goods to be exported.

Risk covered: This guarantee covers the risk of a loss to a commercial bank arising from granting the credit to the exporters.

Guarantee coverage: A certain percentage of the principal amount and interest of the credit extended by a commercial bank. This coverage does not exceed the amount of maximum guarantee commitment.

Guarantee fee: Guarantee fees are calculated on the basis of maximum guarantee commitment determined by Turk Eximbank depending on the terms of the credit.

2.3.4   Post–shipment credit guarantee

Aim: To enable commercial banks to extend post–shipment credits to exporters through the discounting of export bills.

Risk covered: It covers the risk of a loss to a commercial bank arising from the granting of the post–shipment credit to the exporter.

Guarantee coverage: A certain percentage of the principal and interest of the credit extended by a maximum guarantee commitment.

Guarantee fee: Guarantee fees are to be determined by taking into account the terms of credit and the risk of the export transaction.

2.3.5   Overseas contracting servicing credit guarantee

Aim: To enable domestic and foreign financial institutions to extend credits to Turkish contractors in connection with their overseas business.

Risk covered: It covers the risk of a loss to a financial institution arising from the granting of the credit to the contractor.

Guarantee coverage: A certain percentage of the principal and interest of the credit extended by a commercial bank. This coverage does not exceed the amount of maximum guarantee commitment.

Guarantee fee: To be determined by considering the terms of credit, commercial risks and political risks.

2.3.6   *Overseas investment credit guarantee*

Aim: To facilitate extension of credits by commercial banks to Turkish entrepreneurs in connection with their viable overseas investments.

Risk covered: This guarantee covers the risk of a loss to a financial institution arising from the granting of a credit to the contractor.

Guarantee coverage: A certain percentage of the principal amount and interest of the credit extended by the commercial bank and does not exceed the amount of maximum guarantee commitment.

Guarantee fee: To be determined by the Turk Eximbank depending on the maximum guarantee commitment amount.

3.   EXPORT FINANCE PROGRAMMES

3.1   Direct Credits

3.1.1   *Types of contract available*

— Short term export credit

Aim: To meet both the preshipment and post–shipment financial requirements of exporters entering new markets with their products.

Credit limit: To be determined by Turk Eximbank, but does not exceed a specific portion of export FOB value.

Term of credit: Maximum one year.

Repayment: The interest should be paid quarterly; the principal amount should be paid at the end of the term period.

Currency: Turkish Lira or convertible currency.

— Export preparation credit

Aim: To provide financial facilities to exporters for the export preparation period, which must exceed one year.

Credit limit: The maximum amount of credit may not exceed the remaining part of FOB value after the down/advance payment.

Term of credit: 1 to 5 years.

Repayment: Twice yearly through the foreign exchange earnings.

Currency: Turkish Lira or convertible currency.

— Supplier's credit

Aim: To encourage exporters to sell non–traditional products to potential markets with medium and long term credits and to enable Turkish exporters to compete in international markets.

Limits: The maximum amount of credit may not exceed the remaining part of FOB value after the advance payment (minimum 15 per cent of contract value).

Term of credit: 1 to 5 years for medium term; 5 to 10 years for long term.

Repayment: In twice yearly instalments along with interests over the credit period.

Currency: Convertible currency
Security:

1. Guarantee:
— from a bank in the importer's country, or
— from government if the importer is a government department, or
— from an international bank outside the importer's country.

2. An undertaking from the Central Bank of the importing country for prompt remittance of the foreign exchange for repayment of instalment and interest.

Suppliers' credits can also be offered as refinance through a commercial bank or cofinancing with a commercial bank.

— Lines of credit to overseas borrowers

Aim: To promote the export of capital goods/industrial manufactures to developing countries on a deferred payment basis with no risk of payment to exporters.
Credit limit: The lines of credit are negotiated between Turk Eximbank and the foreign government or financial institution.
Term of credit: Normally long term credit.
Repayment: Depends on the general agreement between Turk Eximbank and the foreign government. The repayment period should not exceed that of the foreign buyer to the financial institution or government.
Currency: Convertible currency to be agreed upon.

Security:
— If the loan is extended to a government, security will be in the form of promissory note/bills of exchange.
— If the loan is extended to a financial institution, security will be in the form of a government guarantee.

— Relending to overseas borrowers

Aim: To promote the export of capital goods/equipment or services from Turkey to both developed and developing countries.
Borrower: Leading international commercial banks/merchant banks and investment banks with a worldwide network of branches.
Credit limit: To be decided by negotiations between Eximbank and the borrowing bank. A limit is fixed depending upon the potential for use.
Term of credit: 1 to 5 years.
Repayment: In bi–annual instalments along with interest over the credit period.
Currency: Loans under the credit line to the borrowing bank as well as repayment will be in a convertible currency.

— Buyer's credit

Aim:
— To enable exporters to offer deferred payment for capital goods and other industrial goods in foreign tenders and to enable individual buyers to import from Turkey on a deferred payment basis.

— To support the export of large value supply contracts and/or turnkey projects to developing countries on deferred credit terms.

Credit limit: The remaining part of the FOB value of the contract after advance/down payment.

Term of credit: 1 to 5 years for medium term; 1 to 10 years for long term.

Repayment: In biannual instalments along with interest over the credit period.

Currency: Convertible currency agreed upon.

Security:

— Letter of credit for advance payment and freight and insurance charges.
— Letter of credit or guarantee from an acceptable bank in the importer's country or in a third country.
— Government guarantee.

3.1.2   *Eligibility*

As described in 3.1.1.

3.1.3   *Resulting interest rates*

Interest rates are determined by Turk Eximbank. Suppliers' credit rates are set considering the cost of funds and OECD guidelines, at a level which keeps exporters competitive. For lines of credit and buyers' credits, the creditworthiness of the borrowing country is taken into account.

3.2   Refinancing

3.2.1   *Type of contract available*

— *Export L/C rediscounting credit (preshipment)*

Aim: To meet the financial needs of exporters entering new markets.

Credit limit: To be made available against notes of up to 6 months' maturity.

Repayment: The principal payment to be made by the commercial bank after receiving the foreign exchange earnings. Interest to be paid quarterly by the commercial bank.

Currency: Turkish Lira.

— *Export bill rediscounting*

Aim: To meet the short term post–shipment cash requirements of the exporters.

Credit limit: To be determined by Turk Eximbank; must not exceed a specific portion of export FOB value.

Term of credit: Up to 3 months.

Repayment: The principal payment to be made by the commercial bank after receiving the foreign exchange earnings. Interest to be paid quarterly by the commercial bank.

Currency: Turkish Lira.

3.2.2   *Eligibility*

As described in 3.2.1.

3.2.3   *Resulting interest rates*

To be determined by Turk Eximbank.

4.   AID FINANCE PROGRAMMES

Turkey has no system for combining aid and other funds.

Chapter 25

ARRANGEMENT ON GUIDELINES
FOR OFFICIALLY SUPPORTED EXPORT CREDITS

This revised text of the Arrangement was adopted in March 1988, and has been further amended to include agreed changes up to November 1989.

TABLE OF CONTENTS

266

ARRANGEMENT ON GUIDELINES
FOR OFFICIALLY SUPPORTED EXPORT CREDITS

I. FORM AND SCOPE OF THE ARRANGEMENT

1. Export Credit Transactions Covered

a) Participants shall apply the guidelines contained in this informal Arrangement to officially supported (*) export credits with a repayment term (*) of two years or more relating to contracts for sales of goods and/or services or to leases equivalent in effect to such sales contracts.

b) Special Guidelines apply to the following sectors in accordance with the provisions of paragraph 9:

    1. Ships
    2. Nuclear Power Plants
    3. Power Plants other than Nuclear Power Plants
    4. Aircraft

c) This Arrangement does not apply to export credits relating to exports of:

    1. Military Equipment
    2. Agricultural Commodities

2. Participation

Present participants are listed in Annex I to this Arrangement. Countries willing to apply these Guidelines may become participants upon the prior invitation of the then existing Participants.

II. GUIDELINES FOR BASIC EXPORT CREDIT TERMS AND CONDITIONS

3. Cash Payments

Participants shall require purchasers of exported goods and services receiving officially supported export credits to make cash payments (*) at or before the starting point (*) equal to a minimum of 15 per cent of the export contract value (*).

Participants shall not provide official support for such cash payments other than insurance and guarantees against the usual pre–credit risks.

4. Repayment

Participants shall apply the following Guidelines for the repayment of export credits that are officially supported by way of direct credit, refinancing, eligibility for an interest subsidy, guarantee or insurance.

a) Maximum Repayment Term

For the three categories of countries (*) of destination, the following maximum repayment terms shall apply. The export credit agreement and ancillary documents shall not permit the extension of the relevant repayment term.

Countries of destination	Maximum repayment terms
Category I : Relatively rich	Five years; but after prior notification in accordance with paragraph 14 b) 1), eight and a half years;
Category II : intermediate	Eight and a half years[1];
Category III : relatively poor	Ten years

b) Repayment of Principal and Payment of Interest

1. Principal of an export credit shall normally be repaid in equal and regular instalments not less frequently than every six months commencing not later than six months after the starting point. In the case of leases, this repayment procedure may be applied either for the amount of principal only or else for the amount of principal and interest combined.

2. Interest (*) as set forth in paragraph 5 below shall normally not be capitalised during the repayment term but shall be payable not less frequently than every six months commencing not later than six months after the starting point.

3. If a participant intends not to follow the normal practices for repayment of principal or for payment of interest set forth in 1) and 2) above, the participant shall give prior notification in accordance with the procedure set forth in paragraph 14 b) 1).

5. Minimum Interest Rates

Participants providing official financing support by way of direct credit, refinancing or interest rate subsidy shall apply the following minimum rates of interest:

a) Matrix rates

1. Without prejudice to b) below, the following minimum annual interest rates (matrix rates) shall apply:

Countries of destination	Repayment periods	
	2–5 years	*Over 5 years*
Category II	SDR(2) + 105 bp	SDR(2) + 155 bp
Category III	SDR(2) + 20 bp	SDR(2) + 20 bp

2. SDR base rates for the above matrix interest rates are reviewed semi–annually and subject to adjustment on the 15th of January and July according to the following method:

   i) An adjustment is made if the SDR–weighted average of the monthly interest rates referred to in footnote[2] for the immediately preceding December or June respectively differs by 50 basis points or more from the SDR–weighted average interest rate underlying the preceding adjustment in matrix rates. When such a change occurs, the levels of the matrix rates set out above shall be adjusted by the same number of basis points as the difference in the SDR–weighted averages, the recalculated matrix rates being rounded off to the nearest five basis points[3].

   ii) The interest rates for the currencies constituting the SDR–weighted average are the secondary market yields of financing instruments reported to the OECD pursuant to paragraph 18 *a)* i).

b) Commercial Interest Reference Rates (*)

For countries of destination in Category I, participants shall apply the relevant commercial interest reference rate. Notwithstanding *a)* above, participants may also choose to apply these commercial interest reference rates for countries of destination in Categories II and III. If the terms of such official financing support are fixed before the date of contract, a premium of 20 basis points is added to the commercial interest reference rate[4]. This commercial interest reference rate is also used to compute the discount rate to be used in the calculation of the concessionality level of tied and partially untied aid financing in accordance with paragraph 22 *m)*.

c) Interest Rate System Choice

Participants are prohibited from taking any action that allows banks to offer throughout the life of a floating rate loan the option of either 1. the matrix rate, 2. the CIRR (at time of the original contract) or 3. the short–term market rate, whichever is lower.

6. Local Costs (*)

a) Category II or Category III Countries

Participants shall not finance, guarantee or insure credit for more than 100 per cent of the value of the goods and services exported, including goods and services supplied by third countries. Thus, the amount of local costs supported on credit terms and conditions will not exceed the amount of the cash payment. They shall not grant such support for local costs financed on conditions more favourable than those supported for the exports to which such local costs are related.

b) Category I Countries

The provisions of a) above shall apply, provided that any official support is confined to insurance or guarantees.

7. Maximum Period of Validity of Commitments (*), Prior Commitments and Certain Aid Commitments

a) Participants shall not fix credit terms and conditions for an individual export credit or credit line (*), whether new or being renewed or prolonged, for a period exceeding six months. Commitments that were in effect prior to a modification of the Guidelines of the Arrangement and that became non-conforming because of this modification may not remain in effect for more than six months following the date of the modification.

b) Participants shall not fix for more than one year credit terms and conditions for individual tied or partially untied aid credits that have a concessionality level below the appropriate minimum in paragraph 12 b) below. Aid protocols, aid credit lines or similar agreements may not be valid for more than two years after their signature.

8. Tied and Partially Untied Aid Financing (*)

If a participant intends to support tied or partially untied aid financing, the participant shall, without prejudice to official development assistance procedures administered by the Development Assistance Committee, give notification in accordance with the procedures set forth in paragraphs:

a) 14 c) 1), if the concessionality level (*) is less than 50 per cent;
b) 14 d), if the concessionality level is 50 per cent or more.

9. Special Sectors

Participants shall apply the following special Guidelines to the sectors listed below:

a) Ships

The Guidelines of this Arrangement shall apply to ships not covered by the OECD Understanding on Export Credits for Ships (Annex II to this Arrangement). Efforts shall be pursued to arrive at common provisions for all ships. Until common provisions for all ships are agreed upon, if for any type of ships that is covered by that Understanding and therefore not by the Guidelines of the Arrangement, a participant intends to support terms that would be more favourable than those terms permitted by this Arrangement, the participant shall notify all other participants of such terms in accordance with the procedure set forth in paragraph 14 b) 1).

b) Nuclear Power Plants

This Arrangement shall apply; except that where relevant, the provisions of the Sector Understanding on Export Credits for Nuclear Power Plants (Annex III to this

Arrangement), which complements this Arrangement, shall apply in lieu of the corresponding provisions of the Arrangement.

c) Power Plants other than Nuclear Power Plants (*)

This Arrangement shall apply; except that the maximum repayment term shall be twelve years. If a participant intends to support a repayment term longer than five years in transactions with Category I countries or a repayment term longer than the relevant maximum term set forth in paragraph 4 a) for Category II and III countries, the participant will give prior notification in accordance with the procedure set forth in paragraph 14 b) 1).

d) Aircraft

This Arrangement shall apply; except that where relevant, the provisions of the Sector Understanding on Export Credits for Civil Aircraft (Annex IV to this Arrangement), which complements this Arrangement, shall apply in lieu of the corresponding provisions of the Arrangement.

10. Best Endeavours

a) Objectives

1. The Guidelines set out in this Arrangement represent the most generous credit terms and conditions that participants may offer when giving official support. All participants recognise the risk that in the course of time these Guidelines may come to be regarded as the normal terms and conditions. They therefore undertake to take the necessary steps to prevent this risk from materialising.

2. In particular, if in an individual branch of trade or industrial sector to which this Arrangement applies, credit terms and conditions less generous to buyers than those set forth above in the Arrangement are customary, participants shall continue to respect such customary terms and conditions and shall do everything in their power to prevent these from being eroded as a result of recourse to the credit terms and conditions set forth in this Arrangement.

b) Firm Undertaking

In keeping with the objectives in a) above, the Participants, recognising the advantage which can accrue if a clearly defined common attitude toward the credit terms and conditions for a particular transaction can be achieved, firmly undertake:

1. to respect strictly the existing procedures for notification and in particular to give prior notification at the latest at the stipulated moment before commitment as well as to supply all the information in the detail called for in the form set forth in Annex V;

2. to make maximum use of *the Framework for Information Exchange (see Annex VI)* at an early stage with a view of forming a common line towards credit terms and conditions for particular transactions;

3. to consider favourably face–to–face consultations if a participant so requests in the case of important transactions as set out in the protocol to this Arrangement.

c) Maximum Delays for Replies

If, in an exchange of information referred to under *b)* above, a participant informs another participant of the credit terms and conditions that it envisages supporting for a particular transaction and requests similar information from the other participant, then, in the absence of a satisfactory reply within seven calendar days, the enquiring participant may assume that the other will support the transaction on the most favourable credit terms and conditions permitted by these Guidelines. In cases of particular urgency, the enquiring participant may request a more rapid reply.

11. Matching

A participant has the right to match credit terms and conditions notifiable under paragraph 14, as well as credit terms and conditions offered by a non-participant. The validity of a matching commtiment may not exceed the termination date of the commitment being matched. Participants shall match by offering terms that comply with this Arrangement unless the initiating offer does not comply with this Arrangement. A participant intending to match credit terms and conditions:

  a) notified by another participant shall follow the procedures set forth in paragraph 15 *a)* or *c)* as appropriate;
  b) offered by a non-participant shall follow the procedures set forth in paragraph 15 *b)*.

12. No-derogation Engagement

Participants shall not:

  a) derogate with respect to maximum repayment terms (whatever the form of support), to minimum interest rates or to the limitation of the validity of commitments to a maximum of six months or extend the relevant repayment term through an extension of the grace period before the start of the repayment beyond the normal practice of six months after the starting point; or
  b) avail themselves of the possibilities provided under paragraph 14 *c)* 1) of this Arrangement to support tied or partially untied aid financing having a concessionality level of less than 35 per cent, or 50 per cent if the beneficiary country is a least developed country (LLDC) as defined by the United Nations.

13. Action to Avoid or Minimise Losses

The provisions of this Arrangement are without prejudice to the right of the export credit or insurance authority to take appropriate action after the export credit agreement and ancillary documents become effective to avoid or minimise losses.

III. PROCEDURES

14. Prior and Prompt Notifications

a) Derogations: Procedure for Prior Notification and Discussion

1. If a participant intends to take the initiative to support terms and conditions not in conformity with this Arrangement, the participant shall notify all other participants of the terms and conditions it intends to support at least ten calendar days before issuing any commitment. If any other participant requests a discussion during this period, the initiating participant shall wait an additional ten calendar days before issuing any commitment on such terms. Normally this discussion will be by telex.

2. If the initiating participant moderates or withdraws its intention to support the notified non-conforming terms and conditions, it must immediately inform all other participants accordingly.

3. A participant intending to match notified derogating terms and conditions shall follow the procedure set forth in paragraph 15 a) 1).

b) Deviations: Procedure for Prior Notification without Discussion

1. A participant shall notify, at least ten calendar days before issuing any commitment, all other participants of the terms and conditions if it intends:

   i) to support a credit with a repayment term of more than five but not exceeding eight and a half years to a relatively rich country;

   ii) not to follow normal payment practices with respect to principal or interest referred to in paragraph 4 b);

   iii) to support a credit for a power plant other than a nuclear power plant with a repayment term longer than the relevant maximum set forth in paragraph 4 a), but not exceeding twelve years or

   iv) to support, for any kind of ship to which the OECD Understanding on export credits for ships applies, credit terms and conditions that would be more favourable than those credit terms and conditions permitted by this Arrangement.

2. If the initiating participant moderates or withdraws its intention to give such support to the notified deviating credit conditions, it must immediately inform all other participants accordingly.

3. A participant intending to match notified deviating terms and conditions shall follow the procedure set forth in paragraph 15 a) 2).

c) Procedures for Prior Notification of Aid Financing

1. The procedures set out in paragraph 14 b) shall apply where a participant intends to provide or support tied aid or partially untied aid financing involving a concessionality level of less than 50 per cent; except that wherever paragraph 14 b) refers to a period of ten calendar days, a period of twenty working days shall apply and that participants intending to match shall use the procedures of paragraph 15 a) 3).

2. A participant shall notify all other participants of the terms it intends to support at least twenty working days before issuing any commitment if the participant intends to provide or support trade related aid financing transactions involving a grant

element of less than 50 per cent that are fully and freely available to finance procurement from the recipient country, from substantially all other developing countries and from participating countries. Participants intending to match such financing shall use the procedures of paragraph 15 *a)* 3).

d) Procedure for Prompt Notification (*)

As soon as a participant commits itself to support a tied or partially untied aid financing transaction having a grant element of 50 per cent or more, the participant will promptly notify all other participants accordingly.

e) Exception for Small Projects and Technical Assistance

The reporting requirements of paragraphs 12 *b)* and 14 *c)* and *d)* do not apply to the following transactions:

1. Aid financing where the official development aid component consists solely of technical co-operation that is less than either 3 per cent of the total value of the transaction or one million US dollars, whichever is lower, and

2. Capital projects of less than one million US dollars that are funded entirely by development assistance grants.

15. Procedures for Matching

a) Matching Terms and Conditions Notified in Accordance with Para. 14

1. *Matching of notified derogations:* On and after the expiry of the first ten calendar day period referred to in paragraph 14 *a)* 1) if no discussion is requested (or on and after the expiry of the second ten calendar day period if discussion is requested) and unless the participant intending to match has received notice from the initiating participant that the latter has withdrawn its intention to support non-conforming terms and conditions, any participant will have the right to support:

> *i)* in a case of "identical matching", terms and conditions that include the identical non-conforming element but that otherwise conform to the Guidelines; provided that the matching participant gives as early as possible notification of its intention to match; or

> *ii)* in a case of "other support" prompted by the initial derogation, any other non-conforming element of the terms subject to the restrictions of paragraph 11; provided that the responding participant introducing a fresh derogation, initiates a five calendar day prior notification and five calendar day discussion procedure and awaits its completion. This period can run concurrently with that of the prior notification and discussion procedure initiated by the originally derogating participant but cannot elapse before the end of the applicable ten or twenty calendar day period referred to under paragraph 14 *a)* 1).

2. *Matching of notified deviations:* On and after the expiry of the ten calendar day period referred to in paragraph 14 *b* 1) and unless the matching participant has received notice from the initiating participant that the latter has withdrawn its intention to support the terms and conditions notified in accordance with paragraph 14 *b)* 1), any participant will have the right to support:

i) in a case of "identical matching", terms and conditions that include the identical element notified in accordance with paragraph 14 *b)* 1) but that otherwise conform to the Guidelines; provided that the matching participant gives notification as early as possible of its intention to match.

ii) in a case of "other support", any other element of the terms which does not conform to the Guidelines subject to the restrictions of paragraph 11; provided that the responding participant initiates a five calendar day prior notification procedure without discussion and awaits its completion. This period may run concurrently with that of the prior notification procedure started by the initiating participant, but may not elapse before the end of the ten calendar day period referred to under paragraph 14 *b)* 1).

3. *Matching of a prior notification of aid financing:* The procedures set out in paragraph 15 *a)* 2) shall apply where a participant intends to match aid financing; except that where paragraph 15 *a)* 2) refers to a period of ten calendar days, a period of twenty working days shall apply.

4. *Matching of a prompt notification:* No prior notification need be given if a participant intends to match terms and conditions that were subject to a prompt notification according to paragraph 14 *d)*.

5. *Discount rate in matching:* In matching aid financing, identical matching means matching with an identical concessionality level recalculated with the discount rate in force at the time of matching.

b) Matching Export Terms and Conditions offered by a non–Participant

1. Before considering meeting non–conforming terms and conditions assumed to be offered by a non–participant, a participant shall make every effort to verify that these terms are receiving official support. The participant shall inform all other participants of the nature and outcome of these efforts.

2. A participant that intends to match non–conforming terms offered by a non–participant shall follow the prior notification and discussion procedure under paragraph 14 *a)* 1).

c) Matching Non-conforming Prior Commitments

1. A participant intending to match a prior commitment shall make reasonable efforts to determine whether the non–conforming terms and conditions of the individual transaction or credit line in question will be used to support a particular transaction. This participant will be considered to have made such reasonable efforts if it has informed by telex the participant assumed to offer such non–conforming terms and conditions of its intention to match but in reply to the telex has not been informed within three working days, exclusive the day of reception, that this prior commitment will not be used to support the transaction in question.

2. A prior credit line may be matched by an individual transaction or by means of a credit line. In both cases, the dates of expiry of the matching offer shall not be later than that of the credit line being matched.

3. A participant intending to match another participant's non–conforming prior commitment shall, in the case of:

> i) "identical matching", follow the procedure set forth in paragraph 15 *a*) 1) *i*) when matching a derogation and paragraph 15 *a*) 2) *i*) when matching a deviation;
>
> ii) "other support", follow the procedure set forth in paragraph 15 *a*) 1) *ii*) when matching a derogating prior commitment and the procedure set forth in paragraph 15 *a*) 2) *ii*) when matching a deviating prior commitment.

16. Information on Commitments

As soon as a participant commits credit terms and conditions that it had notified in accordance with paragraph 14 or 15, it shall, in all cases, inform all other participants accordingly by including the notification reference number on the relevant Berne Union 1c form.

17. Information to be Supplied under the Notification and Matching Procedures

The notifications called for by the above procedures shall be made in accordance with and contain the information set out in the "standard form" in Annex V and be copied to the Secretariat of the OECD.

IV. OPERATIONAL PROVISIONS

18. Regular notification and Circulation of Information on Selected Interest Rates

a) Yields on Government or Public Sector Bonds

1. Participants whose currencies constitute the IMF's Special Drawing Right shall notify by telex each month to the Secretariat for distribution to all participants the monthly information on yields of government or public sector bonds as reported in the OECD Financial Statistics under reference number II.2.b, that is:

France: Public and semi–public sector bonds on the secondary market
Germany: Public sector bonds on the secondary market (8–15 years)
Japan: Central government bonds on the secondary market
U.K.:   Government bonds on the secondary market (10 years)
U.S.A.:   US government notes and bonds on the secondary market (composite: over 10 years)

This information shall reach the Secretariat at the latest five days after the end of the month covered by this information.

2. Upon receipt of this information, the Secretariat shall calculate the SDR–weighted average of interest rates for immediate circulation to all participants.

3. At the beginning of July and of January, the Secretariat will in accordance with the method set forth in paragraph 5 *a*) 2), calculate on the basis of the

SDR–weighted averages the semi–annual adjustments to be made to the matrix minimum interest rates set forth in paragraph 5 *a)* 1).

b) Commercial Interest Reference Rates

1. Commercial interest reference rates for currencies that are subject to the provisions of paragraph 5 *b)* shall be telexed at least monthly to the Secretariat for circulation to all participants.

2. Such notification shall reach the Secretariat not later than five days after the end of each month covered by this information. The Secretariat shall then inform immediately all participants of the applicable rates. Any changes in these rates shall enter into effect on the fifteenth day after the end of each month.

3. When market developments require the notification of a change in a commercial interest reference rate in the course of a month, the changed rate shall be implemented ten days after the date of receipt of the notification of this change.

19. Reviews

a) Annual Review

1. The Participants shall review at least annually the functioning of the Arrangement. The reviews will normally take place in the northern spring of each year. In the review, they shall examine *inter alia* notification procedures, derogations, implementation and operation of the differentiated discount rate system, questions of matching, prior commitments, practices on credits for agricultural commodities and possibilities of wider participation in this Arrangement. They shall also review possible modifications of the matrix rates, notably with the aim to bring them closer to market interest rates.

2. These reviews shall be based on information on participants' experience and on their suggestions for improving the operation and efficacy of the Arrangement and shall take account of the objectives of the Arrangement and the prevailing economic and monetary situation. The information and suggestions that participants wish to put forward to this end shall reach the Secretariat not later than forty–five days before the date of review.

b) Review of Commercial Interest Reference Rates

1. The Participants shall review periodically the operation in practice of the commercial interest reference rates with a view to ensuring that the notified rates reflect current market conditions and meet the aims underlying the establishing of the rates in operation. Such reviews shall also cover the premium to be added when these rates are applied.

2. Any participant may submit to the Chairman a substantiated request for an extraordinary review in case this participant considers that the commercial interest reference rates for one or more currencies no longer reflect current market conditions.

20. Validity and Duration

The provisions of this Arrangement are applicable without time limit, unless revised as a result of the review referred to in paragraph 19.

21. Withdrawal

Any participant may withdraw from this Arrangement upon not less than sixty calendar days prior written notice to the other participants.

V. DEFINITIONS AND INTERPRETATIONS

22. For the purposes of this Arrangement, the Participants agreed to the following definitions and interpretations:

a) Cash Payments means payments to be received for goods and services exported by the completion of the exporter's contractual obligations, the date of completion being determined by the starting point.

The quantum of the minimum cash payments is established by reference to the total export contract value; except that in the case of a transaction involving some goods or services supplied from outside the exporter's country, the total export contract value may be reduced proportionately if the official support from which the exporter benefits does not cover those goods and services.

Retention payments due after the latest appropriate starting point referred to under *k)* below do not count as cash payments for the purpose of conformity with the Guidelines.

b) Export Contract Value means the total amount to be paid by the buyer; exclusive of interest in the case of an export sale of goods and/or services or to be paid by the lessee, exclusive of the portion of the lease payment equivalent to interest in the case of a cross border lease.

c) The *Classification of Countries* into categories in paragraph 4 *a)* and 5 *a)* is based on the following criteria:

Cat. I:	Countries with a GNP per capita income of over $4,000 p.a. according to the definite 1979 figures shown in the 1981 World Bank Atlas.
Cat. II:	Countries not classified with Categories I or III.
Cat. III:	Countries eligible for IDA credits plus any other low income countries or territories, the GNP per capita of which would not exceed the IDA eligibility level.

d) Repayment term and interest rates

1. *Repayment Term* means the period of time commencing at the starting point and terminating on the contractual date of the final payment.

2. *Interest* excludes:

   i) any payment by way of premium or other charge for insuring or guaranteeing supplier credits or financial credits;

   ii) any other payment by way of banking fees or commissions associated with the export credit, other than annual or semi–annual bank charges payable throughout the repayment term; and

   iii) withholding taxes imposed by the importing country.

3. In the case of an export through a *relay country*, the relevant interest rate and repayment term set out in paragraphs 4 and 5 are those corresponding to the country of final destination in cases:

i) where the "relay country" makes payment, if and when received from the country of final destination, to the exporting country on the basis of the latter's portion in the total export value; or

ii) where there is security or payment by the country of final destination.

e) Commercial Interest Reference Rate means an interest rate established in accordance with Annex VII to this Arrangement.

f) Local Costs means expenditure, excluding commissions payable to the exporter's agent in the buying country, for the supply from the buyer's country of goods and services, that are necessary either for executing the exporter's contract or for completing the project of which the exporter's contract forms part.

g) Commitment means any arrangement for or declaration on credit conditions, in whatever form, by means of which the intention or willingness to refinance, insure or guarantee supplier credits or to grant, refinance, insure or guarantee financial credits is brought to the attention of the recipient country, the buyer or the borrower, the exporter, or the financial institution.

h) Line of Credit means any understanding or statement, in whatever form, whereby the intention to grant credit benefiting from official support up to a ceiling and in respect of a series of transactions, linked or not to a specific project, is brought to the attention of the recipient country, the buyer or the borrower, or the financial institution.

i) Tied aid financing[5] is defined as loans or grants or associated financing packages involving a concessionality level greater than zero per cent that is in effect tied to procurement of goods and services from the donor country. *Partially untied aid financing*[5] is defined as loans or grants or associated financing packages involving a concessionality level greater than zero per cent that is in effect tied to procurement of goods and services from the donor country and from a restricted number of countries[6].

1. Such financing can take the form of either:

i) Official Development Assistance loans;

ii) Official Development Assistance grants;

iii) Other Official Flows (including grants and loans but excluding officially supported export credits that are in conformity with this Arrangement); or

iv) Any association in law or in fact[7] either in the hands of the donor, lender or borrower among two or more of the following:

— Official Development Assistance loans;

— Official Development Assistance grants;

— Other Official Flows (including grants and loans but excluding officially supported export credits that are in conformity with this Arrangement);

— An export credit that is officially supported by way of direct credit, refinancing, eligibility for an interest subsidy, guarantee or insurance to which this Arrangement applies, other funds at or near market terms or cash payments from the buyer's own resources.

2. Such financing is defined to be in effect tied to procurement of goods and services from one or a restricted number of countries as soon as:

i) one of the financial components listed above is not freely and fully available to finance procurement from the recipient country, substantially all other developing countries and from participating countries, whether by a formal or informal understanding to that effect between the recipient and the donor country, or

ii) it involves practices that the Development Assistance Committee of the OECD or the Participants may determine to result in such tying[8].

3. The definition of "Official Development Assistance" is identical to that in the "DAC Guiding Principles for Associated Financing and Tied and Partially Untied Official Development Assistance".

j) Prompt Notification means a maximum delay of two working days following the date of commitment within which notification is to be given.

k) Starting Point is the same as the Berne Union definition currently in use and is as follows:

1. In the case of a contract for the sale of capital goods consisting of individual items usable in themselves (e.g. locomotives), the starting point is the mean date or actual date when the buyer takes physical possession of the goods in his own country.

2. In the case of a contract for the sale of capital equipment for complete plant or factories where the supplier has no responsibility for commissioning, the starting point is the date when the buyer is to take physical possession of the entire equipment (excluding spare parts) supplied under the contract.

3. In the case of construction contracts where the contractor has no responsibility for commissioning, the starting point is the date when construction has been completed.

4. In the case of any contract where the supplier or contractor has a contractual responsibility for commissioning, the starting point is the date when he has completed installation or construction and preliminary tests to ensure that it is ready for operation. This applies whether or not it is handed over to the buyer at that time in accordance with the terms of the contract and irrespective of any continuing commitment which the supplier or contractor may have, e.g. for guaranteeing its effective functioning or for training local personnel.

5. In the case of paragraphs 2), 3) and 4) above where the contract involves the separate execution of individual parts of a project, the date of the starting point is the date of the starting point for each separate part, or the mean date of those starting points or, where the supplier has a contract, not for the whole project but for an essential part of it, the starting point may be that appropriate to the project as a whole.

l) Interest Rate and Official Support: Apart from agreement on the definition of interest set forth in paragraph 22 *d)* 2) it has not proved possible to establish common definitions of interest rate and official support in the light of differences between long–established national systems of export credit and export credit insurance now in operation in the participating countries. Efforts shall be pursued to elaborate solutions for these definitions. While such definitions are being elaborated, these guidelines do not prejudice present interpretations. In order to facilitate these efforts, notes concerning actual practices in this area, including information on annual or semi–annual bank charges payable throughout the repayment term and considered as part of interest, as they result from the different national systems, were transmitted to the Secretariat of the OECD and distributed to all participants in document TD/CSUS/78.12 and Addenda.

m) 1. *Concessionality level* is very similar in concept to the "grant element" used by the Development Aid Committee (DAC) of the OECD. In the case of grants, it is 100 per cent. In the case of loans, it is the difference between the nominal value of the loan and the discounted present value of the future debt service payments to be made by the borrower, expressed as a percentage of the nominal value of the loan, and is calculated in accordance with the method of calculating the grant element used by the DAC, except that:

> *i)* The discount rate used in calculating the concessionality level of a loan in a given currency is subject to change on an annual basis on the 15th of January and calculated as follows:
>
> *CIRR* + 1/4 (10−*CIRR*). In this formula, *CIRR* is the average of the monthly CIRRs valid during the six−month period extending from the 15th of August of the previous year through the 14th of February of the current year. The calculated rate is rounded to the nearest 10 basis points.
>
> *ii)* The base date for the calculation of the concessionality level is the starting point as defined in paragraph 22 *k).*

2. For the purpose of calculating the overall concessionality level of an associated financing package, the concessionality levels *i)* of export credits that are in conformity with this Arrangement, *ii)* of other funds at or near market rates, *iii)* of other official funds with a concessionality level of less than the minimum permitted by paragraph 12 *b)* above, except in cases of matching[9], or iv) of cash payments that are from the buyer's own resources, are considered to be zero. The overall concessionality level of a package is determined by dividing *i)* the sum of the results obtained by multiplying the nominal value of each component of the package by the respective concessionality level of each component by *ii)* the aggregate nominal value of the components.

3. The discount rate for a given aid loan is the rate that is in effect at the time of notification[10], except in cases of prompt notification, where the discount rate is the rate in effect at the time of commitment. A change in the discount rate during the life of a loan does not change its concessionality level.

4. Without prejudice to 3) above, when calculating the concessionality level of individual transactions initiated under an aid credit line, the discount rate is the rate that was originally notified for the credit line.

n) Power plants other than nuclear power plants are complete power stations not fueled by nuclear power — or parts thereof — comprising all components, equipment, materials and services, including the training of personnel, directly required for the construction and commissioning of such non−nuclear power stations. Not included are items for which the buyer is usually responsible, in particular, cost associated with land development, roads, construction village, power lines, switchyard and water supply, as well as costs arising in the buyer's country from official approval procedures (e.g. site permit, construction permit, fuel loading permit).

NOTES AND REFERENCES

(*)   The asterisk refers to the relevant definitions or interpretations set forth in paragraph 22.

1.   For countries in Category II that were classified in Category III before 6th July 1982, the maximum repayment term shall be ten years; the minimum interest rate applicable for repayment term of over eight and a half to ten years being the same as that for repayment terms of over five to eight and a half years.

2.   SDR means the IMF Special Drawing Right weighted average of the interest rates notified pursuant to paragraph 18 a). These currencies are the US dollar, Deutsche mark, Japanese yen, French franc and pound Sterling. In the calculation of the average interest rate, each currency shall be given the weight set by the IMF for the valuation of the Special Drawing Right.

3.   After any semi-annual period, a change in the SDR-weighted average interest rate shall be computed only on the basis of the IMF weightings of the SDR valuation basket in effect at the end of the semi-annual period.

4.   For the US dollar, this premium shall be increased to 40 basis points if the pre-contract period exceeds three months. For the Swiss franc, this premium shall be added whenever official financing support is provided.

5.   It is understood that the terms "tied aid financing" and "partially untied aid financing" exclude aid programmes of multilateral or regional institutions.

6.   These definitions do not prejudge the distinctions made in the DAC on the quality of aid as concerns tied, partially untied and untied aid.

7.   Associated financing transactions may take various forms — such as "mixed credit", "mixed financing", "joint financing", "parallel financing" or single integrated transactions. Their main characteristic is that the concessional component is linked in law or in fact to the non-concessional component, that either the non-concessional or the concessional component or the whole financing package is in effect tied or partially untied and that the availability of concessional funds is conditional upon accepting the linked non-concessional component.

Association or linkage "in fact" is determined by such factors as the existence of informal understandings between the recipient and the donor authority, the intention by the donor through the use of ODA to facilitate the acceptability of a financing package, the effective tying of the whole financing package to procurement in the donor country, the tying status of ODA and the modality of tender and/or of the contract of each financing transaction or any other practice, identified by the DAC or the Participants in which a de facto liaison exists between two or more financing components.

None of the following practices shall prevent the determination that an association or linkage "in fact" exists: contract splitting through the separate notification of component parts of one contract; splitting of contracts financed in several stages; non-notification of interdependent parts of a contract; non-notification arising from the partial untying of a financing package.

8.   In cases of uncertainty as to whether a certain financing practice falls within the scope of the above definition, the donor country shall furnish evidence in support of any claim to the effect that such a practice is untied.

9.   In identical matching, the concessionality level of any OOF in the initiating participant's offer shall be included in the calculation of the initial offer's concessionality level if the matching offer contains an OOF that is included in its concessionality level, even if the OOF in the initial offer has a concessionality level below the minimum permissible concessionality level.

10.   If a change of currency is made before the contract is concluded, a revision of the notification is required. The discount rate used to calculate the concessionality level will be the one applicable at the time of the revision. However, if the alternative currency is indicated in the original notification and all necessary information is provided, a revision is not necessary.

PROTOCOL

The Participants to the Consensus,

Whereas at the OECD Ministerial meeting of 17th–18th May 1983, the Ministers enjoined the competent bodies of the Organisation for Economic Co–operation and Development to take prompt action to improve existing arrangements so as to strengthen transparency and discipline in the area of aid and trade related concessional finance by all appropriate means;

Whereas the Participants to the Consensus recognise the advantage which can occur if a clearly defined common attitude toward the credit terms for a particular transaction can be achieved and if maximum use is made of the existing arrangements for exchanging information at an early stage;

Whereas the OECD Framework for Information Exchange (Annex VI) lays down rules for exchanging information amongst members of the OECD Group on Export Credits and Credit Guarantees;

Whereas this Framework outlines procedures to be followed in the event that all members taking part in an exchange of information agree to accept that the credit terms for a particular transaction should be the subject of a binding obligation;

Whereas at a meeting of the OECD Consensus Group in April 1984 all Participants firmly undertook to consider favourably face–to–face consultations if a participant so requests in the case of important transactions;

Whereas this undertaking was motivated by the unsatisfactory functioning of existing procedures for exchanging information in a number of important transactions;

Whereas the implementation of the provisions of the Consensus can be jeopardised if procedures for exchanging information do not function efficiently;

Whereas any weakening in Consensus discipline risks provoking wasteful export credit and/or tied aid credit competition and increasing subsidies;

Whereas the search for a common attitude does not prejudice the possibility for participants to retain their rights and liberty as to whether to insure or finance credits for a particular transaction, in the framework of their international obligations.

Have decided as follows:

Within the framework of existing procedures in the field of officially supported export credits and tied aid credits, and with a view to improving transparency, the Participants:

1) Confirm that they will strive to provide the fullest possible details on the credit terms and conditions which they may be considering offering for any transaction which is the subject of an exchange of information;

2) Acknowledge that the interests of all participants are best served if agreement can be reached at an early stage on a common attitude on the export credit conditions for a particular transaction and if the provisions of that agreement are maintained;

3) Reaffirm, therefore, the need to promote common attitudes; particularly on important transactions;

4) Recognise that in certain instances, notably when existing exchange of information procedures are perceived to be functioning in an unsatisfactory manner, face–to–face consultations could facilitate the adoption of a common line;

5) Undertake, in such circumstances, to respond favourably to any such request for early face–to–face consultations and to attend any meeting arranged in order to reach a common attitude on credit terms in conjunction with other interested participants. In this respect, particular attention will be paid to the observance and common interpretation of the guidelines;

6) Confirm moreover the importance they attach to a strict observation of the formal notification procedures provided for in the Arrangement.

Annex I

LIST OF PARTICIPANTS

Australia

Austria

Canada

European Economic Community[1]

Finland

Japan

New Zealand

Norway

Sweden

Switzerland

United States

---

1. Composed of the following Member States:
   Belgium, Denmark, France, Germany, Greece, Ireland, Italy, Luxembourg, Netherlands, Portugal, Spain, United Kingdom.

Annex II

UNDERSTANDING ON EXPORT CREDITS FOR SHIPS

I

1.   For any contract relating to any new sea–going ship or any conversion of a ship[1] to be negotiated from 1st December 1979 onwards, participants in this Understanding agree to abolish existing official facilities[2] and to introduce no new official facilities for export credits on terms providing:

  i) a maximum duration exceeding eight and a half years[3] from delivery and repayment other than by equal instalments at regular intervals of normally six months and a maximum of twelve months;

  ii) payment by delivery of less than 20 per cent of the contract price;

  iii) an interest rate of less than 8 per cent, net of all charges[4].

2.   This minimum interest rate of 8 per cent will apply to the credit granted with official support by the shipbuilder to the buyer (in a supplier–credit transaction) or by a bank or any other party in the shipbuilder's counry to the buyer or any other party in the buyer's country (in a buyer–credit transaction) whether the official support is given for the whole amount of the credit or only part of it.

3.   The minimum interest rate will also apply to the credit granted with support by governments participating in the Understanding, in the shipbuilder's country to the shipbuilder or to any other party, to enable credit to be given to the shipowner or to any other party in the shipowner's country, whether this official support is given for the whole amount of the credit or only part of it.

4.   Insofar as other public bodies participate in measures to promote exports, participants agree to use all possible influence to prevent the financing of exports on terms which contravene the above principles.

5.   Participants, recognising that it is highly desirable to set a limit to credit terms for export, also agree to make their best endeavours to ensure that no more favourable terms than those set out above will be offered to buyers by any other means.

6.   Any participant in the Understanding which wishes, for genuine aid reasons, to concede more favourable terms in a particular case is not precluded from doing so, provided that adequate notice of this decision is given to all the parties to the Understanding in accordance with the procedure established for this purpose. For these cases "adequate notice" shall be interpreted as requiring that notification be made to

all participants if possible at least six weeks before a promise is given, at any stage of the negotiations, to commit the use of funds for that purposee, and in any case at least six weeks before authorisation is given so to commit them.

7. Prior notice shall also be given in accordance with the procedure agreed between the participants of any decision taken for exceptional reasons other than those specified in Clause 6, to support terms more favourable in any way than those of the Understanding. Support (including the provision of aid) will be refused for any order finally placed[5] on more favourable terms before all other participants in the Understanding have been given prior notice in accordance with the procedure agreed.

8. Any participant in the Understanding may, provided that it applies the procedures agreed between the participants, support more favourable terms in a particular substantiated case to match terms of officially supported transactions, or contravention of the above terms by other participants, or competitive from non–participating countries.

II

9. Any participant in the Understanding may obtain information from any other participant on terms of any official support for an export contract in order to ascertain whether the terms contravene this Understanding. Participants undertake to supply all possible information requested with all possible speed. According to the rules and practices of the OECD, any participant may ask the Secretary–General to act on its behalf in the aforementioned matter and to circulate the information obtained to all participants in the Understanding.

10. Each participant undertakes to notify the Secretary–General of its system for the provision of official support and of the means of implementation of the Understanding.

III

11. This Understanding becomes effective as soon as all Members of Working Party No. 6 have notified the Secretary–General of their adherence to it or as soon as participants having so notified the Secretary–General decide that they constitute a representative majority of Members of Working Party No. 6; any participant which disagrees as to what constitutes a representative majority would not be bound by the others' decision. The Understanding is open to other Member countries of the OECD.

12. This Understanding shall be subject to review as often as requested by participants, and in any case at intervals not exceeding one year. Any participant may withdraw from this Understanding upon giving to its partners three calendar months' notice of its intention to do so. Within this period, at the request of any of these partners, there shall be a meeting of Working Party No. 6 to review this Understanding, and any other participant, on notification to its partners, may withdraw from this Understanding at the same effective date as the participant which first gave notice.

NOTES AND REFERENCES

1. Ship conversion means any conversion of sea-going vessels of more than 1.000 grt. on condition that conversion operations entail radical alterations to the cargo plan, the hull or the propulsion system.

2. Official facilities are those which enable credits to be insured, guaranteed or financed by governments, by governmental institutions, or with any form of direct or indirect governmental participation.

3. Given the special nature of the transactions for vessels transporting liquefied natural gas, the duration of authorised credit for this type of ship only is increased to ten years.

4. Interest rate, net of all charges, means that part of the credit costs (excluding any credit insurance premia and/or any banking charges) which is paid at regular intervals throughout the credit period and which is directly related to the amount of credit.

5. An order shall be deemed to have been finally placed as soon as the buyer has committed himself irrevocably under a written and signed agreement to buy from the exporter and to pay according to specified terms, even if the agreement is subject to reservations which can be withdrawn only by the exporter.

Annex III

SECTOR UNDERSTANDING ON EXPORT CREDITS FOR NUCLEAR POWER PLANTS[1]

A. Form and Scope

This Sector Understanding
— complements the Arrangement on Guidelines for Officially Supported Export Credits;
— sets out the particular Complementary Guidelines which are applicable to officially supported export credits relating to new contracts for the export of complete nuclear power stations or parts thereof, comprising all components, equipment, materials and services, including the training of personnel, directly required for the construction and commissioning of such nuclear power stations[2].
— does not apply to items for which the buyer is usually responsible, in particular, costs associated with land development, roads, construction village, power lines, switchyard and water supply, as well as costs arising in the buyer's country from official approval procedures (e.g. site permit, construction permit, fuel loading permit).

B. Credit Terms and Conditions

a) Maximum repayment term

The maximum repayment terms of an officially supported credit shall be 15 years.

b) Minimum interest rate

i) Cat. I destination countries

Special commercial interest reference rate (SCIRR)

ii) *Cat. II and Cat. III destination countries*

Current Arrangement matrix rate plus 100 basis points or SCIRR, where the "matrix rate" is defined as the relevant minimum interest rate specified in paragraph 5 *b)* of ther Arrangement applicable to credits with the longest repayment terms destined for Cat. II and Cat. III, respectively.

iii) Notwithstanding sub–paragraphs *(i)* and *(ii)* above, in cases where the fixed interest rate commitment is limited initially to a maximum period not exceeding 15 years starting from the date of contract award, the minimum interest rate for that period shall be the current Arrangement matrix rate plus 75 basis points or the SCIRR. For the remaining period until the complete repayment of the loan, official support shall be limited to guarantees or interest rate support at the appropriate SCIRR prevailing at the time of rollover. In no event shall the maximum repayment period exceed fifteen years.

iv) For all currencies that are used by participants in officially supported export credits, the special commercial interest reference rates (SCIRRs) are the appropriate Arrangement CIRRs plus 75 basis points[3]. If a currency has more than one CIRR, the CIRR for the longest term shall be used.

c) *Local cost and capitalisation of interest*

Official financing support at rates other than SCIRRs for both local cost and capitalisation of interest accruing before the starting point taken together shall not cover an amount exceeding 15 per cent of the export value.

C. Official Support for Nuclear Fuel[4]

i) The initial fuel load shall consist of no more than:
- The initially installed nuclear core, plus
- Two subsequent reloads, together consisting of up to two–thirds of a nuclear core.

Official support for the initial fuel load shall cover a maximum repayment term of four years from delivery. The minimum interest rate on the initial fuel load shall be at the rates in the Arrangement.

ii) Official support for subsequent reloads of nuclear fuel shall be made available without interest rate support (i.e. only guarantees or financing at CIRRs may be offered) and shall be on repayment terms no longer than two years from delivery. It is understood that repayment terms of over 6 months are exceptional in recognition of which the procedures of paragraph 14 a) of the Arrangement will apply.

iii) Reprocessing and spent fuel management (including waste disposal) shall be paid for on a cash basis.

D. Free Fuel or Services

Participants shall not provide free nuclear fuel or services.

E. Tied Aid Credits

Participants shall not provide tied aid credits, associated financing (as defined by the DAC), aid loans or grants or provide any other kind of financing at credit conditions that are more favourable than those set out in this Understanding.

F. Prior Notification and Consultation

Participants shall notify and consult each other under the terms agreed upon in the Appendix to this Understanding.

G. Review

The provisions of the Sector Understanding are subject to review each year, normally at the spring meeting of the Participants.

NOTES AND REFERENCES

1. All outstanding offers not in conformity with this Sector Understanding and their repayment term, interest rate, and expiry date are identified in document TD/CSUS/84.33. Upon their expiry, any outstanding offer will then be brought into conformity with this Sector Understanding.

2. Where a partial supplier provides equipment for which he has no responsibility of commissioning he may offer CIRRs as an alternative, providing that the maximum period from date of contract does not exceed 10 years.

3. Except that for the Japanese yen, the SCIRR is the Arrangement CIRR plus 40 basis points.

4. It is understood that for the time being the separate provision of Uranium Enrichment Services shall not be subject to financing conditions more favourable than those applicable to the provision of nuclear fuel.

Appendix

PRIOR CONSULTATIONS ON TERMS OF EXPORT CREDITS FOR NUCLEAR POWER PLANTS

1. In the light of past practical experience with one major project and taking into account the progress which has been made in certain respects in the current negotiation the Participants recognise the advantages which can accrue if, pending agreement on a formal Arrangement on export credits for Nuclear Power Plants, a common attitude toward the credit terms can be achieved for particular export credit transactions of such plant. They therefore agreed as an interim measure to engage in prior consultations in all cases a participant intends to give support to such a transaction.

2. To this end the participant initiating the consultation shall notify by telex at least ten days before taking a final decision all other participants of the terms he intends to support specifying, inter alia, the following details:

    a) Cash payments;

    b) Repayment term (including starting point of credit, frequency of instalments for repaying principal amount of credit, and whether these instalments will be equal in amount);

    c) Currency and value rating of the contract (in accordance with paragraph 7 of Annex VI);

    d) Interest rate;

    e) Support for local costs (including the total amount of local costs expressed as a percentage of the total value of goods and services exported, the terms of repayment, and the nature of the support to be given);

    f) Portion of project to be financed, with separate information for initial fuel load, when appropriate;

    g) Any other relevant information including references to related cases.

3. Each participant having received the initial notification by the consulting participant shall in the following ten days not take a final decision on the terms he will support, but shall within five days exchange with all other participants in the consultation views on the appropriate credit terms for the transaction in question with the objective of achieving a common attitude on such terms.

4. If by these exchanges of views by telex a common attitude is not achieved within ten days after the receipt of the initial notification the final decision of each participant in the consultation will be delayed an additional ten days during which period further efforts to achieve a common attitude will be made at face to face consultations.

Annex IV

SECTOR UNDERSTANDING ON EXPORT CREDITS FOR CIVIL AIRCRAFT

Chapter I. LARGE COMMERCIAL AIRCRAFT

1. Form and Scope

This Chapter complements the Arrangement on Guidelines for Officially Supported Export Credits. It sets out the particular complementary guidelines that are applicable to officially supported export credits for financing sales or leases of large civil aircraft listed in the Appendix and supersedes the terms of the OECD "Standstill" (TC/ECG/M/75.1, item 6 and Annex III–A) with respect to such aircraft.

2. Objectives of this Chapter

The objective of this Chapter is to establish a balanced equilibrium that, on all markets:
- equalises competitive financial conditions between participants;
- neutralises finance among participants as a factor in the choice among competing aircraft; and
- avoids distortions of competition.

3. Credit Terms and Conditions

a) Cash payments

The minimum cash payment is 15 per cent of the aircraft's total price (the price of the airframe and any installed engines plus the spare engines and spare parts described in paragraph 9). Participants shall not provide official support for such cash payments other than insurance and guarantees against the usual pre–credit risks.

b) Maximum repayment term

The maximum repayment term of an officially supported credit is twelve years.

4. Minimum Interest Rates

a) Notwithstanding the provisions of paragraph 5 below, the following minimum interest rates, inclusive of credit insurance premia and guarantees, apply where participants are providing official financing support by way of direct credit, refinancing or interest rate subsidy:

1. *Financing in US dollars*

Number of years in maximum repayment term

Up to 10 years	*Over 10–12 years*
TB 10 + 120 basis points	TB 10 + 175 basis points

where TB + 10 means ten–year Treasury bond yields at constant maturity, averaged over the previous two calendar weeks.

2. *Financing in the currencies of the currency cocktail (DM, FF, £, ECU)*[1]

A currency cocktail package, based on ten–year government bond yields for DM, FF, and £[2], plus a margin applies. This margin, calculated as a weighted average of the margins applicable to each currency, is equal to the margin applicable in the case of financing in US dollars.

In the case of financing in ECU, the minimum rate applicable is the long–term ECU bond yield[3] less 20 basis points plus a margin equal to the margin applicable in the case of financing in US dollars.

b) Interest rate adjustments

An adjustment is made to the minimum rates of interest set out in a) above if the two–weekly average of the ten–year government bond yields at constant maturity at the end of each two–week period differs by 10 basis points or more from the average of the ten–year government bond yield at constant maturity at the end of the last two calendar weeks of June 1985. When such a change occurs, the levels of the minimum rates of interest set out above are adjusted by the same number of basis points and the recalculated minimum rates are rounded off to the nearest 5 basis points. Subsequently, minimum rates of interest are adjusted on a two–weekly basis according to the aforementioned method if there is a change of ten basis points or more in the interest rate underlying the preceding change in minimum rates of interest. Similar provisions apply to the ECU in the case of changes in the ECU bond yield.

c) Special adjustments

1. If a participant believes that at least two significant sales in any six–month period:

i) for which participants are direct competitors; and

ii) on which offers have been made with official financial support [see paragraphs 5a) and b)] have been concluded on a pure cover basis, other than PEFCO, at a fixed interest rate below the applicable minimum interest rates specified in this Chapter;

the participants shall consult immediately in order to determine the interest rates on the basis of which the sales have been concluded and, if necessary, to find a permanent solution that ensures that the objectives of paragraph 2 are fully met.

2. If during these consultations:

    i) it cannot be determined whether the interest rates for the sales in question were at, above, or equivalent to the applicable minimum interest rates specified in this Chapter; and

    ii) if a solution cannot be found within thirty days from the start of the consultations;

then the minimum interest rates specified in paragraph 4 a) 1) are reduced by 15 basis points, unless the participants agree that the sales concerned are not significant. In no case is the interest rate for the ten–year option reduced below TB 10 plus 105 basis points. Such adjustments are made without prejudice to continuing consultations to find a solution, including the possibility of a recoupment in the event that additional cases do not occur.

3. If, in any six–month period, two or more sales for which participants are direct competitors are concluded on a floating–rate pure cover basis, consultations to ensure that the objectives of paragraph 2 are fully met shall be held at the request of any participant.

d) Differential between ten and twelve year financing options[4]

1. If, subject to the conditions outlined below, at the end of the period between 1st July 1985 and 1st July 1986, 66 per cent or more of all sales of aircraft, financed either by means of official support or by PEFCO, have been concluded on a ten–year term, then the minimum interest rate on the ten–year financing option shall be increased by 15 basis points.

If, during the following year, 66 per cent or more of all sales of aircraft, financed either by means of official support or by PEFCO, have been concluded on a ten–year term, then the participants shall review the differential between ten and twelve–year financing options with a view to finding a permanent solution to the problem of equating the differential between the two options. If, on the other hand 66 per cent or more of the above sales have been concluded under the ten to twelve–year financing option, then the minimum interest rate on the ten–year financing option shall be decreased by 10 basis points.

2. If, subject to the conditions outlined below, at the end of the period 1st July 1985 and 1st July 1986, 66 per cent or more of all such sales have been concluded on a ten to twelve–year term then the minimum interest rate on the ten–year financing option shall be decreased by 15 basis points.

If, during the following year, 66 per cent or more of all sales of aircraft have been concluded under the ten to twelve–year term, then the participants shall review the differential between ten and twelve–year financing options with a view to finding a permanent solution to the problem of equating the differential between the two options. If, on the other hand, 66 per cent or more of the above sales have been concluded under the ten–year option, then the ten–year minimum interest rate shall be increased by 10 basis points.

e) Date of determination of interest rate offer

A participant may offer the borrower a choice of one of the two following methods for selecting the date on which the minimum interest rate [as defined in paragraph 4 a) *et seq.*] on official fixed interest rate financing [see paragraph 5 a) below] and on PEFCO financing [see paragraph 5 b) below] is determined. The selection by the borrower is irrevocable. The minimum rate is:

> i) the minimum rate prevailing on the date of the offer by the lender, or
> ii) the minimum rate prevailing on whichever one of a series of dates may be selected by the borrower. The date selected shall in no event be later than the date of delivery of the aircraft.

5. Amount of Financing

a) *Official fixed interest rate financing*

1. The maximum percentage of the aircraft total price [as that term is defined in paragraph 3 a)] that may be financed at the fixed minimum rates specified in paragraph 4 a) by means of official financing support is 62.5 per cent when repayment of the loan is spread over the entire life of the financing and 42.5 per cent when repayment of the loan is spread over the later maturities. Participants are free to use either repayment approach, subject to the ceiling applicable to that pattern. A participant offering such a tranche shall notify the other participants of the amount, the interest rate, the date on which the interest rate is set, the validity period for the interest rate and the pattern of repayment.

2. The Participants will review the two ceilings at the time of each review pursuant to paragraph 16 to examine whether one ceiling provides more advantages than the other with a view to adjusting the more advantageous so that a balance is more evenly struck.

b) *PEFCO financing*

1. Fixed–rate funds may be officially financed in a manner comparable to that provided by the Private Export Funding Corporation (PEFCO). Weekly information on PEFCO's borrowing costs and applicable lending rates, exclusive of official guarantee fees on fixed–rate finance for immediate disbursement and for disbursements over a series of dates, for contract offers and for bid offers, shall be communicated to the other participants on a regular basis. A participant offering such a tranche shall notify the other participants of the amount, interest rates, date on which interest rate is set, validity period for the interest rate and pattern of repayments. Any participant matching such financing offered by another participant shall match it in all of its terms and conditions other than the validity period of offers of commitment (see paragraph 6).

2. These rates as notified shall be applicable by all participants as long as the twenty–four month disbursement interest rate does not exceed 225 basis points above TB 10 (see paragraph 4). In the event the twenty–four month rate exceeds 225 basis points, participants are free to apply the rate of 225 basis points for twenty–four months disbursement and all the corresponding rates and shall consult immediately with a view to finding a permanent solution.

c) *"Pure cover" tranche*

Official support by means of guarantees only ("pure cover") is permitted subject to the ceiling specified in d) below. However, a participant offering such a tranche shall notify the other participants of the amount, term, pattern of repayments, and, where possible, interest rates.

d) Total official support

The total amount of funds benefitting from official support pursuant to paragraphs 5 a), b) and c) above shall not exceed 85 per cent of the total price as defined in paragraph 3 a) above.

6. Validity Period of Commitments

The duration of fixed interest rate offers of commitment on the tranches of financing defined in paragraphs 5 a) and 5 b) shall not exceed three months.

7. Fees

Commitment and management fees are not included in the interest rate.

8. Security

Participants retain the right to decide upon security acceptable to themselves autonomously and will communicate fully to other participants on this point, as requested or when deemed appropriate.

9. Spare Engines and Spare Parts

The financing of these items is provided as a function of the size of the fleet of each specific aircraft type, including aircraft being acquired, aircraft already of firm order or aircraft already owned, on the following basis:

- *For the first five aircraft of the type in the fleet:* 15 per cent of the aircraft price (airframe and installed engines);
- *For the sixth and subsequent aircraft of that type in the fleet:* 10 per cent of the aircraft price (airframe and installed engines).

Participants reserve the right to change their practice and match the practices of competing participants in matters of detail relating to the timing of the first repayment with respect to spare engines and spare parts.

10. Tied Aid Credits

Participants shall not provide tied or partially untied aid financing, or provide any other kind of financing on credit conditions that are more favourable than those set out in this Chapter.

11. Prior Commitments

Participants reserve the right to honour all financing commitments made prior to 1st July 1985 and the dates of all subsequent changes in interest rates. They reserve the right to match offers made by other participants.

12. Model Changes

It is understood that when a loan contract has been concluded on one type of aircraft, the terms contained therein cannot be transferred to another type bearing a different model designation.

13. Leases

It is also understood that a participant may match a twelve–year officially supported lease transaction with a twelve–year repayment term and 85 per cent credit financing support, subject to the other terms and conditions of this Chapter.

14. Competition Reference Point

In the event of officially supported competition, aircraft that are in the list of large civil aircraft in the Appendix and that compete with other aircraft may benefit from the same export credit terms and conditions.

15. Procedures

The procedures outlined in the Arrangement on Guidelines for Officially Supported Export Credits apply to this Chapter. In addition, should any participant believe that another participant is offering an officially supported export credit that is not in conformity with the Guidelines without giving advance notice, consultations shall be held within ten days upon request.

16. Review

The information procedures and conditions outlined in this Chapter are subject in principle to an annual review. However, the Participants shall review the provisions of this Chapter whenever requested, notably in relation to the possible development of certain financing and interest rate trends [see paragraphs 4 c) and d)].

Chapter II. ALL AIRCRAFT EXCEPT LARGE COMMERCIAL AIRCRAFT

17. Form and Scope

This Chapter complements the Arrangement on Guidelines for Officially Supported Export Credits. It sets out the particular complementing Guidelines that are applicable to officially supported export credits financing contracts for the international sale or lease of new (not used) aircraft and, if ordered concurrently with the aircraft or if ordered for manufacturing or assembly into such aircraft, engines, sub–assemblies and spare parts of aircraft not covered by Chapter I of this Chapter. It does not apply to hovercraft.

18. Participation

The rules on participation of the Arrangement shall apply.

19. Best Endeavours

The provisions of this Chapter represent the most generous terms that participants are allowed to offer when giving official support. Participants shall however continue to respect customary market terms for different types of aircraft and shall do everything in their power to prevent these terms from being eroded.[5]

20. Categories of Aircraft

The following categories have been agreed upon in view of the competitive situation:

- A. — Turbine–powered aircraft — including helicopters — (e.g. turbo jet, turbo-prop, and turbo–fan aircraft), with generally between 30 to 70 seats. In case a new large turbine–powered aircraft with over 70 seats is being developed, immediate consultations shall be held upon request with a view to agree on the classification of such an aircraft in this category or in chapter I of this Understanding in view of the competitive situation.
- B. — Other turbine–powered aircraft, including helicopters.
- C. — Other aircraft, including helicopters.

An illustrative list of aircraft in categories A and B is in the Annex.

21. Credit Terms and Conditions

Participants undertake not to support credit terms more favourable than those set out in this paragraph.

Category A.	ten years at matrix rates for recipient countries classified in categories II and III[6] or respective CIRRs.
Category B.	seven years at matrix rates for recipient countries classified in categories II and III[6] or respective CIRRs.
Category C.	five years at matrix rates for recipient countries classified in categories II and III[6] or respective CIRRs.

22. Sales or Leases to Third Countries (relay countries)

In cases where the aircraft are to be on–sold or on–leased to an end–buyer or end–user in a third country, the interest rate shall be that applicable to the country of final destination.

23. Matching Provisions

In the event of officially supported competition, aircraft competing with those from another category or chapter shall for a specific sale be able to benefit from matching of the same export credit terms and conditions. Before making the matching offer, the matching authority shall make reasonable efforts to determine the export credit terms and conditions the competing aircraft benefits from. The matching authority will be considered to have made such reasonable efforts if it has informed by telex the authority assumed to offer the terms it intends to match of its intention to do so but has not been informed within three working days that the terms it intends to match will not be used to support the transaction in question.

24. Insurance Premiums and Guarantee Fees

Participants shall not waive in part or in total insurance premiums or guarantee fees.

25. Tied Aid Credits Prohibition

Participants shall not provide tied aid financing, partially untied aid financing, or any other kind of financing on credit conditions that are more favourable than those set out in this Chapter.

26. Consultation and Notification Procedures

The procedures of the Arrangement shall apply to officially supported export credits not in conformity with the terms of this Chapter. In addition, should any participant believe that another participant may be offering an officially supported export credit not in conformity with this Chapter without giving advance notice, consultations shall be held within ten days upon request.

27. Review

The provisions of this Chapter are subject to review annually, normally during the spring meeting of the Participants of the Arrangement. In the review, the Participants will examine possible modifications of the provisions, notably in order to bring them closer to market conditions.[7] In addition, if market conditions or customary financing practices change considerably, any participant is entitled to ask for a special review of the provisions.

NOTES AND REFERENCES

1. The "currency cocktail" financing for the A 300 and A 310 consists of the following percentages of the following currencies:
    — Deutschemark or ECU   40 per cent
    — French franc or ECU   40 per cent
    — UK pound sterling, or
        US dollar or ECU   20 per cent

    For the A 320, the "currency cocktail" consists of the following percentages of the following currencies:
    — Deutschemark or ECU   33.7 per cent (provisional)
    — French franc or ECU   40.0 per cent (provisional)
    — UK pound sterling, or
        US dollar or ECU   26.3 per cent (provisional)

2. At constant maturity, averaged over the previous two calendar weeks.

3. As published by the Luxembourg Stock Exchange — long term bond series, averaged over the previous two calendar weeks.

4. For the operational purposes of this paragraph, it is understood that:
    — The test sample will include only those cases in which the two financing options have been offered by at least one participant;
    — The activation of an interest rate adjustment may take place only if 66 per cent of sales of aircraft according to one option have been concluded under two or more separate transactions;
    — The term "sales of aircraft" signifies that each separate aircraft sold is included in the sample.

5. Best endeavours shall be made *inter alia* with respect to the willingness to respond favourably to the invitation by another participant to consult on possibilities of achieving conditions as close to the market as possible, for example in matching.

6. Before the 15th of July 1988, applicable matrix rates may also be used for recipient countries classified in category I, the minimum interest rate applicable for repayment terms of over 8.5 and up to ten years being the same as for repayment terms of over 5 and up to 8.5 years.

7. Pending the review on official support for export of used aircraft and conditions for maintenance, spare parts and service contracts, these goods and services are covered by the Arrangement on Guidelines for Officially Supported Export Credits. The tied aid credits prohibition in paragraph 25 of this Chapter applies.

Appendix

ILLUSTRATIVE LIST

All other similar aircraft that may be introduced in the future shall be covered by this Sector Understanding and shall be added to the appropriate list in due course. These lists are not exhaustive and serve only to indicate the type of aircraft to be included in the different categories where doubts could arise.

LARGE CIVIL AIRCRAFT

Manufacturer	*Designation*
Airbus	A 300
Airbus	A 310
Airbus	A 320
Airbus	A 321
Airbus	A 330
Airbus	A 340
Boeing	B 737
Boeing	B 747
Boeing	B 757
Boeing	B 767
British Aerospace	BAe 146
Fokker	F 100
McDonnell Douglas	MD–80 Series
McDonnell Douglas	MD–11

CATEGORY A AIRCRAFT

Turbine–powered aircraft — including helicopters — (e.g. turbo jet, turbo–prop and turbo–fan aircraft), with generally between 30 to 70 seats. In case a new large turbine–powered aircraft with over 70 seats is being developed, immediate consultations shall be held upon request with a view to agree on the classification of such an aircraft in this Category or in Chapter I of this Understanding in view of the competitive situation.

Manufacturer	Designation
Aeritalia	G 222
Aeritalia/Aérospatiale	ATR 42
Aeritalia/Aérospatiale	ATR 72
Aérospatiale/MBB	C160 Transall
Boeing Canada	Dash 8
Boeing Vertol	234 Chinook
Broman (U.S.)	BR 2000
British Aerospace	BAe ATP
British Aerospace	BAe Jetstream 41
Canadair	CL 215T
Canadair	RJ
Casa	CN235
Dornier	DO 328
EH Industries	EH–101
Embraer	EMB 120 Brasilia
Fokker	F 50
Gulfstream America	Gulfstream 1–4
Lockheed	L 100
Saab	SF 340
Short	SD 3–30
Short	SD 3–60
Short	Sherpa
etc.	

CATEGORY B AIRCRAFT

Other turbine–powered aircraft, including helicopters.

Aérospatiale	AS 332
Beech	1900
Beech	Super King Air 300
Beech	Starship 1
Bell Helicopter	206B
Bell Helicopter	206L
Bell Helicopter	212
Bell Helicopter	412
Boeing	F 406
British Aerospace	BAe Jetstream 31
British Aerospace	BAe 125
British Aerospace	BAe 1000
British Aerospace	BAe Jetstream Super 31
Canadair	Challenger 601
Canadair	CL 215 (water bomber)
Casa	C 212–200
Casa	C 212–300
Cessna	Citation
Cessna	441 Conquest III

Claudius Dornier	CD2
Dassault Breguet	Falcon
Dornier	Do 228–200
Embraer/FAMA	CBA 123
Fairchild	Merlin/300
Fairchild	Metro 25
Fairchild	Metro III V
Gates Learjet	20, 30 and 55 series
Gulfstream America	Gulfstream III and IV
IAI	Arava 101 B
Mitsubishi	Mu2 Marquise
Piaggio	P 180
Pilatus Britten–Norman	BN2T Islander
Piper	PA–42–100 (Cheyenne 400)
Piper	PA–42–720 (Cheyenne III A)
Reims	Cessna–Caravan II
SIAI–Marchetti	SF 600 Canguro
Westland	W30
etc.	

Annex V

STANDARD FORM FOR NOTIFICATIONS REQUIRED UNDER PARAGRAPHS 14 AND 15

Points to be covered in each and every notification:

1. Name of authority/agency responsible under the Arrangement for making notifications.

2. Reference number (country indication, serial number, year).

3. We are notifying

   — under paragraph (choose one) of the Arrangement
     — 14 *a)* 1) derogation
     — 14 *b)* 1) *i)* "long term" credit to a Category I country
     — 14 *b)* 1) *ii)* "abnormal" payment practices
     — 14 *b)* 1) *iii)* "long term" credit for a conventional power plant
     — 14 *b)* 1) *iv)* "derogating" credit for ship
     — 14 *c)* 1) tied or partially untied aid credit, concessionality level less than 50%
     — 14 *c)* 2) untied aid credit, concessionality level less than 50%
     — 14 *d)* tied or partially untied aid credit, concessionality level 50% or more
     — 15 *a)* 1) *i)* identical matching of a derogation
     — 15 *a)* 1) *ii)* matching by other support of a derogation
     — 15 *a)* 2) *i)* identical matching of a transaction notified under paragraph 14 *b)* 1) [specify *i) – iv)*]
     — 15 *a)* 2) *ii)* matching by other support of a transaction notified under paragraph 14 *b)* 1) [specify i) – *iv)*]
     — 15 *a)* 3) matching a transaction notified under paragraph 14 *c)* 1) (specify "identical" or "by other support")
     — 15 *a)* 4) matching of a transaction notified under paragraph 14 *d)*
     — 15 *b)* 2) matching terms offered by a non–participant
     — 15 *c)* 3) *i)* identical matching of a prior commitment
     — 15 *c)* 3) *ii)* matching by other means of a prior commitment
   — under the Understanding on Export Credits for Nuclear Power Plants
   — under the Sector Arrangement for Civil Aircraft.

4. Country of buyer/borrower.

5. Name, location and status (public/private) of buyer/borrower.

6. Nature of project/goods to be exported; location of project; closing date of tender if relevant, expiry date of credit line.

7. a) Contract value;
   b) Value of the credit or credit line;
   c) Value of exporter's national share;
   d) Minimum contract value of credit line.

   These values shall be stated as follows:
   — The exact value in the denominated currency for a line of credit;
   — The value of an individual project or contract should be disclosed in terms of value ratings in accordance with the following scale in Special Drawing Rights (SDRs):

Category I	:	up to	1 000 000	SDRs		
Category II	:	from	1 000 000		to	2 000 000 SDRs
Category III	:	from	2 000 000		to	3 000 000 SDRs
Category IV	:	from	3 000 000		to	5 000 000 SDRs
Category V	:	from	5 000 000		to	7 000 000 SDRs
Category VI	:	from	7 000 000		to	10 000 000 SDRs
Category VII	:	from	10 000 000		to	20 000 000 SDRs
Category VIII	:	from	20 000 000		to	40 000 000 SDRs
Category IX	:	from	40 000 000		to	80 000 000 SDRs
Category X	:	from	80 000 000		to	120 000 000 SDRs
Category XI	:	from	120 000 000		to	160 000 000 SDRs
Category XII	:	from	160 000 000		to	200 000 000 SDRs
Category XIII	:	from	200 000 000		to	240 000 000 SDRs
Category XIV	:	from	240 000 000		to	280 000 000 SDRs
Category XV	:	exceeding	280 000 000	SDRs*		

   * Indicate actual level within multiples of 40 000 000 SDRs

   When using this scale please indicate currency of the contract.

8. Credit terms which reporting organisation intends to support (or has supported):
   a) Cash payments;
   b) Repayment term (including starting point of credit, frequency of instalments for repaying principal amount of credit, and whether these instalments will be equal in amount);
   c) Interest rate;
   d) Support for local costs (including the total amount of local costs expressed as a percentage of the total value of goods and services exported, the terms of repayment, and the nature of the support to be given).

9. Any other relevant information including references to related cases and where relevant:

a) Justification for: matching (specify reference number of notification matched or other references) or granting long term credits for Category I countries or conventional power plants, etc.

b) The overall concessionality level of the tied and partially untied aid financing calculated in accordance with paragraph 22 *m)* and the discount rate used to calculate that concessionality level;

c) Treatment of cash payments in the calculation of the concessionality level;

d) Development aid or premixed credit or associated finance;

e) Restrictions on use of credit lines.

Annex VI

FRAMEWORK FOR INFORMATION EXCHANGE (FIE)

1. Scope

The Framework for Information Exchange (FIE) concerns credit terms and conditions for any export credit or credit guarantee transactions that are covered by paragraph 1 *a)* of the Arrangement, as well as any aid transaction that is covered by the notification procedures of paragraph 14.

2. Information exchange

a) A participant:
— may address to another participant an enquiry on the attitude it takes in respect of a third country, of an institution in a third country or of a particular method of doing business;
— who has received an application for official support, may address an enquiry to another participant giving the most favourable credit terms that the enquiring participant would be willing to support; or
— who has received allegations that another participant has offered official support that derogates from the guidelines of the Arrangement, may address an enquiry to another participant, stating the details of any such allegation.

If an enquiry is to more than one participant, it shall contain a list of addressees. A copy of all enquiries shall be sent to the Secretariat.

b) The participant to whom an enquiry is addressed shall respond within seven calendar days with as much information as is available at that time. The reply shall include, if possible, the best indication that the participant can give of the decision likely to be taken. If necessary, the full reply shall follow as soon as possible. Copies shall be sent to the other addressees of the enquiry and to the Secretariat.

c) If an answer to an enquiry subsequently becomes invalid because an application has been made, changed or withdrawn, because other terms are being considered, or for any other reason, a follow-up reply shall be made at once and copied to all other addressees of the enquiry and to the Secretariat.

d) All communications shall be made between the designated contact points in each country by means of instant communication (e.g. electronic mail, telex, telefax) and shall be confidential.

3. Special arrangements to prevent a "fait accompli"

a) The information exchange or face–to–face consultations (see the Protocol to the Arrangement) may lead to a common line.

- When a date deadline for bids has been set, the intention to submit a bid that is more favourable than agreed in the common line must be notified to all participants concerned and to the Secretariat at least seven calendar days before the date deadline or the conclusion of negotiations.
- In other cases, such a notification shall be sent to all participants concerned and to the Secretariat not later than the date of commitment.

b) In cases of matching, bids more favourable than agreed in the common line may be submitted even if the deadlines specified in 3 *a)* above cannot be observed if a participant informs all participants concerned and the Secretariat of the need to match and if it observes a waiting period of at least 48 hours before commitment.

Annex VII

DETERMINATION OF COMMERCIAL INTEREST REFERENCE RATES

1.   The Participants have accepted the following aims for evaluating specific commercial interest reference rates (CIRRs):

   i) The CIRR should be representative of final commercial lending rates of interest in the domestic market of the currency concerned;

   ii) The CIRR should closely correspond to a rate for a first class domestic borrower;

   iii) The CIRR should be based, where appropriate, on the funding cost of fixed interest–rate finance over a period of not less than five years;

   iv) The CIRR should not lead to a distortion of domestic competitive conditions;

   v) The CIRR should closely correspond to a rate available to first–class foreign borrowers.

2.   In view of these aims, the Participants have decided that CIRRs shall be set at a fixed margin above their respective base rates.

   a) The base rate is the yield on the secondary market for government bonds with a residual maturity of five years except where the Participants have agreed otherwise.

   b) The fixed margin is 100 basis points, except where the Participants have agreed otherwise.

3.   For all CIRRs, especially those for currencies that are not calculated according to the standard rules laid out in paragraph 2 above for determining the base rate and the fixed margin, the Participants shall continue consultations as provided elsewhere in this Arrangement.

WHERE TO OBTAIN OECD PUBLICATIONS
OÙ OBTENIR LES PUBLICATIONS DE L'OCDE

Argentina – Argentine
Carlos Hirsch S.R.L.
Galería Güemes, Florida 165, 4° Piso
1333 Buenos Aires
Tel. 30.7122, 331.1787 y 331.2391
Telegram: Hirsch–Baires
Telex: 21112 UAPE–AR. Ref. s/2901
Telefax:(1)331-1787

Australia – Australie
D.A. Book (Aust.) Pty. Ltd.
11-13 Station Street (P.O. Box 163)
Mitcham, Vic. 3132   Tel. (03)873.4411
Telex: AA37911 DA BOOK
Telefax: (03)873.5679

Austria – Autriche
OECD Publications and Information Centre
4 Simrockstrasse
5300 Bonn (Germany)   Tel. (0228)21.60.45
Telex: 8 86300 Bonn
Telefax: (0228)26.11.04
Gerold & Co.
Graben 31
Wien 1   Tel. (0222)533.50.14

Belgium – Belgique
Jean De Lannoy
Avenue du Roi 202
B-1060 Bruxelles
Tel. (02)538.51.69/538.08.41
Telex: 63220 Telefax: (02)538.08.41

Canada
Renouf Publishing Company Ltd.
1294 Algoma Road
Ottawa, Ont. K1B 3W8 Tel. (613)741.4333
Telex: 053-4783 Telefax: (613)741.5439
Stores:
61 Sparks Street
Ottawa, Ont. K1P 5R1   Tel. (613)238.8985
211 Yonge Street
Toronto, Ont. M5B 1M4 Tel. (416)363.3171
Federal Publications
165 University Avenue
Toronto, ON M5H 3B9   Tel. (416)581.1552
Telefax: (416)581.1743
Les Publications Fédérales
1185 rue de l'Université
Montréal, PQ H3B 1R7   Tel.(514)954-1633
Les Éditions La Liberté Inc.
3020 Chemin Sainte-Foy
Sainte-Foy, P.Q. G1X 3V6
                        Tel. (418)658.3763
Telefax: (418)658.3763

Denmark – Danemark
Munksgaard Export and Subscription Service
35, Nørre Søgade, P.O. Box 2148
DK-1016 København K
                      Tel. (45 33)12.85.70
Telex: 19431 MUNKS DK
              Telefax: (45 33)12.93.87

Finland – Finlande
Akateeminen Kirjakauppa
Keskuskatu 1, P.O. Box 128
00100 Helsinki   Tel. (358 0)12141
Telex: 125080 Telefax: (358 0)121.4441

France
OECD/OCDE
Mail Orders/Commandes par correspon-
dance:
2 rue André-Pascal
75775 Paris Cedex 16   Tel. (1)45.24.82.00
Bookshop/Librairie:
33, rue Octave-Feuillet
75016 Paris   Tel. (1)45.24.81.67
                           (1)45.24.81.81
Telex: 620 160 OCDE
Telefax: (33-1)45.24.85.00
Librairie de l'Université
12a, rue Nazareth
13602 Aix-en-Provence Tel. 42.26.18.08

Germany – Allemagne
OECD Publications and Information Centre
4 Simrockstrasse
5300 Bonn   Tel. (0228)21.60.45
Telex: 8 86300 Bonn
                Telefax: (0228)26.11.04

Greece – Grèce
Librairie Kauffmann
28 rue du Stade
105 64 Athens   Tel. 322.21.60
Telex: 218187 LIKA Gr

Hong Kong
Government Information Services
Publications (Sales) Office
Information Service Department
No. 1 Battery Path
Central   Tel. (5)23.31.91
Telex: 802.61190

Iceland – Islande
Mal Mog Menning
Laugavegi 18, Pósthólf 392
121 Reykjavik   Tel. 15199/24240

India – Inde
Oxford Book and Stationery Co.
Scindia House
New Delhi 110001   Tel. 331.5896/5308
Telex: 31 61990 AM IN
Telefax: (11)332.5993
17 Park Street
Calcutta 700016   Tel. 240832

Indonesia – Indonésie
Pdii-Lipi
P.O. Box 269/JKSMG/88
Jakarta12790   Tel. 583467
Telex: 62 875

Ireland – Irlande
TDC Publishers – Library Suppliers
12 North Frederick Street
Dublin 1   Tel. 744835/749677
Telex: 33530 TDCP EI Telefax : 748416

Italy – Italie
Libreria Commissionaria Sansoni
Via Benedetto Fortini, 120/10
Casella Post. 552
50125 Firenze   Tel. (055)645415
Telex: 570466 Telefax: (39.55)641257
Via Bartolini 29
20155 Milano   Tel. 365083
La diffusione delle pubblicazioni OCSE viene
assicurata dalle principali librerie ed anche
da:
Editrice e Libreria Herder
Piazza Montecitorio 120
00186 Roma   Tel. 679.4628
Telex: NATEL I 621427
Libreria Hoepli
Via Hoepli 5
20121 Milano   Tel. 865446
Telex: 31.33.95 Telefax: (39.2)805.2886
Libreria Scientifica
Dott. Lucio de Biasio "Aeiou"
Via Meravigli 16
20123 Milano   Tel. 807679
Telefax: 800175

Japan – Japon
OECD Publications and Information Centre
Landic Akasaka Building
2-3-4 Akasaka, Minato-ku
Tokyo 107   Tel. 586.2016
Telefax: (81.3)584.7929

Korea – Corée
Kyobo Book Centre Co. Ltd.
P.O. Box 1658, Kwang Hwa Moon
Seoul   Tel. (REP)730.78.91
Telefax: 735.0030

Malaysia/Singapore –
Malaisie/Singapour
University of Malaya Co-operative Bookshop
Ltd.
P.O. Box 1127, Jalan Pantai Baru 59100
Kuala Lumpur
Malaysia   Tel. 756.5000/756.5425
Telefax: 757.3661
Information Publications Pte. Ltd.
Pei-Fu Industrial Building
24 New Industrial Road No. 02-06
Singapore 1953   Tel. 283.1786/283.1798
Telefax: 284.8875

Netherlands – Pays-Bas
SDU Uitgeverij
Christoffel Plantijnstraat 2
Postbus 20014
2500 EA's-Gravenhage Tel. (070)78.99.11
Voor bestellingen: Tel. (070)78.98.80
Telex: 32486 stdru Telefax: (070)47.63.51

New Zealand –Nouvelle-Zélande
Government Printing Office
Customer Services
P.O. Box 12-411
Freepost 10–050
Thorndon, Wellington
Tel. 0800 733-406   Telefax: 04 499-1733

Norway – Norvège
Narvesen Info Center – NIC
Bertrand Narvesens vei 2
P.O. Box 6125 Etterstad
0602 Oslo 6
         Tel. (02)67.83.10/(02)68.40.20
Telex: 79668 NIC N Telefax: (47 2)68.53.47

Pakistan
Mirza Book Agency
65 Shahrah Quaid-E-Azam
Lahore 3   Tel. 66839
Telex: 44886 UBL PK. Attn: MIRZA BK

Portugal
Livraria Portugal
Rua do Carmo 70-74
1117 Lisboa Codex   Tel. 347.49.82/3/4/5

Singapore/Malaysia
Singapour/Malaisie
See "Malaysia/Singapore"
Voir "Malaisie/Singapour"

Spain – Espagne
Mundi-Prensa Libros S.A.
Castello 37, Apartado 1223
Madrid 28001   Tel. (91) 431.33.99
Telex: 49370 MPLI Telefax: (91) 275.39.98
Libreria Internacional AEDOS
Consejo de Ciento 391
08009 -Barcelona   Tel. (93) 301-86-15
Telefax: (93) 317-01-41

Sweden – Suède
Fritzes Fackboksföretaget
Box 16356, S 103 27 STH
Regeringsgatan 12
DS Stockholm   Tel. (08)23.89.00
Telex: 12387 Telefax: (08)20.50.21
Subscription Agency/Abonnements:
Wennergren-Williams AB
Box 30004
104 25 Stockholm   Tel. (08)54.12.00
Telex: 19937 Telefax: (08)50.82.86

Switzerland – Suisse
OECD Publications and Information Centre
4 Simrockstrasse
5300 Bonn (Germany)   Tel. (0228)21.60.45
Telex: 8 86300 Bonn
Telefax: (0228)26.11.04
Librairie Payot
6 rue Grenus
1211 Genève 11   Tel. (022)731.89.50
Telex: 28356
Maditec S.A.
Ch. des Palettes 4
1020 Renens/Lausanne Tel. (021)635.08.65
Telefax: (021)635.07.80
United Nations Bookshop/Librairie des Na-
tions-Unies
Palais des Nations
1211 Genève 10
        Tel. (022)734.60.11 (ext. 48.72)
Telex: 289696 (Attn: Sales)
Telefax: (022)733.98.79

Taïwan – Formose
Good Faith Worldwide Int'l. Co. Ltd.
9th Floor, No. 118, Sec. 2
Chung Hsiao E. Road
Taipei   Tel. 391.7396/391.7397
Telefax: (02) 394.9176

Thailand – Thalande
Suksit Siam Co. Ltd.
1715 Rama IV Road, Samyan
Bangkok 5   Tel. 251.1630

Turkey – Turquie
Kültur Yayinlari Is-Türk Ltd. Sti.
Atatürk Bulvari No. 191/Kat. 21
Kavaklidere/Ankara   Tel. 25.07.60
Dolmabahce Cad. No. 29
Besiktas/Istanbul   Tel. 160.71.88
Telex: 43482B

United Kingdom – Royaume-Uni
H.M. Stationery Office
Gen. enquiries   Tel. (01) 873 0011
Postal orders only:
P.O. Box 276, London SW8 5DT
Personal Callers HMSO Bookshop
49 High Holborn, London WC1V 6HB
Telex: 297138 Telefax: 873.8463
Branches at: Belfast, Birmingham, Bristol,
Edinburgh, Manchester

United States – États-Unis
OECD Publications and Information Centre
2001 L Street N.W., Suite 700
Washington, D.C. 20036-4095
                      Tel. (202)785.6323
Telex: 440245 WASHINGTON D.C.
Telefax: (202)785.0350

Venezuela
Libreria del Este
Avda F. Miranda 52, Aptdo. 60337
Edificio Galipan
Caracas 106
           Tel. 951.1705/951.2307/951.1297
Telegram: Libreste Caracas

Yugoslavia – Yougoslavie
Jugoslovenska Knjiga
Knez Mihajlova 2, P.O. Box 36
Beograd   Tel. 621.992
Telex: 12466 jk bgd

Orders and inquiries from countries where
Distributors have not yet been appointed
should be sent to: OECD Publications
Service, 2 rue André-Pascal, 75775 Paris
Cedex 16.
Les commandes provenant de pays où
l'OCDE n'a pas encore désigné de dis-
tributeur devraient être adressées à : OCDE,
Service des Publications, 2, rue André-
Pascal, 75775 Paris Cedex 16.

OECD PUBLICATIONS, 2 rue André-Pascal, 75775 PARIS CEDEX 16
PRINTED IN FRANCE
(22 90 01 1) ISBN 92-64-13358-5 - No. 45143 1990

THE EXPORT CREDIT FINANCING SYSTEMS IN OECD MEMBER COUNTRIES

FOURTH EDITION

(22 90 01 1) ISBN 92–64–13358–5

ERRATUM

These pages cancel and replace Chapter 4 (pages 43 to 51 inclusive) and Chapter 16 (pages 167 to 172 inclusive).

Chapter 4

FRANCE

1.   ORGANISATION AND STRUCTURE

1.1   Insurance and Guarantees

1.1.1   *Representative Organisation*

Compagnie Française d'Assurance pour le Commerce Extérieur
(COFACE)
12 Cours Michelet
La Défense 10, Cédex 51
92065 Paris La Défense.

Telephone: (33 1) 49 02 20 00
Telex: 614884 F
Telefax: 47 73 81 97
           47 73 86 49

1.1.1.1   *Function*

The Compagnie Française d'Assurance pour le Commerce Extérieur (COFACE),
set up in 1946, is a semi–public, joint stock company. Its function is to operate a
public credit insurance service and to provide a performance guarantee on all foreign
trade transactions. Depending on the circumstances or on the risks involved, it acts
either on its own account or on behalf of the government (see 1.1.1.5).

1.1.1.2   *Summary of organisation*

Governing board

— Chairman Managing Director
— Director–General

The formulation of government policy and the co–ordination of offical support in
this area are the province of the Direction des relations économiques extérieures

(DREE — External Economic Relations Directorate) of the Ministry for Economic Affairs, Finance and the Budget.

Technical Directorates

— Short term
— Medium term
— Market development insurance

Operational Directorates and Departments

— General Secretariat

  • Public Relations and Administration
  • Finance

— Marketing and communications
— Information systems
— Legal and Technical Affairs

1.1.1.3   *Resources*

COFACE's capital, totalling FF 30 million, is held by the Caisse des dépôts et consignations, the Crédit national, the Banque française du commerce extérieur (BFCE), the Société française d'assurance pour favoriser le crédit and the major nationalised banks and insurance companies.

1.1.1.4   *Other organisations involved*

The formulation of government policy concerning export credits is the province of the Ministry for Economic Affairs, Finance and the Budget.

The Commission des Garanties et du Crédit du Commerce Extérieur (CGCE) has the task of advising the Director for External Economic Relations in his examination of the transactions submitted to him. The CGCE comprises representatives of the Ministry for Economic Affairs, Finance and the Budget, the Ministry for Foreign Affairs, the technical ministries concerned, COFACE, the Bank of France and the BFCE.

1.1.1.5   *Relations with the State*

Cover of risks is shared between the government and COFACE as follows: COFACE covers short term commercial risks (credits up to 3 years) on its own account, except for "extraordinary" (*) commercial risks. All other risks are covered by COFACE on behalf of the government: short, medium and long term political risks, the commercial risks of the whole transaction in the case of credits with maturities exceeding 3 years, "extraordinary" commercial risks.

---

* Any risk exceeding a certain amount per transaction and per buyer.

All applications for guarantees are submitted to COFACE. For risks insured on behalf of the government, decisions are taken in principle by the Director for External Economic Relations after consulting the CGCE [see 1.1.1.4]. COFACE is, however, empowered to delegate decision making to a fairly large extent.

COFACE keeps separate accounts for the two types of business (i.e. insurance on its own account and on behalf of the government).

For short term transactions covered by COFACE on its own account (short term commercial risk), the French Treasury gives COFACE excess–of–loss cover in consideration of an annual payment of 0.5 per cent of the premiums received.

1.1.1.6   *Relations with the private sector*

Relations with the private sector are not institutionalised. However, for various special reasons, co–insurance agreements with other insurance companies are sometimes concluded.

COFACE has no monopoly in law, so may sometimes be in competition with the private sector as regards both political and commercial risks. Currently, however, this does not happen very often.

1.2   Export finance

1.2.1   *Representative organisation*

Banque Française du Commerce Extérieur (BFCE)
21 Boulevard Haussmann
75009 PARIS.

1.2.1.1   *Function*

The government participates, via the BFCE, in the financing of export credits with maturities exceeding two years in order to stabilize credits financed in French francs or in a foreign currency.

In France export credit financing involves close co–operation between the commercial banks and two public institutions: the BFCE and COFACE [see 1.1]. Like COFACE, the BFCE acts both on its own behalf, and is hence subject to general banking rules, and on behalf of the government, either as the manager of the stabilization mechanism, when this is applied, or as the direct supplier of credits with maturities exceeding 7 years for countries in Consensus Categories II and III.

1.2.1.2   *Summary of organisation*

Governing board

— Chairman
— Director–General
— Deputy Director–General

General Secretariat

Six Directorates:

— International
— Medium and long term export credits
— France
— Legal affairs
— Financial affairs and treasury
— Development.

1.2.1.3   Resources

The BFCE raises the necessary resources on national and international financial markets on behalf of the government, which provides surety for debenture loans.

The commercial banks draw the necessary funds from their normal resources, either their own resources deriving from the surplus of deposits on credits arranged or resources raised on the French money market or on national and international financial markets.

1.2.1.4   Other bodies involved

None.

1.2.1.5   Relations with the State

See 1.2.1.1.

1.2.1.6   Relations with the private sector

The BFCE holds the monopoly for the financing of government–subsidised long term export credits (with maturities exceeding 7 years). As regards the financing of medium and short term credits, it is in competition with the private sector.

1.3   Aid finance

The Ministry of Co–operation is responsible for granting capital subsidies and technical assistance to some forty independent countries in sub–Saharan Africa, the Indian Ocean and the Caribbean. ODA credits granted to these countries (and to a few others) are managed by the Caisse centrale de coopération économique (CCCE). ODA to countries other than those dealt with by the CCCE is granted by the Treasury (Ministry for the Economy, Finance and the Budget).

2.   INSURANCE AND GUARANTEE PROGRAMMES

2.1   Cover for exporters

2.1.1   *Policies available*

COFACE offers a wide range of insurance schemes covering both commercial and political risks, both during the period of manufacture and the period of the credit. COFACE insurance policies are always conditional (compensation is paid only if damage through one of the risks covered occurs) and the proportion covered is always less than 100 per cent.

In the case of supplier credits the proportions covered are in principle as follows, whatever the type of policy:

— For commercial risks, 85 per cent; this proportion may be raised to 90 per cent if the transaction is guaranteed by a bank approved by COFACE ;
— For political risks, 90 per cent (in the case of buyer credits it is 95 per cent for all risks).

For *heavy capital goods and major projects*, the insurance provided by COFACE takes the form of individual policies covering commercial and political risks.

For *mass produced or light manufactured goods*, there are two options:

— The exporter may take out a comprehensive policy, in which case he must see to it that all transactions of this type are guaranteed against commercial risks. As regards political risks, he remains free to decide the country of destination to be covered by the guarantee ;
— The exporter may take out an open policy, in which case he is entirely free to decide the risks he wishes to cover (political and/or commercial) and the transactions he wishes to guarantee.

Exports of *consumer goods, raw materials and equipment,* for which credit maturities do not usually exceed 6 months, are covered by comprehensive policies. These cover the total export sales figure, taking the following factors into account: private or public–sector buyer, commercial or political risks. The policyholder may, however, if he wishes, exclude certain risks as regards certain countries (political risks or public–sector buyer risks).

In accordance with the rules of the OECD Arrangement, the best terms for private credits guaranteed by COFACE are in principle the following:

— *Repayment period* (unless specific agreements have been reached):
  — For heavy capital goods and major projects: 5 to 10 years, depending on the amount of the contract and the country of destination.
  — For light manufactured goods: depending on the amount of the contract, up to 3 years at the most.
  — For consumer goods: 6 months.
  — Repayment of principal *in equal half-yearly instalments* with no grace period.
— Generally, *minimum cash payments* of 15 per cent, or up to 20 or 25 per cent depending on the country and the buyer.
— *Local costs* are covered and financed up to the amount of the cash payments and on the same terms as the export credit for the portion that may

be repatriated. Assistance with local costs is provided only in exceptional cases and in accordance with the OECD Arrangement.

2.1.2   *Criteria for accepting cover*

2.1.2.1   *Eligibility*

Transactions are considered principally in the light of the following criteria:
— Creditworthiness of the buyer's country.
— Where applicable, availability of funds up to the ceiling set for the country concerned.
— The amount of the transaction, the terms of payment requested.

2.1.2.2   *Nationality requirements*

Transactions insured by COFACE may, in principle, include a foreign content equivalent of up to 40 per cent of the contract value provided the foreign component originates from another EEC country. Foreign content originating from a non–EEC country may constitute up to 30 per cent of the total contract price if there is a reciprocal agreement between France and that country, otherwise a maximum of 10 per cent is allowed.

2.1.3   *Cost of cover*

In the case of cover against political risk during the period of the credit for a private buyer, the premium for a five–year credit may be from 0.34 per cent to 2.28 per cent of the amount of the credit, depending on country risk. If application is also made for cover against commercial risk for the same credit, the premium may be from 1.48 per cent to 10.05 per cent.

2.2   Guarantees for banks

The cover available to banks takes several forms.

2.2.1   *Direct cover*

— For **buyer credits** (i.e. when the bank grants the foreign buyer a loan to enable him to pay cash for the export), COFACE insures the bank directly, issuing a policy covering it against credit risks (commercial risks, political risks or public sector buyer risks). In all cases, the proportion guaranteed is 95 per cent. This cover can be offered to French and, in some circumstances, foreign banks.
— For **discounting without recourse** by the bank of debts incurred on account of a supplier credit, COFACE issues to the discounting bank a policy providing cover against credit risk. Terms are much the same as for buyer credit, but the facility is available only for exports to a limited number of countries (OECD + Persian Gulf).
— For **debenture loans** launched on the international markets by French or foreign institutions in order to finance French exports, the institution raising the loan may also be provided with direct cover.

2.2.2   *Indirect cover*

For supplier credit, the exporter may, by agreement with COFACE, transfer compensation rights to the bank financing the transaction.

2.3   Other insurance programmes

2.3.1   *Foreign exchange risk insurance*

French exports may be denominated in foreign currencies. For this reason, COFACE offers exchange risk insurance subsidiary to that obtained on the forward market.

Foreign exchange risks are covered whether or not the contract is insured by COFACE.

Whatever the type of cover offered, the following common principles are complied with:

— Cover must be applied for prior to the date chosen for the determination of the exchange rate to be guaranteed;
— An application for cover is irrevocable as from the date on which the exchange rate to be guaranteed is set;
— From the outset, the amount of the cover in French francs corresponding to the amount denominated in a foreign currency is set. COFACE indemnifies the insured for any exchange losses, but reclaims from the insured the value of any foreign exchange gains that may accrue.

Most of the main convertible currencies used in international trading can be covered by COFACE.

The amount of the premium depends on the type of cover, the time during which risks are covered and the currency concerned.

2.3.2   *Cost escalation insurance*

This insurance gives the exporter partial cover against any abnormal increase in his various production costs during the period in which the contract runs.

Such cover is available only for major contracts for capital goods or services where the lead time exceeds 12 months. Transactions with EEC buyers cannot be insured in this way.

The insurance normally covers that portion of the contract to be carried out by the exporter himself, but may be extended to cover portions sub–contracted to French nationals or nationals of another EEC Member State.

Price increases affecting production costs are determined according to a price review formula whereby actual cost increases are compensated above a threshold corresponding to the rises in prices normally to be expected in the manufacturing country.

The premium is 1.15 per cent per year of the amount covered.

2.3.3   *Bond insurance*

COFACE can provide cover against calling in the event of some political upheaval and against the risk that the bond holder may, without justification, refuse to return any sums deposited.

Broadly speaking, three types of bond are guaranteed by COFACE:
— Bid bonds deposited on tendering. Cover is provided case by case, by means of individual policies.
— Bonds guaranteeing the restitution of down–payments.
— Performance bonds.

The two latter types of bond are guaranteed under the standard credit insurance policy.

2.3.4   *Risks involving equipment belonging to the exporter*

Where an exporter carries out abroad a project requiring the use of equipment which the exporter intends to repatriate afterwards, COFACE can cover the following risks (if they ensue from political events):
— Destruction or arbitrary seizure of equipment during the period of the project.
— Impossibility of re–exporting equipment once the contract has been completed.

This cover can be provided only if the export transaction itself has been insured; it is then considered to be an extra guarantee accessory to the cover of manufacturing risks.

2.3.5   *Risk of inability to repossess leased property*

This guarantee covers confiscation or arbitrary seizure of leased property. It is operative only if the reasons for inability to repossess are political.
It can be provided independently of cover of credit risks incurred in leasing.

3.   EXPORT FINANCE PROGRAMMES

Procedures for export credit financing are of two quite different kinds, depending on the maturity of the credit concerned. Credits with maturities of between 2 and 7 years are considered to be medium term credits. Those with maturities exceeding 7 years are considered to be long term credits. Short term credits are not eligible for preferential treatment and are financed and refinanced entirely by commercial banks at market rates.

3.1   **Direct credits**

Long term buyer credits in French francs or foreign currencies are financed directly by the BFCE (see also 3.3).

3.2   **Refinancing**

Long term supplier credits in French francs or foreign currencies are financed by the BFCE through refinancing by banks discounting the commercial claim (see also 3.3).

3.3   Interest subsidies

3.3.1   *Types of contract available*

Medium term export credits and the medium term portion of long term credits financed in French francs are stabilized by the BFCE on behalf of the Treasury. The BFCE compensates the difference between a reference rate (TRIBOR for credits denominated in French francs and PIBOR for those denominated in foreign currencies), to which is added the current bank margin and the cost of financing (the "taux de sortie") in accordance with the OECD Arrangement. This stabilization system is symmetrical, since the BFCE recoups any gains accruing from refinancing; it is also optional, with the bank free to decide whether or not to exercise this option before the credit is first used.

3.3.2   *Eligibility*

The system is used only for exports to countries that are not members of the EEC.

3.3.3   *Resulting interest rates*

The cost of financing (the "taux de sortie") for medium and long term credit varies depending on whether or not the rate is officially subsidised:

— In the case of medium or long term French franc or foreign currency credits for Consensus Category II (repayment period only) and Category III countries, the cost is the rate applicable under the OECD Arrangement, including the bank margin, to which should be added the credit guarantee premium and the initial commission and management charges levied by the banks.

— In the case of medium or long term French franc or foreign currency credits for Consensus Category I and II countries (for the portion of the credit extended prior to the repayment period), the banks receive no official financing subsidy and are free to set the interest rate at the level they deem appropriate. The cost of the credit hence depends on that rate, to which should be added a margin, the credit guarantee premium and the initial commission and management charges.

Short term credits are generally extended at rates akin to money market rates or the bank base rate (which corresponds to the "prime rate") plus an average of 1 per cent for bank charges and the cost of the COFACE premium when these credits are insured. The base rate is adjusted fairly frequently. In March 1989 it stood at 9.60 per cent.

3.4   Other credit operations

Credits denominated in foreign currencies may be stabilized by the BFCE on behalf of the government. This stabilization compensates the difference between a reference rate (PIBOR), to which is added the current bank margin and the cost of financing in accordance with the Arrangement. Here, too, the system is symmetrical, any gains from refinancing being recouped. At end December 1988, foreign currency credit amounts outstanding represented 13 per cent of total export credits.

4.   AID FINANCE PROGRAMMES

4.1   Associated financing (mixed credits)

4.1.1   *Funds available*

Treasury loans are usually combined with private export credits guaranteed by the government in the framework of a mixed credits system set up in the early 1960s. A mixed credit is granted under an agreement (protocol) negotiated with the developing country concerned. The protocols set the amount and terms of the aid granted and specify the purposes for which it is to be used (list of projects), as well as stating how much of the total amount is aid and how much export credits.

The development aid component is granted on concessional terms. The private credit is extended on Arrangement terms. The overall grant element of these tied aid credits is in line with the OECD Arrangement guidelines. The funds lent are tied to purchasing in France but can, if necessary, be used to finance local expenses.

4.1.2   *Eligibility*

Prior evaluation is systematic and is the responsibility of the DREE, which employs for this purpose either its own services or outside consultants.

On their completion projects are evaluated by the Treasury and the DREE. Assessments are based on reports sent in by French diplomatic services in the countries concerned and on surveys carried out on the spot by independent consultants.

The process involves the application of development criteria.

4.2   Integrated credits

Where certain recipient countries request it, France sometimes grants "monobloc" credits amalgamating funds from the official development aid budget and funds raised on the markets in a single overall loan. Criteria and procedures for evaluating projects and decision–making are the same as for mixed credits. These loans are negotiated by the Treasury and the DREE with the country concerned. A monobloc loan, like a mixed credit, is tied to the purchase of goods from France.

4.3   Other tied or partially untied aid

The Caisse Centrale de Coopération Economique (CCCE) grants some forty independent countries in sub–Saharan Africa, the Indian Ocean and the Caribbean concessional loans funded from the official development aid budget, as well as commercial loans at Arrangement terms. The CCCE also co–finances development aid projects in association with the various international financial institutions.

Chapter 16

NORWAY

1.   ORGANISATION AND STRUCTURE

1.1   Insurance and Guarantees

1.1.1   *Representative organisation*

Garanti–Instituttet for Eksportkredit
Postboks 1763 Vika
0122 Oslo 1

Telephone: (47 2) 832835
Telex: 8121153
Telefax: (47 2) 832445

1.1.1.1   *Function*

The Guarantee Institute for Export Credits (GIEK) is a State agency responsible to the Ministry of Foreign Affairs. GIEK was re–organised in 1960 in continuation of Statens Eksportkredittkommisjon and set up under its present name.

1.1.1.2   *Summary of organisation*

GIEK is organised in two departments dealing with commercial and political risks, respectively. There are also legal and administrative services. Applications regarding exports to developed countries are handled by the commercial risk department, whereas applications regarding exports to developing or state trading countries are dealt with by the political risk department.

1.1.1.3   *Resources*

The guidelines for operation of GIEK's general guarantee scheme are to cover indemnities and operating expenses. GIEK's own funds for operation of this scheme were depleted in 1981 due to heavy losses. Funding is now provided by the government according to need.

The operation of the general guarantee scheme is subject to an underwriting ceiling, which is revised annually. The present ceiling is NKr 13 billion.

GIEK's special scheme of guarantees for export credits to, or investments in, developing countries was abolished as from 31st December 1987.

1.1.1.4   *Other organisations involved*

GIEK is administered by a Board of ten members comprising representative
of the Ministries of Foreign Affairs, Finance and Industry, the banks, the confederation of Norwegian Business and Industry, the national Trade Union, the Export Council as well as independent members and the Managing Director of GIEK itself.

An additional Board member representing the Norwegian Agency for Development Aid (NORAD) participates when cases concerning indemnities under the special scheme for developing countries are dealt with.

1.1.1.5   *Relations with the state*

The state provides funds for GIEK and sets underwriting ceilings.

1.1.1.6   *Relations with the private sector*

Private banks and insurance companies can provide some forms of cover. Risk sharing between GIEK and private banks or insurance companies is no longer obligatory for credits covering political risks over NKr 10 million, but still obligatory for commercial risks.

1.2   **Export Finance**

1.2.1   *Representative organisation*

A/S Eksportfinans (Forretningsbankenes finansierings–og eksportkredittinstitutt)
Dronning Mauds gate 15
0250 Oslo 1

Telephone: (47 2) 830100
Telex: 78213 "Exfin m"
Telefax: (47 2) 832237

1.2.1.1   *Function*

A/S Eksportfinans (The Financing and Export Credit Institute of the Norwegian Commercial Banks) was incorporated in Norway on 2nd May 1962 with limited liability. It is a private company owned by the commercial banks of Norway. The objective of the company is to grant medium and long term loans for export promotion and for manufacturing trade and handicraft. In addition to extending credits on commercial terms, the company is authorised to give export credit with governmental support.

The principal business of the company is the provision of medium and long term credits mainly in connection with Norwegian exports, but also in connection with the substitution of domestically produced goods for imports.

The company is required by its articles of associaiton to operate in accordance with sound commercial principles. Like other Norwegian financing corporations, the company is governed by the company's act of 4th June 1976 and the Financing Activities Act of 10th June 1988.

1.2.1.2   *Summary of organisation*

Not available.

1.2.1.3   *Resources*

The company has a share capital of NKr 107.5 million, which is subscribed by the shareholding banks.   The funds needed for the company's financing activities are raised by borrowing in the medium and long term domestic and international capital markets.

The company's bonds in the United States have been granted AAA rating by Standard Poor's and Aa by Moody's.   The company has access to all the international capital markets.

There is no government guarantee on its borrowings, and the company has no special government supported funding resources.

From 1962 to 1978, Eksportfinans only granted purely commercial credits.   In 1978, the government entrusted the company with the administration of an officially supported export credit system.   The company has continued its commercial activities in parallel.

1.2.1.4   *Other organisations involved*

None.

1.2.1.5   *Relations with the state*

Officially supported export credits are extended under an agreement with the Ministry of Finance.   The operating policies and the results are reviewed annually by Parliament.

1.2.1.6   *Relations with the private sector*

There is basically a free market, but officially supported export credits are only available through Eksportfinans.

1.3   Aid Finance

1.3.1   *Representative organisation*

Royal Norwegian Ministry of Development
Cooperation (MDC)

2.   INSURANCE AND GUARANTEE PROGRAMMES

2.1   Cover for Exporters

2.1.1   *Policies available*

GIEK offers several forms of cover for both pre–shipment and post–shipment risks.   The form in which insurance is given depends upon a number of variables such as credit amount, payback period, risk level and type of transaction. For short term credits, wholeturnover cover from GIEK is available for both political and commercial risks. GIEK also offers cover in co–operation with domestic banks, where the bnaks provide funding and also absorb a share of the credit risk.

For credits tied to exports of capital goods, GIEK may cover both political and commercial risks. Insurance for credits less than NKr 10 million to foreign or domestic lenders covers 100 per cent of the credit. This applies to both suppliers' and buyers' credits, with a 10–20 per cent recourse to the exporter being the norm. Recourse for political risk to exporters may be dropped altogether after three years provided there has been no payment default during this period. Recourse for comercial risk may be dropped after eight years. For these credits, GIEK's guarantee is available without a need to share the risk.

For political risks covering credits of NKr 10 million or larger, risk sharing with commercial banks is no longer obligatory. For insurance given on a pro rata basis, GIEK and other guarantors normally have identical securities, third party guarantees, mortgages, etc. GIEK's share of the commercial risk may not exceed 75 per cent of total guaranteed credit. GIEK's share of the political risk may not exceed 90 per cent of total guaranteed credit. However, if the private guarantee market totally withdraws from a market, GIEK may increase cover to 100 per cent with a 10 per cent recourse to the exporter.

Cover is not available for exporters using the "cash contract scheme".

2.1.2   Eligibility

The exporter is required to make sufficient credit information available before application for cover is processed. Securities in the form of government or central (state) bank guarantee may allow for an increased percentage of cover. GIEK provides cover for credits that are in accordance with terms normal for the trade in question. In general, the following limits are respected:

— For consumer goods/raw materials, credit period up to six months is accepted. Certain exceptions are allowed within Berne Union agreements;
— For capital goods, credit period, downpayment, repayment terms and level of local cost financing must be within the limits of the OECD Arrangement.

Up to 30 per cent of foreign components may be accepted in contracts underwritten by GIEK. For components of Nordic origin the percentage may be increased to 40.

2.1.3   Cost of cover

Premiums/fees are calculated as a percentage of the direct amount of the transaction.

The premium depends upon variables such as: credit period, public or private buyer, securities available and general creditworthiness. For purposes of setting premia for political risks countries are classified in five categories.

2.2   Guarantees for Banks

GIEK may provide cover to Norwegian or first class international banks or other financial institutions.

2.3   Other Insurance Programmes

GIEK may accept liabilities in a foreign currency and pay claims in the same currency. Risk exposure can be covered either on domestic or international forward markets.

3.   EXPORT FINANCE PROGRAMMES

3.1   Direct Credits

3.1.1   *Types of contract available*

Only post–shipment credits are extended.

3.1.2   *Eligibility*

The criteria for granting credits are determined by a set of detailed regulations. The main rule is to support Norwegian exporters facing officially supported credit competition. Credits may be extended either from A/S Eksportfinans' official or commercial windows.

For the export credits offered under the officially supported sector, lending terms are determined by the Arrangement and the Understanding on Export Credits for Ships. The financing of foreign components is limited to 30 per cent of the contract.

For the commercial lending sector of A/S Eksportfinans, the lending terms are determined by the cost of funds plus a normal commercial margin. The rate of interest is fixed on the day of lending. Currency risk exposures, if any, are carried by the company.

3.1.3   *Resulting interest rates*

Medium and long term credits are financed by A/S Eksportfinans. Eksportfinans finances post shipment credits through its official window up to 85 per cent of the transaction value at the agreed Arrangement minimum rates. The interest rate is fixed at the time of commitment in accord with the Arrangement Guidelines.

There is no government support available for short term credits. They are financed directly by exporters or refinanced with the commercial banks at market rates. The interest rate is fixed at time of disbursement.

3.2   Refinancing for banks

Not available.

3.3   Interest subsidies

Not available.

3.4   Other credit operations

Because of the narrowness of the Norwegian capital market, foreign funding in connection with medium and long term export credit transactions has been encouraged by the government. Exporters and banks may freely extend foreign currency provided that the conditions are in conformity with normal commercial practices. Buyers' credits extended by Norwegian financial institutions require formal approval by the Bank of Norway or the Ministry of Foreign Affairs.

4.   AID FINANCE PROGRAMMES

4.1   Associated Financing (Mixed credits)

4.1.1   *Funds available*

Norway operates a mixed credit scheme administered by the Royal Norwegian Ministry of Development Corporation (MDC). The scheme is based on aid principles. The grant element may be given either in form of interest subsidies for commercial bank credits or a cash grant. In the former case, the credit will usually be in a pre–mixed form and extended either by Eksportfinans or another financial institution.

4.1.2   *Eligibility*

The purpose of the scheme is to increase the amount of finance available for investment in high priority projects of developing countries. Eligible recipients are, from July 1987 onward, low income (including LLDCs) and lower middle–income countries. The funds can be used for matching and are normally tied to procurement from Norway, but third country procurement is possible for up to 30 per cent. As far as possible, international competitive bidding is used. For the time being, the new scheme is restricted to smaller supply contracts (below NKr 50 million), in order to limit the budget funds required.

4.1.3   *Resulting terms and interest rates*

These are in accordance with Arrangement guidelines.

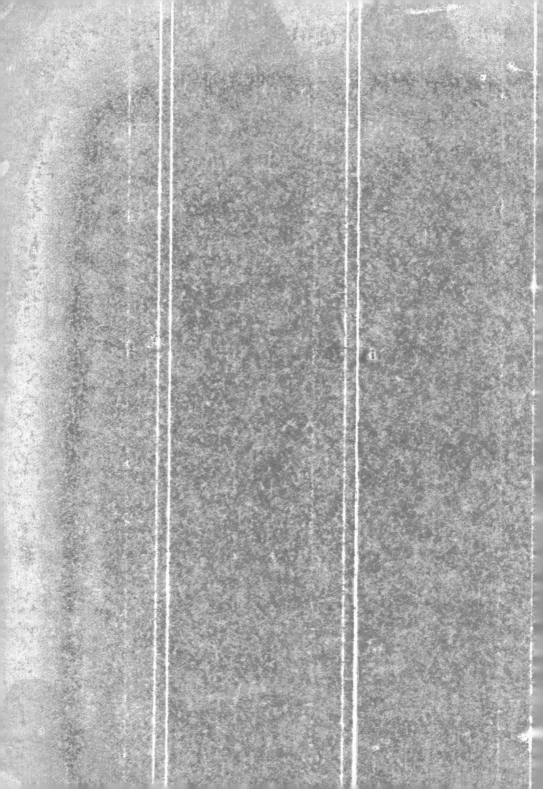